Bibliografische Information der Deutschen Nationalbibliothek:
Die Deutsche Nationalbibliothek verzeichnet diese Publikation in der Deutschen Nationalbibliografie; detaillierte bibliografische Daten sind im Internet über http://dnb.d-nb.de abrufbar.

Impressum:
Lektorat: Benedikt Brendel
Copyright © 2016 ScienceFactory
Ein Imprint der GRIN Verlag GmbH
Druck und Bindung: Books on Demand GmbH, Norderstedt, Germany
Coverbild: wikimedia.org

Körper, Sexualität und Gender.
Zur (De)Konstruktion von „Männlichkeit" und „Weiblichkeit" im Werk von William Shakespeare

Inhaltsverzeichnis

Monstrous Bodies – Körper und Männlichkeit bei Shakespeare 7

Einleitung 8

Wahrnehmung und Signifikanz außergewöhnlicher Körper in der Renaissance-Gesellschaft 19

Konzepte sexueller Identität in der Frühen Neuzeit 28

Richard III. – Ein „Monster" auf dem Thron 35

Caliban – Das „Tier" im Mann und die Jungfrau 47

Falstaff – Die Weiblichkeit des fetten Mannes 72

Schlussbetrachtung 89

Bibliographie 92

The Construction of Feminity and Masculinity in Shakespeare's *Macbeth* 97

Foreword 98

The Sources of the Play 99

Masculinity in Shakespeare's *Macbeth* 101

The Values of Chivalry 102

The Duties of Chivalrous Knights 103

King Duncan's "Natural Order" 105

Macbeth's Development from Scotland's Saviour to Scotland's Criminal King and Bloody Tyrant 108

Sterility as the Underlying Reason for Macbeth's Violence 112

Banquo: Perfect Knight or Villain? 116

Macduff: The Epitome of Chivalry? 122

Malcolm: Hope for a Restored "Natural Order"? 125

Femininity in Shakespeare's *Macbeth* 132

The Elizabethan Housewife 133

Humble Lady Macduff 135

Witches as a Social and Political Problem in Shakespeare's England 138

Between the Genders: The Witches in *Macbeth* 139

Macbeth and Lady Macbeth: Marital Fulfillment in Regicide 152

Conclusion 158

Works Cited 160

Gender Politics in *Macbeth* **165**

Introduction 166

Gender ideology 167

Gender stereotyping in *Macbeth* 171

Gender conflict in *Macbeth* 177

Conclusion 189

Bibliography 191

Körper- und Spiegelmetapher und ihre Funktion in ausgewählten Sonetten William Shakespeares **193**

Einleitung 194

Die Entwicklung des Sonetts bis in die elisabethanische Zeit 195

Das Sonett bei William Shakespeare 199

Körper- und Spiegelmetapher in der Literatur 203

Betrachtung einzelner Sonette 209

Zusammenfassung 216

Literaturverzeichnis 217

Einzelbände **219**

Monstrous Bodies – Körper und Männlichkeit bei Shakespeare

Verena Ludwig, 2008

Einleitung

Jahrhunderte bevor der Begriff *Gender* und der dazugehörige wissenschaftliche Diskurs sich entwickelten, verhandelten William Shakespeares Dramen bereits Probleme sexueller Identität, dysfunktionale Familienbeziehungen und Formen des Aufbegehrens gegen traditionelle Geschlechterrollen. In der neueren Shakespeare-Forschung wurden diese Themen im Zuge der sich aus der Frauenforschung entwickelnden *Gender Studies* vor allem an den weiblichen Charakteren der Dramen behandelt. Erst in den letzten Jahren erhält auch die wissenschaftliche Untersuchung von „Männlichkeit" eine erhöhte Aufmerksamkeit, die angesichts der durch die Frauenforschung ins Rollen gebrachten Verschiebungen und Umbrüche der traditionellen Geschlechterrollen und -vorstellungen dringend notwendig wurde. Während die *Gender Studies* sich anfangs vornehmlich auf das Herrschaftsverhältnis zwischen Männern und Frauen konzentriert haben, rücken nun auch die Machtgefüge unter Männern und verschiedenen „Männlichkeiten" unter den Bedingungen der patriarchalischen Gesellschaft in den Mittelpunkt des wissenschaftlichen Interesses.

Der stetige Zwang zur Aufrechterhaltung des individuellen und gesellschaftlichen *Gender*-Konstruktes hat nicht nur für die Frauen als der männlichen Herrschaftsstrukturen untergeordnetes „anderes" Geschlecht, sondern auch für die beteiligten Männer schmerzliche Konsequenzen und führt zur Diskriminierung und Ausgrenzung derjenigen, die der symbolisch überfrachteten Männlichkeitsnorm nicht entsprechen können.

Diese Grundannahmen werden von der Geschlechterforschung den männerdominierten Gesellschaftsstrukturen zu allen Zeiten als gegeben zugrunde gelegt, wenn auch unter sich jeweils wandelnden biologischen und ästhetischen Vorzeichen. Durch die festgeschriebenen Forderungen und Rollenzuschreibungen einer als „patriarchalisch" gekennzeichneten Gesellschaft befanden sich Männer seit jeher unter einem konstanten Druck, ihre „Männlichkeit", ihre soziale und sexuelle Identität zu finden und ihren Geschlechtsgenossen gegenüber durch unterschiedliche kulturelle Praktiken zu beweisen.

Dreihundert Jahre bevor Psychoanalyse und *Gender Studies* die Untersuchungsmethoden und wissenschaftlichen Begriffe für diese inneren und äußeren Konflikte entwickelt haben, hat Shakespeare sie erkannt und in seinen Dramen seinen Mitmenschen vor Augen geführt. In einer vormodernen Welt, die durch die Taten und Gedanken von Männern bestimmt war, einer Gesellschaft, deren Ordnung sich aus der Macht des Vaters ableitete, interessierte der Dramatiker sich für den

Kampf des (männlichen) Individuums, sich in dieser Ordnung zu behaupten, zum
„Mann" zu werden und den damit verknüpften Anforderungen zu entsprechen.
Die Frau, „das Weibliche", dient dabei zumeist als Gegenentwurf, entweder als
„Suffocating Mother", von der er sich lösen muss, um seine männliche Identität
entwickeln zu können[1], oder als idealisierte Jungfrau, die die Projektionsfläche
seiner sexuellen und machtpolitischen Wunschvorstellungen ist.

Die Risse und Veränderungen im traditionellen Geschlechterverhältnis, die wir in
unserer Gesellschaft aktuell beobachten, wurden auch in der elisabethanischen
Gesellschaft empfunden. Die Thronbesteigung Elizabeths I. im Jahr 1558 brachte
eine enorme Erschütterung der patriarchalischen Herrschaftslegitimation mit sich:
Eine Frau an der Spitze des Patriarchats, ein weiblicher „body natural" als Verkörperung des männlichen „body politic", stellte die „von Gott gewollte" Geschlechterhierarchie auf den Kopf und barg die Gefahr des völligen Zusammen-
bruchs des Patriarchats und des damit einhergehenden Verständnisses von „Männlichkeit".

Körper und „Männlichkeit"

Was aber ist „männlich"? Das Konzept „Männlichkeit" scheint vor allem durch
den Ausschluss von „Nicht-Männlichem" konstituiert zu sein, an erster Stelle der
zwanghaften Abgrenzung vom „Weiblichen" und damit assoziierten Eigenschaften wie Schwäche, Emotionalität, und Weichheit. Eine positive Definition von
„Männlichkeit" ist hingegen nur schwer herstellbar:

> Männer haben schon immer gewusst was ein ‚ganzer Kerl' ist, wer
> dazu gehört und wer nicht, woran man seinesgleichen erkennt (...) Nur,
> wenn man Männer auffordert zu beschreiben, was Männlichkeit ist,
> stellt man sie vor große Schwierigkeiten.[2]

Ein greifbares Feld zur Untersuchung von „Männlichkeit" ist der Körper. Wie
„Weiblichkeit" als Objekt des in erster Linie von Männern hergestellten Attrakti-
vitäts- und Rollendiskurses, ist auch „Männlichkeit" untrennbar mit dem Körper

---

[1] Der Untersuchung der allmächtigen, „erdrückenden" Mutterfigur als Bedrohung maskuliner
Identität in Shakespeares Werken hat sich vor allem Janet Adelman in *Suffocating Mothers*
gewidmet. (Adelmann, Janet, *Suffocating Moterhs. Fantasies of Maternal Origin in Shakespeare's Plays, "Hamlet" to "The Tempest"*. New York/London, 1992)

[2] Michael Meuser, *Geschlecht und Männlichkeit, Soziologische Theorie und kulturelle Deutungsmuster*. Opladen, 1998, S. 130.

verbunden, als „Ort der Selbst- und Weltdeutung", als „zentrale Kategorie menschlicher Sinndeutung und Handlungsorientierung".[3]

In den späten sechziger Jahren, gewissermaßen als Folgeerscheinung der Entwicklung der Geschlechtergeschichte, entstand erstmals eine kulturwissenschaftliche Debatte um den Körper. Angeregt von feministischer Theorie und den Arbeiten Michel FOUCAULTS wurde diese Debatte im Verlauf der achtziger und neunziger Jahre vom unaufhaltsamen Aufstieg der Genetik als Schlüssel zum letzten Geheimnis des Körpers und der Möglichkeit seiner künstlichen Erschaffung, aber auch durch die Verbreitung der neuen Krankheit AIDS und in jüngster Zeit durch die neue Körperästhetik in Zeiten der plastischen Chirurgie, befeuert.[4]

Körpergeschichte als wissenschaftliche Disziplin verspricht eine neue, fruchtbare Zugriffsweise auf vergangene Mentalitäten und Lebensweisen. Nicht mehr nur als materielle Existenzform, als Gegenstand biologischer, medizinischer, demographischer oder ernährungswissenschaftlicher Fragestellungen, sondern als soziales Konstrukt und Symbolsystem wird der Körper seither in verschiedenen akademischen Bereichen unter den Aspekten von Körpersymbolik, Körperbildern und Körpererfahrung untersucht.[5]

Auch der Weg zu einem solchen „integrativ verstandenen"[6] Körperbegriff verlief zunächst über die wissenschaftlich, institutionell und politisch übergreifende Frauen- und Geschlechtergeschichte. Als Folge dieser ursprünglichen Verankertheit der neuen Körperforschung in den *Gender Studies* kreisen die Untersuchungen zur sozialen und symbolischen Signifikanz von Körpern vor allem um das

---

[3] Clemens Wischermann, „Geschichte des Körpers oder Körper mit Geschichte?", in: Clemens Wischermann & Stefan Haas (Hrsg.), *Körper mit Geschichte*. Münster/Konstanz, 2000.

[4] Valentin Groeber, „Körper auf dem Markt. Söldner, Organhandel und die Geschichte der Körpergeschichte", in: Mittelweg 36. Zeitschrift des Hamburger Instituts für Sozialforschung, (Dezember 2005), S. 69.

[5] Eine der frühesten und wegweisendsten Veröffentlichungen zur Körpergeschichte sind die von Michael Feher, Ramona Nadaff und Nadia Tazi herausgegebenen *Fragments for a History of the Human Body* (3 Bde, New York, 1989). Die erste deutschsprachige Zusammenfassung zur Körpergeschichte hat Maren Lorenz mit *Leibhaftige Vergangenheit. Eine Einführung in die Körpergeschichte* vorgelegt (Tübingen, 2000) und mit *Reizbare Maschinen. Eine Geschichte des Körpers 1765-1914* (Frankfurt/M., 2001) hat Philipp Sarasin zuletzt eine grundlegende Arbeit zur Konzeption des Körpers in Übergangszeit zwischen Früher Neuzeit und Moderne geschaffen.

[6] Wischermann, S. 12.

Feld der Geschlechterdifferenz. Andere Konzepte wie Ethnie oder Alterszugehörigkeit stehen deutlich dahinter zurück.

In den folgenden Ausführungen zu Körper und Männlichkeit bei Shakespeare soll es um einen Bereich von „Körperlichkeit" gehen, der bisher wenig Aufmerksamkeit erhalten hat und im öffentlichen Diskurs noch immer weitgehend tabuisiert wird: der „behinderte", von der medizinischen und gesellschaftlichen, und hier besonders von der „männlichen" Norm abweichende Körper.[7]

Innerhalb der gesellschaftlichen Konstruktion von Männlichkeit steht beim Mann seit jeher vor allem die Leistungsfähigkeit seines Körpers im Vordergrund. Nur ein leistungsfähiger Körper ist wirklich „männlich", denn er erlaubt es dem Mann, seine maskulinen Qualitäten öffentlich zu inszenieren, sich im Wettkampf, etwa im Sport, mit seinen Geschlechtsgenossen zu messen, oder seine Attraktivität auf Frauen als „Trophäen" seiner Potenz zur Schau zu stellen:

> Die Dimension des Körpers bleibt in der sozialen Praxis gegenwärtig. Nicht als ‚Basis', aber als Objekt der Praxis. Männlichkeit stattet den Körper aus.[8]

Was ist aber mit den Individuen, die den gesellschaftlichen Forderungen an eine funktionsfähige männliche Identität, sozial und sexuell, von vorneherein nicht entsprechen, die aus dem Patriarchat ausgeschlossen werden müssen, weil sie keine „ganzen Männer" sein können?

Um einer Antwort auf diese Frage näher zu kommen, sollen in dieser Arbeit drei von Shakespeares zahlreichen außergewöhnlichen Körpern untersucht werden, drei Charaktere, die sich gerade wegen ihrer außergewöhnlichen Korporealität seit ihrem ersten Erscheinen auf einer Bühne besonderer Popularität erfreuen und Gegenstand zahlreicher Interpretationsansätze sind: Richard III., Caliban und Falstaff.

---

[7] David T. Mitchell und Sharon L. Snyder kritisieren die Vernachlässigung des behinderten Körpers im akademischen Körper-Diskurs: *"The current popularity of the body in critical discourse seeks to incorporate issues of race, gender, sexuality and class while simultaneously neglecting disability."* ("Disability Studies and the double bind of representation", in: David T. Mitchell and Sharon L. Snyder (eds.), *The Body and Physical Difference: Discourses of Disability.* Michigan, 1997, S. 1)

[8] R.W. Connell u.a., „Ansätze zu einer neuen Soziologie der Männlichkeit", in: BauSteineMänner (Hrsg.), *Kritische Männerforschung, Neue Ansätze in der Geschlechtertheorie.* Berlin, S. 66.

Bucklig, verkrüppelt, missgestaltet, mehr Tier als Mensch, grotesk fettleibig – diese drei Männer sind Gegenentwürfe zu den idealen Vertretern patriarchalischer Männlichkeit, wie sie ihnen in ihren jeweiligen Stücken als Antagonisten, als Herrscher oder als Schützlinge begegnen. Dennoch sind sie weit mehr als bloße „Antihelden", ist ihre besondere Körperlichkeit mehr als das äußere Zeichen innerer Verkommenheit, hat Shakespeare seine „Monster" nicht aus reiner Effekthascherei auf die Bühne gebracht.

An diesen durch ihre außergewöhnlichen Körper gekennzeichneten Charakteren soll der Zusammenhang zwischen *disability*, verstanden als jegliche von der Norm abweichende Körperlichkeit, und „Männlichkeit", sowohl in sexueller als auch in sozialer Hinsicht, untersucht werden. Welchen Einfluss hatte körperliche Andersartigkeit auf die Sexualität und die „Männlichkeit" einer Person im Verständnis des frühneuzeitlichen Beobachters, und welche neuen Erkenntnisse können wir aus der historischen Rezeption für unser heutiges Verständnis dieser Figur gewinnen?

Durch die Analyse der „Behinderungen" dieser drei Charaktere sollen die historischen, sozialen und mythologischen Faktoren aufgezeigt werden, die sie als von traditionellen sozialen Kreisen Ausgeschlossene stigmatisieren und ihrer „Männlichkeit" dadurch besondere Bedeutung geben. Diesen Fragestellungen kann nur entsprechend fundiert nachgegangen werden, wenn kulturelle Voraussetzungen für die zeitgenössische Interpretation von *disabilities*, die Autor und Publikum damals zur Verfügung standen, zuvor geklärt werden. Dazu sollen zunächst frühneuzeitliche Auffassungen sowohl aus den mythologisch-volkstümlichen als auch aus medizinischwissenschaftlichen Diskursen über außergewöhnliche Körper vorgestellt werden.

Welche Assoziationen verband das Publikum dieser Zeit mit bestimmten körperlichen Eigenschaften? Welche anatomischen und medizinischen Erklärungsansätze waren vorherrschend? Grundlegende Einblicke in die Erklärungs- und Deutungsmuster dieser Zeit geben die wissenschaftlich motivierten *prodigy books* von frühneuzeitlichen Universalgelehrten wie Ambroise PARÉ[9] sowie die galenische Humoralpathologie, die zu dieser Zeit die Grundlage der medizinischen Theorie und Praxis bildete; aber auch die an Volksglauben und Sensationslust orientierten

---

[9] Ambroise Paré, *Des monstres et prodiges*. (Paris, 1573), Engl. Übers.: *On Monsters and Marvels*. Translation, Introduction and Notes by J. R. Pallister. Chicago, 1982.

broadsheeds und *broadside ballad*s, in denen „Monster" als Zeichen göttlichen Zorns und bevorstehenden Unglückes gedeutet wurden.

Eine Beschäftigung mit der Bedeutung eines Textes zu seiner Entstehungszeit muss sich immer dem Vorwurf des Historizismus, also der Begrenzung eines Textes auf die ursprüngliche Intentionalität seines Autors, stellen. Diese Verengung auf die vermeintlich historisch „richtige" Bedeutung eines Textes widerspricht natürlich dem poststrukturalistischen Anspruch auf Intertextualität. Andererseits ist das radikale Bestehen auf der totalen Dekonstruktivität eines Textes für die Untersuchung einer bestimmten kulturellen Bedeutungsebene ebenso sinnlos wie seine Historisierung, da man dadurch, so Francis BARKER und Peter HULME, an einem Punkt gelange, *„where the only option becomes a voluntaristic ascription to the text of meanings and articulations derived simply from one's own ideological preferences."*[10]

Wenn also in den folgenden Ausführungen nach den kulturellen Diskursen von körperlichen Devianzen zur Zeit der Entstehung von Shakespeares Werken gefragt wird, soll dies nicht unter Auslassung des heutigen Verständnisses dieser Körper geschehen, sondern im Gegenteil einen Beitrag zur Untersuchung dieser Texte unter modernen Fragestellungen zu *Sex* und *Gender*, „normalen" und „nicht normalen" Körpern leisten:

> A properly political intertextuality would attend to successive inscriptions without abandoning that no longer privileged but still crucially important first inscription of the text.[11]

Ein Aspekt, der von Körperlichkeit nicht trennbar ist, ist dabei der von Sexualität und Geschlechterkonzepte zu dieser Zeit. Was galt als „männlich", was als „weiblich", welche Vorstellungen von männlicher und weiblicher Sexualität gab es und wie hingen sie mit den gängigen Körperkonzepten zusammen? Die einflussreiche Theorie vom frühneuzeitlichen „Ein-Geschlecht-Körper" wurde erstmals durch

---

[10] Francis Barker & Peter Hulme, „Nymphs and reapers heavily vanish: the discursive contexts of *The Tempest*", in: John Drakakis (Hrsg.), *Alternative Shakespeares*. London/New York, 1985, S. 193.

[11] Ebd., S. 193.

THOMAS LAQUEUR in „Making Sex" formuliert.[12] Welche Konsequenzen die Vorstellung von isomorphen Geschlechtsorganen, also einer nicht biologisch festgelegten „Männlichkeit" für die Konstruktion und Zuschreibung von Gender-Zugehörigkeit hat, wenn auch noch der betreffende Körper nicht den gesellschaftlichen ästhetischen und funktionellen Normen entspricht, wird ein wichtiger Teil der zu untersuchenden Signifikanz des männlichen „behinderten" Körpers sein.

Für eine Betrachtung von Korporealität und Gender-Konstruktionen erlaubt die psychoanalytische Untersuchung von Shakespeares Charakteren neue Perspektiven und Erkenntnisse. Janet ADELMANN, Valerie TRAUB und Linda BAMBER zählen zu den VertreterInnen dieses zunächst besonders auf weibliche Gender-Diskurse konzentrierten Ansatzes.

Die nachfolgende literaturwissenschaftliche Beschäftigung mit außergewöhnlichen Körpern soll auf Grundlage der Definition von „Behinderung" und körperlicher „Andersartigkeit" geschehen, wie sie in den Disability Studies formuliert ist. Hierzu soll zunächst ein kurzer Überblick über die Motivationen und Ziele dieses recht neuen wissenschaftlichen Zweiges gegeben werden.

Die Disability Studies als neuer Zweig der Literaturwissenschaft

Die Beschäftigung mit körperlichen Behinderungen als signifikante Kategorie in der Literaturwissenschaft ist ein relativ neues Forschungsfeld, das sich in den siebziger Jahren im Zuge der Cultural Studies in Großbritannien und den USA als eine „sozial- und kulturwissenschaftlich reflexive, aber auch handlungsbezogene und politische Wissenschaft"[13] entwickelt hat. Zwar waren Behinderungen bis zu diesem Zeitpunkt schon lange Gegenstand akademischer und professioneller Disziplinen, jedoch beschränkte sich diese auf die Verwaltung, Behandlung und Pflege von Menschen mit Behinderungen, Menschen, die gemeinhin als mangelhaft und unproduktiv für die soziale Gemeinschaft angesehen werden: So definiert die „EingliederungshilfeVerordnung nach §47 Bundessozialhilfegesetz" Menschen mit Behinderung als „*Personen, bei denen infolge einer körperlichen Regelwidrigkeit die Fähigkeit zur Eingliederung in die Gesellschaft in erheblichem*

---

[12] Die nachfolgenden Ausführungen beziehen sich auf die deutsche Übersetzung: Thomas Laqueur, *Auf den Leib geschrieben. Die Inszenierung der Geschlechter von der Antike bis Freud*. Übers. v. H. Jochen Bußmann, Frankfurt/New York, 1990.

[13] Volker Schönwiese, „Perspektiven der Disability Studies", in: *Behinderte in Familie und Gesellschaft* 5 (2005), S. 16.

Umfange beeinträchtigt ist"[14], eine mehr als unglückliche Formulierung, die dem Behinderten quasi eine Absichtlichkeit in seiner Verletzung der biologischen und gesellschaftlichen „Regeln" für einen eingliederungsfähigen Körper vorwirft.

Weil Behinderung überwiegend als ein behandlungs- und korrekturbedürftiges medizinisches Phänomen kommuniziert wird, hat die Geisteswissenschaft sie lange nicht als grundlegende Kategorie von sozialer Erfahrung und symbolischem Kapital erkannt. So steht der Dominanz von biologischer, sozialer und erkenntnistheoretischer Forschung in diesem Bereich eine auffällige Stille aus den Geisteswissenschaften gegenüber: Während literatur- und kulturwissenschaftliche Forschung im Zuge der Entstehung der *Cultural Studies* soziale Identitäten wie *Gender*, Sexualität, Klasse und Rasse für sich entdeckt und aus der Vernachlässigung durch die sozialen und biologischen Wissenschaften erlöst haben, wurde der Lebenswelt von Menschen mit Behinderungen bisher noch nicht ihre eigene, einzigartige und wertvolle Perspektive zugestanden.[15]

Eine Grundvoraussetzung für eine Verbesserung dieser Lage wäre die Einbindung behinderter Personen und ihrer Perspektive in die wissenschaftliche Arbeit der *Disability Studies,* was zumindest in Deutschland dank „*jahrzehntelanger Versäumnisse in der Bildungs- und Integrationspolitik*" kaum der Fall war, denn „*behinderte WissenschaftlerInnen und Lehrende sind in den Bildungseinrichtungen des deutschsprachigen Raumes kaum zu finden.*"[16]

Auch außerhalb der wissenschaftlichen Beschäftigung, zum Beispiel in den populären Medienproduktionen, sind Behinderte bislang nur unzureichend portraitiert worden, sie tauchen dort höchstens als „Opfer", als Objekte von Mitleid und Rührseligkeit auf, aber selten als Protagonisten mit einer Lebens- und Erfahrungswelt aus eigenem Recht.

Die geisteswissenschaftliche Beschäftigung mit Behinderung könnte einen wichtigen Beitrag dazu leisten, die einzigartige Subjektivität des Begriffes „Behinderung" und der Projektionen, die von der Gesellschaft auf behinderte Menschen in der Geschichte projiziert wurden, aufzuzeigen und in Frage zu stellen:

---

[14] Ernst Klee, *Behindert. Über die Enteignung von Körper und Bewusstsein*. Frankfurt a. M. 1980, online eingestellt unter: http://bidok.uibk.ac.at/library/klee-behindert.html?hls=Klee#id2701497.

[15] Mitchell/Snyder, S. 2.

[16] Schönwiese, S. 18.

> Die Disability Studies bieten den notwendigen Perspektivwechsel zur Veränderung gesellschaftlicher Rahmenbedingungen, indem sie behinderte Menschen zum Subjekt von Wissenschaft machen statt sie, wie bisher üblich, lediglich als zu beforschendes Objekt zu betrachten.[17]

Wie kommt es aber dazu, dass Menschen mit Behinderungen einer derartigen Diskriminierung und Stigmatisierung ausgesetzt sind? Einen Erklärungsversuch bieten David T. MITCHELL und Sharon L. SNYDER in ihrer Einleitung zu „*The Body and Physical Difference*"[18] an: Im Gegensatz zu Krankheit und Altern, die auch mit körperlicher Beeinträchtigung und sozialer Unproduktivität verbunden würden, trage Behindertsein den Stempel eines permanenten biologischen Zustandes wie Rasse und Geschlecht, aus dem das Individuum sich nicht befreien kann. Demnach beinhaltet die behinderte Person mehr als nur eine physische/kognitive Beeinträchtigung oder Andersartigkeit. Ihre Körperlichkeit durchzieht jeden Aspekt ihres sozialen Wesens, denn ihr Zustand wird als im Material ihrer physischen und moralischen Persönlichkeit eingebettet angesehen. Somit wird körperliche Behinderung mit sozialer Identität, Biologie und Persönlichkeit gleichgestellt:

> The physical world provides the material evidence of an inner life (corrupt or virtuous) that is secured by the mark of visible difference[19]

In einer Gesellschaft, die auf der medizinisch garantierbaren Leistungsfähigkeit jedes Einzelnen aufbaut, und in der jeder körperliche Makel, jedes Abweichen von den strengen ästhetischen Vorgaben durch chirurgische Eingriffe korrigiert werden kann, nimmt eine Behinderung, die sich aller Heilung und Rehabilitation widersetzt, einen unnatürlichen Status im medizinischen und sozialen Diskurs ein. Behinderung ist „Schicksal", behinderte Menschen sind nicht korrigierbar und deshalb irgendwie „unmenschlich", sie befinden sich ständig in einer Umgebung der „Andersartigkeit", die sie für immer von den „normalen" Konventionen alltäglicher sozialer und kultureller Handlungen ausschließt.[20]

---

[17] http://www.disability-studies-deutschland.de/dsd.php [18.12.2007]

[18] David T. Mitchell and Sharon L. Snyder (eds.), *The Body and Physical Difference: Discourses of Disability*. Michigan, 1997.

[19] Mitchell/Snyder, S. 3.

[20] Ebd., S. 4.

Die folgenden Ausführungen zu Körperlichkeit und Männlichkeit sollen in diesem Kontext der *Disability Studies* verstanden werden. Bei der Beschäftigung mit Körperlichkeit und Männlichkeit im Rahmen der *disability studies* treten einem rasch Probleme mit Begrifflichkeiten in der deutschen Sprache vor Augen, die sich im englischsprachigen Kontext so nicht ergeben. Worte wie „behindert", „anormal", „missgebildet" sind zutiefst negativ und abwertend geprägt und bieten sich als neutrale Begrifflichkeiten für eine wissenschaftliche Beschäftigung mit diesem Themenkomplex nicht an. Lässt sich die Benutzung des Wortes „behindert" auch nicht ganz vermeiden, soll wann immer möglich im Folgenden, wenn es um die besondere, von der gesellschaftlichen Norm abweichende Körperlichkeit eines Charakters geht, das Wort *disability* benutzt werden, wie es in der Einleitung zu „The Body and Physical Difference" definiert wird:

> we use the term disability to designate cognitive and physical conditions that deviate from normative ideas of mental ability and physiological function.[21]

Eine solchermaßen weit gefasste Definition erkennt an, dass „Behinderung" oder „Beeinträchtigung" mehr bedeuten als ein medizinischer Zustand oder eine „Deformiertheit" des Körpers und dass *disability* vor allem als soziales Konstrukt zu verstehen ist. Richard, dessen Körper wohl noch am ehesten unter das heutige Verständnis von „behindert" fällt, aber auch Caliban mit seinem kaum greifbaren, aber offenbar wenig menschlichen Äußeren und der enorm übergewichtige Falstaff können unter diesen *disability*-Begriff gefasst werden. Sie alle werden von ihrer Gesellschaft aufgrund ihrer Körperlichkeit als „anormal" empfunden, und scheitern im Versuch, ihre Rollen innerhalb des sozialen Gefüges auszufüllen. Sie fallen am Ende derselben Pathologisierung und Aussonderung zum Opfer, wie sie auch in der postmodernen Gesellschaft geschehen wäre, wenn auch vielleicht unter anderen Bedeutungszuweisungen ihrer Körperlichkeit.

Weniger der üblicherweise untersuchte Zusammenhang zwischen körperlichem Defizit und defizitärem Charakter – Richard als *villain*, Caliban als primitiver „Ureinwohner", Falstaff als unmoralischer Feigling –, sondern die Bedeutung ihrer körperlichen Andersartigkeit für ihre Rolle in der patriarchalischen Gesellschaft, ihre „Männlichkeit", soll im Fokus der folgenden Untersuchungen stehen.

---

[21] Mitchell/Snyder, S. 6.

Dazu soll zunächst ein Überblick über die Deutungen, Assoziationen und Erklärungsmodelle folgen, denen *disabilities* in der frühneuzeitlichen Gesellschaft unterworfen waren.

Wahrnehmung und Signifikanz außergewöhnlicher Körper in der Renaissance-Gesellschaft

Wir alle sind von den körperlichen „Anomalien", die uns auf Shakespeares Bühne begegnen, gleichzeitig fasziniert und abgestoßen:

> Physical and cognitive differences mark lives as inscrutable and mysterious, and thus we approach these artistically embellished differences with a distanced curiosity that simulates intimacy while staving off the risk of an encounter.[22]

Die Grundlage dieser Faszination ist, dass eine Erzählung von Andersartigkeit uns unserer eigenen „Normalität" und gesellschaftlichen Zugehörigkeit versichert und ein Bedürfnis nach Klarheit befriedigt, das gerade in der Renaissance, die eine langsame Ablösung von der rigiden, aber auch Halt gebenden mittelalterlichen Weltordnung erlebte, sehr drängend war. Der Mensch befreite sich aus dem ideologischen Korsett der göttlichen Vorbestimmung und erlangte eine neue Selbstständigkeit, ein Prozess, der eine enorme ideologische und individuelle Verunsicherung über den eigenen Platz im Universum mit sich brachte. Teil dieses Zwiespaltes zwischen dem anhaltenden Glauben an göttliche Strafen und Zeichen und der neuen wissenschaftlich-rationalen Beschäftigung mit Mensch und Natur ist die Wahrnehmung und Darstellung vom *monstrous bodies* in der Renaissance-Gesellschaft.

Wonder books, broadside ballads und fairground monsters

„Anormale", außergewöhnliche Körper stellen seit jeher die Konturen und Grenzen dessen in Frage, was wir für „menschlich" halten. Märchen- und Fabelwesen wie Zentauren, Riesen, Werwölfe, Meerjungfrauen und Zyklopen sind uralte kulturelle Zeugnisse unseres Umgangs mit dem fremdartigen und befremdlichen Körper, sie sind mythische Erklärungsversuche für Körperlichkeiten, die unsere Vorstellungen von Normalität sprengen und daher eigentlich nicht existieren dürften.[23]

---

[22] Mitchell/Snyder, S. 15.

[23] Rosemarie Garland Thomson, "Introduction: From Wonder to Error – A genealogy of Freak Discourse in Modernity", in: Dies. (Hrsg.), *Freakery: Cultural Spectacles of the Extraordinary Body*. New York, 1996, S. 1.

Dabei hat die Art und Weise, wie der anormale Körper innerhalb der kulturellen Vorstellung formuliert wird, historische Veränderungen durchgemacht, vom Diskurs des Fantastischen in der Vormoderne bis hin zum Diskurs des Abnormalen in unserer Zeit.

Stets jedoch war er den Projektionen und Sinngebungen der „normalen" Gemeinschaft unterworfen, denn sein Erscheinen deutete immer auf etwas anderes, über seine bloße Materialität Hinausgehendes hin. Aus dieser „Hyperrepräsentativität" rührt die früheste Bezeichnung des außergewöhnlichen Körpers als „Monster", abgeleitet von den lateinischen Begriffen *monstrare*, einer Mischung aus „monstrare", „zeigen, bezeichnen"; und „monere", „warnen und vorhersagen"[24]. Das „Monstrum" ist also eine „Warnung" und „Zeichen": seit der Antike ein Hinweis auf den göttlichen Willen, im Mittelalter eine Strafe Gottes für die moralische Verdorbenheit der Menschen und ein Schlüssel zur Aufdeckung der geheimnisvollen Mechanismen der Natur in der Aufklärung. Gleich unter welchem Erklärungsmuster es verhandelt wird, immer funktioniert das „Monster" als Mittel, um physische Devianzen zu erklären und diese gleichzeitig als „anders" festzulegen.

Die „Monstrosität" eines Körpers ist dabei ganz von kulturellen Sinngebungen und der subjektiven Auffassung des jeweiligen Beobachters abhängig: *„the monstrous designation, it seems, has less to do with what the 'monster' actually possesses and more to do with the manner in which it is perceived."*[25] Aus den etymologischen Ableitungen des „Monsters" von „monstrare" ergibt sich auch die populäre Annahme, dass der abnormale Körper eine Prophezeiung beinhalte. So sollte eine *monstrous birth*, also die Geburt eines missgebildeten Kindes, Erdbeben, Epidemien, Hungersnöte, Kriege und Thronwechsel ankündigen. Es war daher in der Renaissance-Gesellschaft von enormer Wichtigkeit, die vermeintlichen Bedeutungen dieser „prodigies" zu entziffern, da die korrekte Interpretation eine göttliche Botschaft enthüllen konnte.

Das Wort „Monster" selbst hatte im elisabethanischen England dabei eine amorphe, weit gefasste Bedeutung. Noch immer geprägt von der mittelalterlichen Vorstellung einer rigiden Weltordnung, der „chain of beings", konnte „monstrous"

---

[24] Mark Thornton Burnett, *Constructing "monsters" in Shakespearean drama and early modern culture*. Basingstoke 2002, S. 2.

[25] Burnett, S. 3.

alles bezeichnen, was als „unnatürlich" empfunden wurde, also sämtliche Erscheinungsformen, Persönlichkeitsmerkmale und Verhaltensweisen, die sich außerhalb der vorgeschriebenen Parameter befanden.[26]

„Monster" waren daher nicht, wie in der heutigen Zeit, beunruhigend auf Grund ihres unanpassbaren pathologischen Zustandes, sondern wegen der Bedeutungen, die ihren Körpern zugeschrieben wurden: Sie waren von Gott gesandte Zeichen seines Unmutes und zugleich Hinweise auf die Instabilität der Grenzen zwischen „Menschlichem" und „Unmenschlichem":

> By challenging the boundaries of the human and the coherence of what seemed to be the natural world, monstrous bodies appeared as sublime, merging the terrible with the wonderful, equalising repulsion with attraction.[27]

Diese kulturelle Signifikanz von *disabilities* führte zu einer besonderen Popularität des „Monströsen" in der Renaissance-Gesellschaft. Der außergewöhnliche Körper war zu Shakespeares Zeit im Fokus einer intensiven „troubled fascination"[28] und Objekt von *monster ballads*, Reiseberichten und Tagebüchern, öffentlichen Verkündigungen, Satiren und Theaterstücken. Es herrschte ein florierender Handel mit *wonder books*, die die bekanntesten Monster der Zeit illustrierten und interpretierten. Der Jahrmarkt mit seinen „monster booths", der Marktplatz, die Taverne und sogar Privathaushalte waren Orte, wo man für wenige Pennies mit wohligem Grusel die verschiedensten „Monstrositäten" besichtigen konnte.

Der bekannteste und älteste Jahrmarkt Londons war die dreitägige *Bartholomew Fair* in West Smithfield außerhalb der Stadtmauern Londons, die seit dem frühen zwölften Jahrhundert am Vorabend des St. Bartholomew's Day am 24. August eröffnet wurde und zu Shakespeares Zeit schon eine uralte Einrichtung war. Als religiöse Zusammenkunft zur Verehrung des heiligen Bartholomäus gegründet wurde die *Bartholomew Fair* mit der Zeit zu einer monumentalen Ansammlung des Fremden und Exotischen, „*a sort of mecca for monsters*"[29].Die „Monster" erschienen dort in einer karnevalesken Umgebung zusammen mit Seiltänzern,

---

[26] Ebd., S. 2.

[27] Garland Thomson, S. 3.

[28] Ebd., S. 1.

[29] Paul Semonin, "Monsters in the Marketplace: The Exhibition of Human Oddities in Early Modern England", in: Rosemarie Garland Thomson (Hrsg.), *Freakery: Cultural Spectacles of the Extraordinary Body*. New York, 1996, S. 76f.

Puppenspielern, Feuerschluckern und Tierdompteuren. Komische Kurzaufführungen, die „drolls", zeigten Zwerge, dressierte Tiere und Menschen mit körperlichen Anomalien. Das Monströse vermischte sich hier mit dem Theater:

> In many respects, Bartholomew Fair was a theatrical extravaganza in which the monsters were normal and their extraordinary form became part of a spectacle of the unnatural, the grotesque, and the lewd.[30]

Neben der finanziellen Ausschlachtung der Faszination des andersartigen Körpers auf dem Unterhaltungssektor hatte auch die Kirche das „Monster" als wirkungsvolles Instrument für sich entdeckt. *Prodigy literature* und *broadside ballads*, also billige, auf Handzetteln gedruckte Moritaten über die Geburt von monströsen Kindern und Tieren dienten den protestantischen Reformatoren auf verschiedene Weise dazu, die Popularität des „Monsters" für ihre eigenen Zwecke zu verdüstern:

> The ballads sought to instill fear instead of wonder in the hearts of the common people, to whom the dreadful litany of God's wreath must have become a numbing routine.[31]

Mit der sich entwickelnden „wissenschaftlichen" Beschäftigung mit *disabilities* wurde das „Monster" zum umkämpften Phänomen. Es herrschte ein Konflikt zwischen kirchlichen Predigern, die „monstrous births" vor allem als ominöse Zeichen von Gottes Unmut über sündiges Verhalten verstanden wissen wollten, und der aufkeimenden wissenschaftlichen Mentalität, die jede religiöse Signifikanz des „Monsters" ausradieren und es in einem rein medizinischen Erklärungszusammenhang zu etablieren versuchten.

Produkt dieses Forschungsinteresses am außergewöhnlichen Körper war die neue Literaturgattung der *wonder literature*, in der die rein religiöse Behandlung monströser Phänomene durch ein enzyklopädisches Interesse an Naturwundern ersetzt werden sollte. Diese „wissenschaftlichen", in Latein verfassten Abhandlungen wurden zwar plagiarisiert und in Umgangssprache übersetzt als preiswertere *prodigy books* auch an die ungebildete, aber zahlungswillige Masse verkauft. Gleichzeitig ist aber sowohl in der wissenschaftlichen als auch in der populistischen Ausrichtung eine deutliche Tendenz zur Säkularisierung des Monströsen zu

---

[30] Semonin, S. 77.
[31] Ebd., S. 72.

erkennen, da die klinischen Beschreibungen von „Monstern" nur noch gelegentlich von Abbildungen mythischer Kreaturen und mystischen Interpretationen abgewechselt wurden.[32] Den *wonder books* sowie den medizinischen Abhandlungen über die Geburten von missgebildeten Kindern und Tieren lag ein starkes Bedürfnis zugrunde, sich vom mittelalterlichen Aberglauben zu lösen und das „Monster" zu erklären, zu rationalisieren und zu entmystifizieren. Das Bedrohliche, Unerklärliche des außergewöhnlichen Körpers sollte seinen Schrecken verlieren, indem dieser in eine vermeintlich kontrollierte, wissenschaftliche Sphäre eingebunden wurde. Weil „monstrosity" eine so weit gefasste Bezeichnung war, bestand der erste „wissenschaftliche" Schritt zunächst darin, Definitionen und Klassifizierungen für dieses Phänomen zu finden, was dem jeweiligen Autor und seinen Ausführungen zusätzlich auch eine gewisse Professionalität und Glaubwürdigkeit verlieh.[33]

Eines der heute bekannteste Exemplare eines *wonder books* und der zu dieser Zeit wohl ehrgeizigste Versuch, das „Monster" zu naturalisieren, ist das bereits erwähnte, 1573 von Ambroise PARÉS verfasste Werk *Des monstres et prodigés*, ein Katalog bunt gemischter Kuriositäten wie siamesische Zwillinge, Giraffen, Hermaphroditen und Meerjungfrauen. Dennoch findet hier noch keine völlige Ablösung von der sublimen Signifikanz des „Monsters" statt: In den Ausführungen des französischen Chirurgen läuft eine klinisch-säkulare Betrachtungsweise teils parallel, teils entgegengesetzt zu religiösen Interpretationen. Sein Ansatz, so Rosemarie GARLAND THOMPSON, „*straddles the seam between wonder and error, between marvelous and medicalized narratives of the anomalous body.*"[34] Paré definiert das „Monströse" noch immer auf der Grundlage eines normativen, göttlichen Standards, nach dem „Monster" „unnatürlich" sind, weil sie nicht diesem Standard entsprechen und die Grenzen des „Normalen" überschreiten.

Von einer solchen Definition des „Monströsen" als „unnatürlich" war es im allgemeinen Verständnis und Sprachgebrauch nur ein kleiner Schritt zu einer enormen Erweiterung des Bedeutungsspektrums dieses Begriffes. Alles, was von der Norm abwich, Menschen, Gewohnheiten und soziale Praktiken, konnte demnach als „monströs" bezeichnet werden; und so wurden in öffentlichen Pamphleten und

---

[32] Semonin, S. 72.

[33] Burnett, S. 24.

[34] Garland Thompson, S. 3.

Veröffentlichungen auch Trunkenheit, Faulheit, Undankbarkeit, Lust, Mord, Prostitution Verrat, Obdachlosigkeit und vieles mehr als „monströs" gegeißelt[35].

Vom „Wunder" zum „Freak" zum „Teratum"

Im 16. Jahrhundert vollzogen Anatomie und Chirurgie entscheidende Fortschritte, denn mit der Ablösung von den mittelalterlichen moralischen und religiösen Beschränkungen wurde die Anatomie in Ansätzen zur empirischen Wissenschaft. Ein neues Körperbewusstsein entwickelte sich, einhergehend mit einer Objektivierung und Wahrnehmung des Körpers als Funktionsgefüge, das mittels der neuen medizinischen Behandlungsmethoden wiederherstellbar und reparierbar schien. Eine abgerücktere, distanzierte Sicht auf den Körper ermöglichte eine neue wissenschaftliche Erforschung. Betrachtet man die Flut von chirurgischen Traktaten, die Masse von Veröffentlichungen auch im Bereich der Anatomie, so drängt sich der Eindruck auf, dass geradezu eine Lust an dieser neuen „Einsicht" in den Körper herrschte.

In den *wonderbooks* des 16. Jahrhunderts ist noch eine gewisse Unentschlossenheit und Spannung zwischen religiösen und wissenschaftlichen Paradigmen zu erkennen: *„On the monstrous body, it might be argued, battled the competing claims of God and science."*[36]

Das Ideal einer rationalen Objektivität, das sich hier noch in den Anfängen befindet, beginnt sich im Verlauf des 17. Jahrhunderts herauszuformen, die *monstrous births* werden nun als biologisch bedingt anerkannt. Mit der Befreiung dieser Phänomene von den althergebrachten, übernatürlichen und moralischen Erklärungsmustern wurde auch die mit der Geburt eines „unnormalen" Kindes einhergehende Stigmatisierung der Eltern seltener.

Das Monster war nun in das Interesse der illustren Intellektuellenszene Londons, besonders in das der Anhänger des Naturalismus gerückt. Seit der Mitte des 17. Jahrhunderts galt der „upper class" die Lust des Volkes am „Monströsen" als eine ignorante, barbarische Vergnügung des Pöbels. Der Besuch der „monster booths" auf der Bartholomew Fair stand nun im Gegensatz zu der – nicht weniger sensationslüsternen – wissenschaftlichen Beschäftigung mit dem „Monster" in Bibliothek und Sezier-Saal, die der gebildete und wohlerzogene Mensch ausübte.[37]

---

[35] Burnett, S. 25.
[36] Burnett, S. 26.
[37] Semonin, S. 72.

In dem Maße, wie die wissenschaftliche Forschung begann, den religiösen und mythischen Anspruch auf das Monster abzulösen und durch öffentliche Sezierungen die Anatomie von außergewöhnlichen Körpern ans Licht brachte, wurde das „Monster" mehr und mehr in klinischen Zusammenhängen betrachtet. „Monster" als Wunder und göttliche Zeichen verschwinden, stattdessen werden andersartige Körper zu „Kuriositäten", zu „Launen" einer Natur, die letzten Endes nur dazu da ist, dem Menschen zu dienen, der sie mit Hilfe der Wissenschaft entschlüsselt und damit beherrscht.[38]

Der französische Zoologe Isidore Geoffroy SAINT-HILAIRE untersuchte Mitte des 19. Jahrhunderts erstmals die biologischen Ursachen für Fehlbildungen bei Embryonen[39] und begründete mit der *Teratologie* die Wissenschaft der endgültigen Entschlüsselung des „Monsters": Das erstaunliche Monster, der wundersame „Freak" wird gezähmt und rationalisiert und ist nun ein pathologisches *Teratum*, *„in brief: wonder becomes error."*[40]

Trotz der Instrumentalisierung des Monströsen für die Zwecke der reformatorischen Prediger, trotz der Entmystifizierung und Rationalisierung des außergewöhnlichen Körpers blieb das Monster doch vor allem ein Teil populärer Unterhaltung. Es ist für die folgenden Überlegungen zur Wirkung des „Bühnen-Monsters" auf das elisabethanische Publikum wichtig zu beachten, dass neben den uns als Quellen erhaltenen wissenschaftlichen und religiösen Dokumentationen mit ihrer Verachtung für den Volksglauben eine Welt von Monster-Mythen existierte, die die kulturelle Sphäre, in der diese Leute lebten, durchzog und mitgestaltete:

> While Protestant divines and naturalists were busy trying to separate humankind from nature, the popular mind still felt at home in a mental world inhabited by fabulous creatures, a realm of natural wonders based upon the ancient assumption that human beings and nature were locked into one interacting world. [41]

Neben solchen Versuchen der Definition und Klassifizierung des „Monströsen" bleibt das wichtigste Element der Beschäftigung mit außergewöhnlichen Körpern,

---

[38] Garland Thomson, S. 3.
[39] Isidore Geoffroy Saint-Hilaire, *Histoire générale et particuliére des anomalies de l'organisation chez l'homme et les animaux ou Traité de tératologie*. Paris/ Brüssel 1832-37.
[40] Semonin, S. 4.
[41] Ebd., S. 74.

ihre Ursachen festzustellen. Es gab eine Vielzahl von Ansätzen, die die Entstehung von „Monstern erklären sollten, von denen einer, das Phänomen der „unnatural birth", im Folgenden näher betrachtet werden soll.

„Unnatural births"

> From forth the kennel of thy womb hath crept A hellhound... (R III., IV.4.47-48)

Das Phänomen der so genannten „unnatural births" hatte eine besonders hohe wissenschaftliche und kulturelle Faszination. Sehr populäre *broadside ballads* und verschiedene Traktate von Gelehrten dieser Epoche über „unnatürliche" Geburten deformierter Kinder und Tiere lösten beim Publikum wohliges Schaudern und abergläubische Furcht aus. Im Volksglauben wurde die Geburt eines missgebildeten Kindes oder auch Tieres stets als unheilverkündend interpretiert, mit schicksalhaften Auswirkungen auf die gesamte Nation. Jede Abnormalität wurde dabei als Zeichen für eine bestimmte Verkommenheit des englischen Volkes gedeutet: Ein missgestalteter Mund beispielsweise stand für verrohte Sprache, eine Hand ohne Finger für Faulheit, Missbildungen am Unterleib folglich für perverse sexuelle Gelüste: „*the hinder part (...) shew vs playne, / Our close and hidden vice.*"[42]

Als Ursachen für „monstrous births" wurden aber nur indirekt die moralischen Abwege des Volkes angeführt. An erster Stelle wurden sie als Folgen sündigen Verhaltens der Eltern, vor allem aber der werdenden Mutter, interpretiert, wie etwa abnormale sexuelle Praktiken während Empfängnis oder Schwangerschaft. Allein die Gedanken der Frau während des Geschlechtsverkehrs konnten seinen Erkenntnissen nach zu Abnormalitäten des Kindes führen: Dachte sie dabei etwa an einen „blackamoore", bestand die Gefahr, dass sie ein dunkelhäutiges Kind zu Welt brachte.[43]

Die so gewonnenen Erkenntnisse waren also nicht objektiv wissenschaftlich im Sinne des heutigen Verständnisses, sondern geprägt von abergläubischen und pseudo-wissenschaftlichen Konzeptionen und Konstrukten vor allem des Weibli-

---

[42] "The forme and shape of a monstrous Child, borne at Maydstone".(London 1586); Joseph Lilly, *A collection of seventy-nine black-letter ballads and broadsides*. London, 1867, S. 19497, online einsehbar unter http://www.openlibrary.org/details/collectionofseve00lillrich [12.12.2007].

[43] Ian Frederick Moulton: *"A Monster Great Deformed": The Unruly Masculinity of Richard III*. Shakespeare Quarterly 47 (3) 1996, S. 263.

chen, das es in einem patriarchalischen Systems beständig als zu Recht unterdrücktes Geschlecht zu bestätigen galt. Die beängstigende Fähigkeit der Frau, Leben zu schenken und die damit einhergehende Macht über das ungeborene Kind in ihr uferte aus in pseudo-medizinischen Theorien über Fähigkeiten, den Fötus zu manipulieren oder gar abzutöten, indem sie es im Uterus quasi „erwürgte". JANET ADELMANN beschreibt in „*Suffocating Mothers*" den in der Frühen Neuzeit herrschenden Glauben, „*that the mother could literally deform fetuses through her excessive imagination, her uncontrollable longings, her unnatural lusts*"[44].

Auch nach der Geburt bestand für den Säugling Gefahr seitens der Mutter: Nach heutigen Erkenntnissen ist eine Ursache für die hohe Kindersterblichkeit dieser Zeit die Mangelernährung als Konsequenz aus der Annahme, die Milch der Mutter sei in der Phase nach der Geburt schädlich für das Kind, da sie aus umgewandeltem Menstruationsblut bestehe.[45] Säuglinge wurden daher zunächst mit Ersatznahrung gefüttert und an eine Amme übergeben, die im Glauben, dass über die Muttermilch dem Kind womöglich auch unerwünschte Eigenschaften der jeweiligen Frau übertragen würden, sorgfältig auf ihre Charaktereigenschaften hin ausgesucht wurde.[46] Abgesehen vom Entzug der lebenswichtigen Muttermilch war damit auch die frühkindliche Bindung an die Mutter, die heute als für eine gesunde psychische Entwicklung grundlegend gilt, zu dieser Zeit sehr häufig nicht gegeben. So wird das Motiv der emotional distanzierten oder erst gar nicht vorhandenen Mutter als Ursache seelischer Konflikte auch in Shakespeares Dramen immer wieder aufgegriffen: „*Love foreswore, me in my mother's womb*" (3HVI 3.2.153).

Nachdem nun die verschiedenen, teils miteinander konkurrierenden Wahrnehmungen und Bedeutungszuweisungen des außergewöhnlichen Körpers in der Frühen Neuzeit dargestellt wurden, sollen im Folgenden zeitgenössische medizinische und (pseudo-)wissenschaftliche Vorstellungen von sexueller Identität gezeigt werden, die grundlegend für das Verständnis und die Analyse der drei zu untersuchenden Charaktere sind.

---

[44] Adelmann, S. 6.

[45] Thomas Laqueur, *Auf den Leib geschrieben. Die Inszenierung der Geschlechter von der Antike bis Freud.* Übers. v. H. Jochen Bußmann, Frankfurt/New York, 1990, S. 123

[46] Adelmann, S. 7.

Konzepte sexueller Identität in der Frühen Neuzeit

Wir haben es im frühneuzeitlichen England mit einer patriarchalischen Gesellschaft zu tun, in der die Legitimierung der männlichen Herrschaft auf von Männern konstruierten Ideologien über geistige und körperliche Fähigkeiten, Anatomie, Sexualität und *Gender* basierte.

Allerdings fehlte zu dieser Zeit der für uns so selbstverständliche – und in seiner Signifikanz von Judith Butler in Frage gestellte – solide biologische Unterbau für das, was als „männlich" oder „weiblich" galt. Wie Will FISHER mit Bezug auf Judith Butlers *Bodies that Matter* argumentiert, gelten unsere modernen Kategorien vom biologischen Geschlecht mit primären und sekundären Geschlechtsmerkmalen nicht für Shakespeares Zeitgenossen:

> The sexual differences that 'mattered' in the early modern period are not neccessarily the same as those that 'matter' today.[47]

Die frühneuzeitlichen medizinischen Vorstellungen von geschlechtskonstituierenden Körpereigenschaften sind durch eine bedrohliche Instabilität gekennzeichnet, bestehen sie doch aus einer prekären Ausbalanciertheit der Körpersäfte und einer Vorstellung von isomorphen Geschlechtsorganen bei Mann und Frau – biologische „Männlichkeit" also als ein Zustand, der sich ständig ins Weibliche umkehren kann.

Sexualität vor dem Hintergrund der Humoralpathologie

Anders als in heute vorherrschenden Assoziationen von *disabilities* wurden diese in der Renaissance weder zwangsläufig mit körperlicher Schwäche in Verbindung gebracht, noch wurde die Sexualität behinderter Menschen tabuisiert oder eine Asexualität vorausgesetzt. Im Gegenteil sahen Universalphilosophen wie Michel de Montaigne (1533-1592) und Francis Bacon (1561-1626) eine medizinische Verbindung zwischen körperlichen Missbildungen und erotischen Fähigkeiten.[48]

Während Montaigne Behinderten oder Missgebildeten beider Geschlechter eine erhöhte sexuelle Kraft und vergrößerte Genitalien beimaß, formulierte Bacon

---

[47] Will Fisher, "The Renaissance Beard: Masculinity in Modern England", in: *Renaissance Quarterly* 54 (2001), S. 156.

[48] Moulton, S. 264.

1625 in seinem Essay „Of Deformity" die Vermutung, physische Deformiertheit sei ein äußeres Zeichen für sexuelle Perversität.[49]

Solche „wissenschaftlichen" Untersuchungen basieren auf der in der Frühen Neuzeit richtungsweisenden Humoralpathologie oder Viersäftelehre, die im 4. Jahrhundert vor Christus von den Hippokratikern entwickelt und von dem Arzt und Anatomen Galenos von Pergamon sechshundert Jahre später in seiner endgültigen, bis ins 19. Jahrhundert einflussreichen Form niedergeschrieben wurde.[50]

Grundlegend ist dabei die Annahme, der Körper sei ein „Behältnis" von vier Körperflüssigkeiten, Blut (= lat.: *sanguis*), gelbe Galle (= griech. *cholé*), schwarze Galle (= *mélas cholé*) und Schleim (= griech. *phlegma*), deren individuelle Zusammensetzung die Grundkonstitution des Menschen bestimmt. Jede Flüssigkeit wird einem Element zugeordnet und entsteht in einem bestimmten Organ. So ist Blut, das im Herzen gebildet wird, der konstituierende Saft der Sanguiniker und dem Element Luft zuzuordnen; gelbe Galle, die aus der Leber stammt, wird den Cholerikern sowie dem Element Feuer zugeordnet; schwarze Galle, die in der Milz und den Hoden produziert wird, bestimmt den Charakter der Melancholiker und gehört zum Element Erde. Schleim zuletzt, der im Gehirn produziert wird, bestimmt das Wesen der Phlegmatiker und hat Bezug zum Element Wasser.

Eine Mischung aus allen vier Körpersäften fließt in den Adern des Menschen[51], erstrebenswert und entscheidend für die physische und psychische Gesundheit – beide sind voneinander untrennbar – ist aber ein Equilibrium der Körpersäfte.

Da das Humoralsystem abhängig von der Temperatur und Menge der Flüssigkeiten im Körper ist, können Krankheiten seelischer und körperlicher Natur durch die Regulation des Säfte-Gleichgewichts geheilt werden, indem man dem Körper heiße, kalte, feuchte oder trockene Substanzen hinzufügt oder entnimmt, wie etwa beim Aderlass. Der Grundzustand beim Mann sollte dabei heiß und trocken sein, bei der Frau kalt und feucht, wobei sich schon andeutet, dass es sich bei dem gesamten Konzept der Humoral-Medizin um ein von vornherein „gegendertes" Prinzip handelt:

---

[49] Francis Bacon, *Essays, Civil and Moral*. Vol. III, Part 1. The Harvard Classics. New York, 1909–14; online unter www.bartleby.com/3/1/ [12.03.2008].

[50] Die folgenden Ausführungen zur frühneuzeitlichen Humoralpathologie basieren auf dem Kapitel „Bodies of rule: embodiment and interiority in early modern England", aus Mark Schoenfeldt, *Bodies and Selves in Early Modern England. Physiology and Inwardness in Spenser, Shakespeare, Herbert, and Milton*. Cambridge, 1999, S. 1-40.

[51] Bruce R. Smith, *Shakespeare and Masculinity*. Oxford 2000, S. 72.

„Männlichkeit" als eine Funktion der Körperchemie ist verbunden mit den edleren Elementen Luft und Wasser und mit den „heißeren", also aktiveren, aggressiven Körpersäften Blut und gelbe Galle. Die „männlichen" Grundtemperamente sind also die des „Sanguinikers", eines lebhaften, leichtblütigen Menschen oder des Cholerikers, im positiven Sinne willensstark und furchtlos. Die Frau dagegen ist bestimmt von den „schweren" Elementen Wasser und Erde, die über die korrespondierenden Säfte Schwarze Galle und Schleim zu den Grundtemperamenten Melancholie und Phlegmatismus, also Schwermütigkeit und Passivität führten.

Auch unterscheidet der weibliche Körper sich vom männlichen insofern, als dass die Frau im Gegensatz zum Mann nicht in der Lage ist, die Balance und den Abfluss ihrer Körperflüssigkeiten zu regulieren. Als Zeichen dafür galt das Menstruationsblut, das offensichtlich keine besondere Funktion im Körper hatte und zudem von vielen als giftig angesehen wurde.[52] Die Tatsache, dass der weibliche Genitalbereich im Vergleich zum männlichen eine „Öffnung" aufweist, diente als Erklärung für die Unfähigkeit, ihren „offenen" Körper als Behälter der verschiedenen humoralen Flüssigkeiten zu kontrollieren. Als symptomatisch für diese Tatsache galt die ständig wechselnde, instabile Gemütslage der Frau, die anders als der Mann unfähig war, ihren Verstand über ihre Körperfunktionen herrschen zu lassen. Das zeigte auch die weibliche Geschwätzigkeit, denn offenbar war eine Frau nicht einmal fähig, die Worte bei sich zu halten, die ihrem Körper entweichen.[53]

Im Gegensatz dazu steht das geschlossene System des männlichen, kontrollierten Körpers mit den wichtigsten männlichen Säften, Galle und Blut. Galle, mit Sitz im Gehirn, repräsentiert die Tatkraft, den Mut, vor allem aber den überlegenen männlichen Verstand. Dennoch: nicht Galle, sondern *„blood is the humour that makes men men"*[54], und das nicht nur, weil es für Stärke, Leidenschaft und Vitalität steht. Der Hauptgrund, warum das männliche Blut eine herausgehobene Wichtigkeit besitzt, besteht darin, dass es die Grundlage zur Produktion von Samen ist. Diese erfordert eine starke Erhitzung des Blutes, was Frauen die Initialrolle in der Fortpflanzung von vornherein unmöglich macht, da sie ja von Natur aus kälter sind. Sperma ist demnach nichts anderes, als durch Hitze veredeltes, weiß gewordenes Blut.

---

[52] Mark Breitenberg: *Anxious Masculinity in Early Modern England.* Cambridge 1996, S. 49.
[53] Smith, S. 16.
[54] Ebd., S. 20.

Hier entsteht, wie Mark BREITENBERG in „Anxious Masculinity" ausführt, ein Dilemma:

> The paradox in this cultural and anatomical code is that if the generation of semen (heated blood) is the most quintessentially masculine moment, it is also, finally, just a moment.[55]

Die Ejakulation als „Höhepunkt" der Männlichkeit ist gleichzeitig der Moment höchster Gefährdung des maskulinen Prinzips, denn was ist sie anderes als der Verlust der Kontrolle über die Körpersäfte und damit ein Rückfall in das weibliche Prinzip? So ist der Samenerguss gleichzeitig der Verlust von Männlichkeit, aber auch medizinische Notwendigkeit, denn ein Übermaß an Sperma im Körper würde das humorale Gleichgewicht und damit die körperliche und geistige Gesundheit stören.

Die Frau als Auslöserin einer erotischen Begierde, der der Mann sich hilflos ausgesetzt sieht, ist die Ursache für diesen Moment des männlichen Kontrollverlustes, sie reißt ihn mit herunter auf ihre niedere, rein körperliche Ebene, die Hierarchie von *Gender* und sozialem Status wird in dieser Situation aufgehoben. „Männlichkeit" war also nicht nur durch einen Verlust der humoralen Balance gefährdet, sondern auch durch die Frau, die den Mann mit ihrer Sexualität zu ihrem Opfer machte.

Mark BREITENBERG stellt in seiner Beschäftigung mit dem frühmodernen England die These auf, dass diese Gesellschaft auf der geschlechterpolitischen Ebene nicht dem viel zitierten elisabethanischen Weltbild, der „great chain of beings" gemäß strikt geordnet, sondern von Konflikten, Unsicherheiten und Ängsten geprägt sei:

> A cauldron of bubbling anxieties, a language of unresolvable contradictions and paradoxes, a world gray and ambivalent rather than clear and recognizable.[56]

Das Patriarchat ist ein soziales System, dessen Fundament eine als „natürlich" vorausgesetzte Ungleichheit seiner Mitglieder ist. Produkt und zugleich antreibende Kraft dieses Systems ist eine ständige Angst derjenigen, deren Überlegenheit auf selbst konstruierten und aufrecht zu erhaltenen Voraussetzungen beruht, vor dem möglichen Verlust ihrer Privilegien.

---

[55] Ebd., S. 50.
[56] Breitenberg, S. 1.

Die Grundsätze der patriarachalen Ordnung müssen, gemäß dem bei FOUCAULT und BUTLER diskutierten regulierenden Ideal, ständig verteidigt und von neuem bekräftigt werden, um die als naturgegeben konstruierte Macht und Autorität des Mannes aufrecht zu erhalten.

Die Angst vor der Zerstörung der machtkonstituierenden Geschlechteridentitäten war dabei eine durchaus materielle, denn ein Element, dass das Konstrukt von „Männlichkeit" und ihrer natürlichen Überlegenheit besonders prekär machte, war die damals vorherrschende Vorstellung vom Ein-Geschlecht-Körper, die im nächsten Schritt umrissen werden soll.

Zwei Körper – ein Geschlecht

Trotz der Fortschritte in der Anatomie, trotz der neuen Lust am Betrachten des Körpers herrschte noch das aus der Antike übernommene Prinzip des „Ein-Geschlecht-Leibes". Das heißt, die für unser heutiges Geschlechterverständnis ganz fundamentale und selbstverständliche biologische Basis der Verschiedenheit von Mann und Frau war zu dieser Zeit nicht gegeben, es gab nur einen einzigen „Grund-Körper", und der war männlich. Die doch scheinbar ganz offensichtlichen körperlichen Unterschiede, die heute als „primäre und sekundäre Geschlechtsmerkmale" bezeichnet werden, erklärten sich in der Unvollkommenheit der weiblichen Version des Körpers, der seit antiker Zeit als schöpferischer „Defekt", als Devianz vom idealen männlichen Körper galt. Anders als zu vermuten wäre widerlegten die neuen empirischen Untersuchungen nicht die antiken Theorien, die weiblichen Geschlechtsorgane seien nur eine innenliegende, quasi umgestülpte Kopie der männlichen, sondern wurden zu ihrer Bestätigung herangezogen. Man ging also davon aus, der Gebärmutterhals sei das Pendant zum Penis und der Uterus entspräche dem Scrotum. Eine eigene dezidierte Terminologie für die weiblichen Genitalien gab es nicht; selbst anatomische „Neuentdeckungen", die von dieser Annahme der Isomorphie der Geschlechtsorgane abwichen, wie etwa die der Klitoris, wurden ohne weitere Erklärungen stillschweigend der Ein-Geschlecht-Theorie untergeordnet.

Man sah das, was man sehen wollte: Auch das Öffnen des Körpers, das Zutagebringen des vermeintlich nun buchstäblich „Offen"-sichtlichen, konnte das Bild vom „misslungenen" weiblichen Körper, das ja unter anderem zur Legitimierung der Beherrschung der Frau diente, nicht ins Wanken bringen, wie Thomas LAQUEUR in „Making Sex" zeigt:

> Die Geschichte der Anatomie während der Renaissance weist darauf hin, dass die anatomische Repräsentation von Mann und Frau nicht

von der Evidenz von Organen, Kanälen oder Blutgefäßen abhängt, sondern von dem soziokulturell geprägten Umgang mit Repräsentation und Illusion.[57]

Die Überzeugung, Mann und Frau seien nicht zwei verschiedene Geschlechter, sondern Versionen des einen männlichen Körpers, barg aber eine bedrohliche Möglichkeit der Transferenz in sich, denn die nach innen gestülpten Genitalien der Frau, die sich nur wegen ihrer kälteren humoralen Konstitution nicht wie beim Mann außerhalb des Körpers befanden, konnten bei einer starken Veränderung des Humoralhaushalts oder durch andere Vorfälle aus dem Körper „herausspringen" und so in einem einzigen Moment die Frau zum Mann machen. Solche Fälle waren keinesfalls abwegig und sogar in der „wissenschaftlichen" Literatur belegt, zum Beispiel bei Montaigne in seiner „Marie-Germain"-Anekdote.[58]

Da ein (Selbst-)Bewusstsein von der biologischen, also der „natürlichen" Unabänderlichkeit des eigenen Geschlechts und damit des eigenen Status in der Gesellschaft der Frühen Neuzeit nicht vorhanden war, war es um so mehr nötig, die Normen und Ideologien, die Männlichkeit und Weiblichkeit definieren sollten, materiell, also nach BUTLER „sozial signifikant" zu machen. Mit dem Ein-Geschlecht-Leib als Grundlage des *Sex*-Verständnisses dieser Zeit wird ihre Theorie des *doing gender*, die ja wegen der weitestgehenden Ausklammerung des tatsächlichen physiologischen Körpers kritisiert wird, umso greifbarer, denn hier ist effektiv keine physiologische, sondern nur eine soziale Geschlechteridentität vorhanden, die ständig durch „gender performance" materialisiert werden muss. Ohne klare Zuschreibungen von Rollen, Verhaltensweisen, Möglichkeiten und Begrenzungen von „Mann-Sein" und „Frau-Sein" war das vormoderne Patriarchat nicht existenzfähig. Körperliche Geschlechtsidentität musste durch bestimmte Requisiten materialisiert werden, die quasi als „Prothesen" für die uneindeutigen Genitalien dienten:

> I would argue that sex was materialized through an array of features and prosthetic parts. A list of some of these parts would have to include clothing, the hair, the tongue, the weapons…[59]

---

[57] Thomas Laqueur, *Auf den Leib geschrieben. Die Inszenierung der Geschlechter von der Antike bis Freud.* Übs. V. H. Jochen Bußmann, Frankfurt/New York 1990, S. 83.

[58] Will Fisher, "The Renaissance Beard: Masculinity in Modern England", in: *Renaissance Quarterly* 54 (2001), S. 157.

[59] Ebd., S. 157.

Hierher rührte wohl auch das gesellschaftliche Unbehagen angesichts der „boy actors" und der modischen Eskapaden einiger Londonerinnen Anfang des 17. Jahrhunderts, die sich wie Männer kleideten und damit einen Sturm der Entrüstung auslösten, der sich in feurigen Predigten, Gedichten und Pamphleten äußerte, darunter auch das „Hic-Mulier"-Pamphlet von 1620. In *„Anxious Masculinity"* schreibt Mark BREITENBERG dazu:

> We may take a step further to say that the primary fear to which these texts respond is the intolerable possibility of sameness between women and men, a possibility that would render meaningless both the gender/status system (and) the individual subjectivities within it.[60]

Die englische Gesellschaft der Renaissance-Zeit befand sich also in einer ständigen Spannung, verursacht durch das Bestehen auf äußeren, als „natürlich" dargestellten *Gender*-Zuschreibungen und einer zugrunde liegenden biologischen Unklarheit der Geschlechter-Unterschiede, die den vermeintlich gottgegebenen privilegierten Status des Mannes jederzeit aufheben könnte. Wenn im Folgenden also Richard III., Caliban und Falstaff als Männer mit *monstrous bodies* innerhalb einer patriarchalischen Gesellschaft betrachtet werden, gilt es, die Signifikanz ihrer Körperlichkeit sowohl aufgrund der mythischen und wissenschaftlichen Zuschreibungen von Monstrosität als auch der pathologischen Bedeutung ihrer *disabilities* für ihre Männlichkeit zu beachten.

---

[60] Breitenberg, S. 153.

Richard III. – Ein „Monster" auf dem Thron

> Sin, death, and hell have set their marks on him,
> And all their ministers attend to him (R III., I.3.292-93)

Die moderne Geschlechterforschung hat bei der Untersuchung von Literatur in den allermeisten Fällen vor allem die weiblichen Figuren im Blick. In *Richard III* scheinen die Frauen, die in den drei *„Henry VI"*-Dramen noch so aktiv und mächtig waren, in den Hintergrund gedrängt, ein *Gender*-Konflikt ist zunächst nicht auszumachen, denn die Handlung scheint sich um die für die Historien typischen politischen Ränkespiele zu drehen: *„Because it is wholly a political world, it, too, offers few metaphysical problems"*.[61] Diese Beobachtung von LINDA BAMBER zu den *history plays* wird *Richard III* jedoch bei weitem nicht gerecht. Viel mehr, als es zunächst den Anschein hat, spielt *Gender*, und ganz besonders die Darstellung und Funktionsweisen von „Männlichkeit", in diesem Drama eine bedeutende Rolle. Denn Richard ist kein geschlechtsloser Krüppel, sondern ein Mann, dessen übersteigerte Männlichkeit – und nicht etwa stereotypische „Bosheit" – zur Gefahr für die Gesellschaft wird.

Dass Richard nicht durch seine „monströse" Körperlichkeit, sondern durch seine Position in der patriarchalischen Gesellschaft, also nicht in erster Linie durch seine *disabilities*, sondern durch seine daraus resultierende verhinderte Männlichkeit zum „Monster" wird, soll im Folgenden gezeigt werden. Zunächst soll aber ein Überblick über das historische Vorbild folgen, nach dem Shakespeare den Bühnencharakter und auch den Körper von Richard III. modelliert hat.

„Villain king?" – Der historische Richard

> As he was small and little of stature, so was he of bodie greatlie deformed; the one shoulder higher than the other; his face was small, but his countenance cruell, and such, that at the first aspect a man would iudge it to sauour and smell of malice, fraud, and deceit. When he stood musing, he would bite and chew busilie his nether lip; as who said, that his fierce nature in his cruell bodie chafed, stirred, and was euer unquiet (Holinshed's Chronicles, 1577)

---

[61] Linda Bamber, *Comic Women, Tragic Men. A Study of Gender and Genre in Shakespeare*. Stanford, 1982, S.23.

Noch fünfhundert Jahre nach seiner kurzen Herrschaft wird die „wahre" historische Person Richard III. in der modernen Geschichtswissenschaft kontrovers diskutiert. Die Tendenz der Erkenntnisse geht inzwischen dahin, dass eine große Zahl der ihm posthum zugeschriebenen Untaten und Grausamkeiten auf einer Art Propaganda der nachfolgenden Tudor-Monarchie beruht, die nach der gewaltsamen Ergreifung der Krone selbst unter einigem Legitimierungsdruck gestanden haben dürfte. Teil dieser gezielten Negativdarstellung war wohl auch die Darstellung des Gestürzten als deformiertes Monstrum, denn in den vorliegenden zeitgenössischen Quellen ist von keinerlei Missbildungen die Rede, die, wären sie tatsächlich so dramatisch gewesen wie später behauptet, doch sicherlich irgendwo hätten Erwähnung finden müssen.

Thomas MORES „*History of King Richard*", herausgegeben 1557 und vermutlich eine der Inspirationsquellen für Shakespeares Bühnencharakter Richard, ist ein für die humanistische Geschichtsschreibung typisches Werk. Anders als heute ging es in vormodernen Geschichtsdarstellungen weniger um historische Akkuratheit als um den moralischen und erzieherischen Wert des Beschriebenen. Die oftmals reichlich ausgeschmückten, großzügig mit fiktiven Elementen garnierten Schilderungen hatten die didaktische Absicht, dem Leser „nachahmenswerte und abschreckende Beispiele aus dem Leben guter und schlechter Menschen vor Augen zu führen".[62] Auf diesen Schilderungen, wie hoch auch immer ihr Wahrheitsgehalt ist, basiert auch Shakespeares Theaterfigur, und gerade die ihm zugeschriebenen „Monstrositäten" mögen seine Person zu einer so geeigneten Vorlage für eine Tragödie beziehungsweise Historie (denn es ist nach wie vor strittig, ob *Richard III* zu den Historien oder Tragödien gezählt werden soll) gemacht haben.

Shakespeares fiktive Darstellung dieses englischen Königs hat über die Jahrhunderte die immer mehr in Vergessenheit geratende historische Person Richard III. ersetzt. Die Fiktion scheint heute greifbarer als die historische Wahrheit, die sich ohnehin nicht mehr vollkommen rekonstruieren lässt, auch wenn einige Wissenschaftler und Hobby-Historiker, die sich zu der „*Richard III Society*" zusammengeschlossen haben, nach wie vor versuchen, Richard von seinem schlechten Image zu befreien und Drama und Geschichte zu trennen.[63]

---

[62] Christine von Eichel-Streiber, *Die Dramatisierung des Konflikts von Individuum und Gesellschaft in Shakespeares Richard III*. Frankfurt a. M. 1982 (Diss.), S. 104.

[63] URL der Richard III Society: http://www.richardiii.net/begin.htm [17.12.2007].

Ob die reale Person Richard nun tatsächlich einen deformierten Körper hatte oder nicht – für den Bühnencharakter Richard III. erzeugt seine körperliche Beschaffenheit von Anfang an eine besondere Wahrnehmung durch das zeitgenössische Publikum, das aufgrund der allgemeinen Kenntnisse über die populäre Schreckgestalt der englischen Geschichte das Drama sicherlich mit gewissen Erwartungen und Konzeptionen gegenüber der Darstellungsweise der Bühnenfigur durch den Schauspieler verfolgte.

Mehr als bei allen anderen Shakespeare-Figuren wird die Aufmerksamkeit des Zuschauers von Anfang an auf Richards Körperlichkeit hingelenkt, beginnend in der allerersten Szene. Im starken Gegensatz zu den Eingangsszenen der vorangegangen Stücke der Tetralogie, in welchen die Bühne von Personen zu wimmeln scheint und in welchen in einer Art Zusammenfassung der bisherige Verlauf der historischen Ereignisse ausführlich geschildert wird, steht Richard völlig allein auf der Bühne und lässt das Geschehene aus eigener Sicht Revue passieren, „*a single figure into which the scope of English history seems to compact itself*"[64].

Die Erwartungshaltung des Publikums wird hier also ausgenutzt, indem man die Korporealität Richards gleich zu Anfang in den Mittelpunkt rückt und dem Betrachter während des langen Monologs genug Zeit gibt, um die physische Beschaffenheit der Figur genau zu studieren. Auch Richards Sprache dient in diesem Monolog so wie während des gesamten Stückes dazu, die Aufmerksamkeit immer wieder auf seinen Körper zu lenken. Er selbst beschreibt seine Monstrosität mit beißender Selbstironie und gesteht seine bösen Absichten nicht nur, sondern begründet sie geradezu mit seiner körperlichen Beschaffenheit: „*cheated of feature by dissembling Nature*"(I.1.19) ist er „*determined to prove a villain*" (I.1.30). Hier wird eine weitere Präkonzeption des Zuschauers aufgenommen und bestätigt, nämlich der Zusammenhang zwischen seiner körperlichen und seiner moralischen Monstrosität, eine Vorstellung, die in der Frühen Neuzeit selbstverständlich war.

Richards Körper in der Diagnose der frühneuzeitlichen Medizin

Wie lassen sich die Konzepte von körperlichen Missbildungen und medizinischen Zusammenhängen, die zur Zeit der Entstehung von *Richard III* im elisabethanischen England kursierten, auf dessen spezielle Korporealität anwenden?

---

[64] Marie A. Plasse, *Corporeality and the Opening of Richard III*. In: Willson, Robert F. Junior, *Entering the Maze: Shakespeare's Art of beginning*. New York, 1995, S. 11.

Folgt man den zeitgenössischen Deutungen der „unnatural births", war schon Richards Geburt ein Zeichen für Unheil, eine Bedrohung für die Gesellschaft, begleitet von düsteren Omen, wie King Henry VI. sich in der Szene seiner Ermordung erinnert:

> The owl shriek'd at thy birth – an evil sign;
> The night-crow cried, aboding luckless time;
> Dogs howl'd, and hideous tempest shook down trees;
> The raven rook'd her on the chimney's top,... (3HVI, 5.6.44-48)

Aus der zeitgenössischen medizinischen Perspektive deutet Richards Deformiertheit schon auf den ersten Blick auf eine ungesunde Veränderung seines erotischen Haushaltes hin. Folgt man Bacon und Montaigne, ist er entweder ein sexueller Akrobat mit großem Genital oder ein durch seine äußerliche Abnormalität gekennzeichneter Perverser. Seine eigenen Aussagen, was das sexuelle Verhältnis zu Frauen angeht, gehen aber weder in die eine noch in die andere Richtung. Mag er aufgrund seiner *disabilities* auch eigentlich für eine gesteigerte Libido veranlagt sein, schätzt er seine Attraktivität für das andere Geschlecht selbst doch eher gering ein:

> I'll make my heaven in a lady's lap, (...) And witch sweet ladies with my words and looks. / O miserable thought! And more unlikely / Than to accomplish twenty golden crowns. (3HVI, 3.2.148-52).

Es sind tatsächlich vor allem die Frauen, die, degradiert zu passiven Schachfiguren in seinem Intrigenspiel, sein abstoßendes Äußeres kommentieren. „*Never hung poison on a fouler toad. / Out of my sight! Thou dost infect mine eyes.*" (RIII, 1.2.147) schleudert ihm Lady Anne während der spektakulären Werbungsszene entgegen, und Queen Margaret bezeichnet ihn als „*lump of foul deformity*" (RIII, 1.2.57), als „*elvish-mark'd, abortive, rooting hog*" (RIII,1.3.228). „Abortive" kann hier als „missgestaltet", aber auch als „unfruchtbar" verstanden werden, könnte also ein Hinweis auf seine Unfruchtbarkeit sein.

In Richards Unfähigkeit, eine sexuelle oder gar Liebesbeziehung zu einer Frau einzugehen, liegt laut Janet ADELMANN auch der Grund für seinen tödlichen Ehrgeiz. Sein Hunger nach Macht ist Ersatz für seine sexuelle Impotenz:

> He will remake himself in the image of a commanding and overbearing political ambition, finding his masculine potency through the substitute heaven of the crown.[65]

Die enorme Tatkraft, die er in der Verfolgung seiner Ziele an den Tag legt, lässt sich auch mit Hilfe der frühneuzeitlichen Medizin erklären. Die angedeutete Impotenz führt zu einer Verlagerung der körperlichen Energien, die sich, da seine Genitalien nicht funktionstüchtig sind, andere Kanäle zur Entladung suchen, und hier liegt laut Ian Frederick MOULTON die soziale Dynamik von Richards Missgestaltetheit: „*That which is unable to raise itself physically may rise socially instead*"[66].

Immer wieder wird Richard von den anderen Personen im Stück mit Blut assoziiert: Richmond nennt ihn einen „*bloody tyrant and a homicide; / one raised in blood, and one in blood established*" (RIII, 5.3.247-8), seine eigene Mutter, die Duchess of York, prophezeit ihm „*Bloody thou art, bloody will be thy end*" (RIII, 4.4.195).

Wenn Richards Körper, wie durch die Reaktionen seiner Umwelt zu vermuten ist, ein Übermaß an Blut aufweist, würde dies auch bedeuten – wenn man zusätzlich noch die durch seine Deformiertheit gesteigerte erotische Kraft mit einbezieht –, dass seine Spermaproduktion gewissermaßen auf „Hochtouren" läuft. Da er aber keine Gelegenheit zu einer für die Balance seiner Humoralkonstitution unumgängliche „Entladung" des Überschusses an Samen beziehungsweise Blut hat, muss man davon ausgehen, dass seine geistige und körperliche Gesundheit leidet. Hinzu kommt eine offensichtlich übersteigerte innere Hitze, auf die er selbst hinweist:

> I cannot weep, for all my body's moisture
> Scarce serve to quench my furnace burning heart;... (3 HVI, 2.1. 79-80)

Eine derart dramatisch gesteigerte Hitze, zugleich ein weiteres Zeichen übersteigerter Männlichkeit, führt laut Viersäftelehre nach und nach zu der Austrocknung der Körperflüssigkeiten, was auch eine Erklärung für Richards Unfähigkeit ist, beim Tod seines geliebten Vaters zu weinen. Auch wenn Weinen in der Situation,

---

[65] Adelmann, S. 2.
[66] Moulton, S. 265.

gerade dieser Situation, in der frühneuzeitlichen Kultur durchaus erlaubt war[67], galt es doch im Allgemeinen als kindisch und „effeminate", denn auch das Vergießen von Tränen bedeutete für den Mann letztendlich einen gefährlichen Verlust der Kontrolle über den Körper: „*Tears then for babes; blows and revenge for me!*" (3HVI, II.1.86).

Da die Körpersäfte in untrennbarer gegenseitiger Abhängigkeit stehen, lässt sich aus der Ausgetrocknetheit seiner Tränen schließen, dass auch sein Samen vertrocknet ist.

So bedeuten allein seine körperliche Beschaffenheit und die Umstände seiner Geburt eine Bedrohung für die Gesellschaft und zugleich eine womöglich perverse, in jedem Falle aber gesteigerte und zugleich verhinderte Sexualität. Da seine sexuelle Kraft, zusätzlich angefeuert durch sein sanguinisches Temperament, in der Praxis nicht zur Entfaltung kommt – sei es, weil er aufgrund seiner körperlichen Handicaps impotent ist oder wegen seiner Unfähigkeit, sich Frauen zu nähern – sucht sich seine Energie andere Ventile im Bereich des politischen Machtkampfes.

Aufgrund der zeitgenössischen kulturellen und medizinischen Deutungsmuster lässt Shakespeares Richard III. sich also als hypermaskuliner Mann charakterisieren, dessen eigentlich sexuelle Energie, seine Leidenschaft kein „Ventil" findet und sich deshalb in seinen aggressiven politischen Ambitionen äußert. Sein humoralpathologischer Haushalt und seine körperliche Beschaffenheit bilden dabei ein gefährliches Paradox: Nicht nur, dass er durch seine Impotenz in ständiger sexueller Frustration lebt, die sich in seiner Misogynie und seiner Verurteilung der Lust als „*bestial appetite*" (III.5.80) äußert. Als „Monster" wird er zusätzlich von der Gesellschaft in die Sphäre des „Anderen", des „Weiblichen" verwiesen, denn als „*diffused infection of a man*" (I.2.78), als „Mängelwesen" ist er nach dem vormodernen Sex-Verständnis ebenso ein von dem Ideal des männlichen Körpers abweichendes Modell wie die Frau.

Damit stellt Richard auf besondere Weise die Renaissance-Vorstellungen der strikten Abgrenzungen von *Gender* und (sexueller) Identität und der Polarität von „männlich" und „weiblich" in Frage. Dies ist ein besonders heikles Thema, wenn man die gesellschaftliche und politische Situation betrachtet, vor deren Hintergrund Shakespeare seine Figur erschaffen hat und die jene Konzepte und Denkmuster enthielt, unter denen *Richard III* vom Publikum gedeutet wurde.

---

[67] Moulton S. 263.

Die Henry VI-Tetralogie als Spiegelung der politischen und *gender*-ideologischen Situation von Elizabeths Herrschaft

A woman's general; what should we fear? (3HVI,1.2.67)

Obwohl Shakespeare mit Richard eine historische Figur als Protagonisten seines Dramas gewählt hat und in dessen Gestaltung von Geschichtschroniken inspiriert wurde, deren Schilderungen er auch zu weiten Teilen im Verlauf des Stückes umsetzt, handelt es sich dabei doch nicht primär um eine Darstellung der Geschehnisse ungefähr einhundert Jahre vor seiner Zeit. *Richard III* ist, wie die überhaupt in der Tudor-Ära sehr populären *history plays*, viel mehr eine Widerspiegelung der sozialen und politischen Konflikte und Fragestellungen, die die Menschen in ihrer eigenen Zeit beschäftigten.

Erst im Licht dieser Gesellschaft wird die eigentliche Monstrosität Richards wirksam. Christine VON EICHEL-STREIBER beschreibt das Drama als einen Konflikt zwischen Individuum und Gesellschaft:

> Das Drama erscheint wie die Thematisierung der Gefahr, die ein einzelner, der seine persönlichen Interessen und seinen Willen über alles stellt, für Staat und Gesellschaft bildet.[68]

Das ist sicherlich richtig, besonders wenn man beachtet, das das Konzept des Individuums in der Renaissance noch neu war, hatte man doch im Mittelalter, einer Zeit, in der das Denken ganz auf ein jenseitiges Leben fokussiert war, den Belangen des Einzelnen nur wenig Beachtung geschenkt.

Richard aber ist nicht nur ein Egoist oder Megalomane, der durch seine Rücksichtslosigkeit und Machtgier in Konflikt mit der Gesellschaft gerät. Der Konflikt zwischen Mensch und Gesellschaft ist doch genau genommen der Grundton eines jeden Dramas; und die von EICHEL-STREIBERS vorgeschlagene Deutung wird den Aspekten, die die Figur Richards und ebenso die beiden anderen hier zu untersuchenden „Monster" in ihrer Korporealität und ihrer daraus resultierenden zeitgenössisch interpretierten Signifikanz so besonders machen, nicht gerecht. Im Folgenden gilt es daher, nachdem bereits zeitgenössische medizinische Hintergründe und Deutungsmuster dargestellt wurden, zu zeigen, unter welchen Konzepten von

---

[68] von Eichel-Streiber, S. 103.

Geschlecht und Gesellschaftsordnung und in welcher politischen Situation Shakespeare seine männlichen „monstrous bodies" erschaffen hat und wie diese seiner „Monstrosität" Bedeutung verleihen.

Die patriarchalische Gesellschaft des frühneuzeitlichen Englands erfuhr am 15. Januar 1559 mit der Thronbesteigung Elizabeths I. eine dramatische Erschütterung ihrer Legitimierungsideologie. Eine Frau auf dem Thron, an der Spitze des Staates, ein weiblicher „body natural" als Herrscherin über den männlichen „body politic", in ihren Händen die männlichste aller Aufgaben, nämlich die Kriegsführung – eine solche Situation stellte die „von Gott gewollte" Geschlechterhierarchie auf den Kopf und war Wasser auf die Mühlen der „anxious masculinity".

Zu allem Überfluss herrschte, wie MOULTON unterstreicht, zur Renaissance-Zeit ohnehin eine gewisse Verwirrung der Männlichkeits-Konzepte, denn die Entwicklung der höfischen Kultur des 16. und 17. Jahrhunderts, die vom idealen Höfling die Beherrschung des eleganten Tanzes, der Poesie und der schönen Worte forderte, stand in krassem Gegensatz zu der althergebrachten, auf Aggressivität und körperlicher Kraft basierenden Männlichkeit, die sich auf dem Schlachtfeld und nicht auf der Tanzfläche äußerte.[69]

Mit der Zeit arrangierte man sich zwar mit seiner Königin, indem man ihre bedrohliche und primitive weibliche Körperlichkeit und Sexualität mit dem Kult-Bild der „chaste queen" übermalte, um ihre Andersartigkeit gegenüber den anderen Frauen zu betonen[70]. Dennoch blieb ihre Weigerung, das einzig Sinnvolle, was eine Königin in den Augen der Vertreter des Patriarchats hätte tun können, nämlich eine vorteilhafte diplomatische Ehe mit einem ihrer zahlreichen politisch potenten „Verehrer" einzugehen und dem Reich wenigstens einen – natürlich möglichst männlichen! – Erben zu schenken, eine weitere Quelle der Verunsicherung. Diese Situation, ein weiblicher Kopf des Patriarchats, eine Frau als Heerführer und eine ungesicherte Thronfolge, schlägt sich nieder in den Henry VI.-Dramen und allen anderen Historien Shakespeares (und nicht nur dort).

Linda BAMBER schreibt in „Comic Women, Tragic Men", die Frau in den Historien sei „*best described as unproblematic*", im Gegensatz zu den weiblichen Figuren

---

[69] Moulton, S. 254.

[70] Philippa Berry, *Of Chastity and Power. Elizabethan Literature and the Unmarried Queen.* London/ New York 1989, S. 62.

in den Tragödien, denn „*[...] whatever role she plays, she never offers any metaphysical complications, never raises issues for the masculine Self.*"[71] Diese These wackelt beträchtlich, wenn man sich den Handlungsverlauf der Henry VI.-Trilogie vor Augen führt, die doch im Kern nichts anderes beschreibt als die Folgen einer verkehrten Geschlechter-Hierarchie. Hier stehen monströs männliche Frauen, allen voran die kriegerische und skrupellose Margaret von Anjou, unfähigen, verweichlichten „effeminate rulers" gegenüber und stellen das männliche Selbstverständnis in Frage, indem sie das „Männliche" manipulieren und dominieren.

Henry VI. besteigt den Thron als kleiner Junge, also in einer Lebensphase, in der er noch nicht als „männlich" gilt und von Mädchen in seinem Alter gendertechnisch noch nicht unterschieden wird – ein „effeminate ruler" von Anfang an, der im Laufe seiner Entwicklung nie wirklich zum Mann heranreift. Weichlich, von seiner Ehefrau bevormundet, unfähig in der Kriegskunst, ist er nicht einmal in der Lage, seinem Erben den Thron zu sichern, sondern gibt die Herrschaft an den Duke of York ab. Aber auch sein Nachfolger, Edward IV., erweist sich als „unmännlich", indem er sich unfähig zeigt, sein Schwäche für Frauen zu zügeln, sich also auf weibische Weise seinen Leidenschaften hingibt und somit in die „Falle" der weiblichen Sexualität tappt, indem er eine unvorteilhafte Ehe eingeht, die das Königreich schwächt.

Bedrohen in den ersten beiden Teilen ehrgeizige Frauen und schwache Männer das Patriarchat, wird im dritten die soziale Grundlage dieser Gesellschaftsform, das Band zwischen Vater und Sohn, zerstört:

> [N]o longer do fathers and sons share the same ideals and fight side by side, instead the hapless king witnesses the horrible spectacle of fathers killing sons and sons killing fathers.[72]

Am Ende dieser Entwicklung, als Fortsetzung der Henry VI-Dramen, steht Richard als Gegenmodell zu den „effeminate men" der anderen Stücke: Er ist ein hypermaskuliner Charakter, der mit seinem Körper die Pervertiertheit des Regimes widerspiegelt und mit seiner übermäßigen, ungelenkten Männlichkeit die endgültige Zerstörung des Patriarchats einläutet, bis Fortuna am Ende die ideale Ordnung in Gestalt Richmonds wiederherstellt.

---

[71] Bamber, S. 21f.

[72] Moulton, S. 258.

Die soziale Signifikanz von Richards Körperlichkeit

Nachdem in den Henriaden also zu sehen war, was geschieht, wenn „das Weibliche" die Macht übernimmt, schildert *Richard III* die Folgen des übermäßig „Männlichen". Es zeigt sich, dass nicht nur Weiblichkeit eine dunkle, monströse Seite hat, sondern auch Männlichkeit, wenn sie außer Kontrolle gerät.

Aber zu welchem Zeitpunkt wird Richards körperliche Erscheinung, seine übersteigerte Männlichkeit eigentlich zur Bedrohung für die Gesellschaft? Die Umstände seiner „unnatural birth" und seine Deformiertheit werden schon in den Henry-Dramen geschildert. Auch dort erscheint er als düstere Figur, dennoch ist er längst nicht als das Monster identifizierbar, als das er in *Richard III* auftreten wird. Im Gegenteil erscheint er dort noch als ein vollwertiges Mitglied der patriarchalischen Gesellschaft: Er kämpft erfolgreich und mutig neben seinen Brüdern für seine Familie in der Schlacht, er ist eingebettet in ein stabiles Vater-Sohn-Verhältnis – die Grundlage des Patriarchats – und zeigt seinem Vater gegenüber sogar eine tiefe Zuneigung, wie aus der stolzen Äußerung *„Methinks 'tis prize enough to be his son"* (3HVI, 3.2.168) abzulesen ist.

Der Auslöser für Richards „Verwandlung" liegt laut MOULTON im Moment der Ermordung seines Vaters durch Margaret und Clifford:

> York's death comes to serve as an emblem for his son Richard's alienation from the patriarchical masculine community, and the change in Richard's social position is manifested by a precise physical change.[73]

Und tatsächlich wird ihm ja in dieser Situation, als er nicht um seinen Vater weinen kann, zum ersten Mal seine extreme innere Hitze bewusst, die, wie zuvor gesagt, auf eine dramatische humorale Veränderung hinweist.

Mit dem Tod des Vaters findet also äußerlich eine Veränderung der sozialen Position satt, die von einer inneren, physikalischen Veränderung seines Wesens begleitet wird. Diese Zerstörung der Humoralbalance bewirkt wiederum eine Unfähigkeit, den Vater so zu betrauern, wie es gesellschaftlich gefordert ist und bestätigt dadurch nach Außen sein vermeintlich „asoziales" Verhalten. Er wendet sich von den männlichen Prinzipien und Ehrvorstellungen ab und hat durch seine Unfruchtbarkeit so oder so keine Chance, Teil des patriarchalischen Grundprinzips der Fortpflanzung zu werden, außer in der brutalen, blutigen Phantasie, die er seiner zukünftigen Schwiegermutter Queen Elizabeth schildert (IV.4.296ff.) .Da er

---

[73] Moulton, S. 260.

ganz und gar unfähig ist, an „normalen" emotionalen und sexuellen Beziehungen teilzunehmen, konzentrieren sich seine Energien völlig auf seinen politischen Ehrgeiz. Allerdings kann er auch in diesem Bereich nicht ganz ohne Frauen auskommen, jedoch ist sein Werben um Lady Anne und später um Elizabeths Tochter allein politisch motiviert, auch wenn er dabei durchaus die Fähigkeit beweist, Zuneigung und erotisches Verlangen vorzutäuschen.

Richard hat keinen Vater mehr, dem er sich unterordnen kann und wird niemals einen Sohn haben, an den er seine Macht und seine Fähigkeiten weitergeben kann. Mit Yorks Tod ist er somit vollkommen und unwiderruflich aus der männlichen patriarchalischen Gesellschaft ausgeschlossen. Seine eigentlich idealen männlichen Qualitäten – Intelligenz, Mut, Aggressivität, Ehrgeiz – werden ohne das regulative Moment der männlichen Bündnisse zur Gefahr. Er stellt sie nur noch in seine eigenen Dienste und ist „unruly", unkontrollierbar, geworden. Andere Menschen interessieren in nur noch in ihrem Nutzen und ihrer Manipulierbarkeit für seine Zwecke. In der Eingangsszene des Dramas steht er deshalb ganz allein auf der Bühne und präsentiert seine düsteren Pläne und seinen missgestalteten Körper, denn erst mit dem Ausschluss aus der Gesellschaft gewinnt dieser Körper soziale Signifikanz. Nicht seine Deformiertheit per se macht ihn also zum „villain", sondern sein Verhalten als „unruly man", der sich außerhalb der patriarchalischen Ordnung bewegt: Richard ist kein *körperliches*, sondern ein *soziales* „Monster":

> I had no father, I am like no father;
> I have no brother, I am like no brother;
> And this word, "love", which graybeards call divine,
> Be resident in men like one another
> And not in me – I am myself alone. (RIII, V.6.80-84)

Richard weiß, dass er durch sein *disabilities* kein „Mann" sein kann, und für immer aus der männlichen Gemeinschaft ausgeschlossen ist. Er trägt einen tiefen Hass auf Frauen in sich, und zwar nicht nur auf seine Mutter, deren *„devilish plots / Of damned witchcraft"* er, ganz dem Prinzip der „monstrous births" entsprechend, für seine Missgestaltetheit verantwortlich macht (III.4.61). Weil er durch seine *disability* dazu verdammt ist, nie einen Platz in der Domäne der patriarchalisch konstruierten „Männlichkeit" einnehmen zu können, befindet er sich automatisch im Bereich des „Weiblichen", dass er als pathologisch hypermaskuliner Mann ebenso fürchtet, wie die „normalen" Männer seiner Gesellschaft. „*The son* *of the female is the shadow of the male*", sagt Falstaff (2HIV,III.2), und ohne Vater, abgeschnitten von männlichen sozialen Bündnissen, ist Richard ganz das Geschöpf seiner Mutter. „*Deformed, unfinished, sent before my time / Into this breathing world, scarce half made up*" (I.1.20-21) wird er sich niemals von ihr lösen können, weil ihm der Zutritt zur „Männlichkeit" verwehrt bleibt, auch wenn er sich in seiner Fantasie durch die Ermordung all seiner Rivalen quasi selbst neu gebären will, mit der Krone als „*the ripe revenue and due of birth*" (III.7.157).

Shakespeares Historien zeigen eine streng hierarchische Repräsentation von *Gender*-Unterschieden auf, in der die Frauen aus allen historischen Prozess ausgeschlossen werden müssen, ein Akt der Unterdrückung des Weiblichen, den eine männlich dominierte Kultur benötigt, um sich zu erhalten und zu reproduzieren. Nachdem der übermächtige weibliche Einflusses der vorangegangenen Henry-Dramen in *Richard III* vermeintlich endlich beseitigt wurde, zeigt sich, dass dieses „Andere", verkörpert in Richards „monströser", zugleich übermännlicher und weiblicher Korporealität, zurückgekehrt ist, um abermals die Gesellschaft ins Chaos zu stürzen.

Das nächste zu untersuchende „Monster", Caliban aus *The Tempest*, entzieht sich der Möglichkeit einer Deutung seines Körpers auf der zeitgenössischen medizinischen und mystischen Ebene aus einem einfachen Grund: Man weiß nicht, wie sein Körper aussieht, welche somatischen Eigenschaften eigentlich seine „Monstrosität" ausmachen. Jedoch ist auch er klar als *disabled* gekennzeichnet und einer dementsprechenden Ausstoßung aus der Gesellschaft unterworfen, und gerade die Undefinierbarkeit seiner Korporealität macht letztendlich seine bedrohliche sexuelle Signifikanz besonders für den Patriarchen Prospero aus.

Caliban – Das „Tier" im Mann und die Jungfrau

Keine andere von Shakespeares Figuren scheint so rätselhaft, so offen für die unterschiedlichsten Lesarten und kulturellen Projizierungen wie Caliban aus *The Tempest*. Menschliche Schildkröte, groteskes Fischmonster, hundeköpfiger Primitivling, Darwins „missing link" und in jüngerer Zeit rebellierendes Opfer von Kolonialisierung, Versklavung und Rassismus – Caliban hat auf der Bühne die unterschiedlichsten Formen angenommen. Sein „monströser" Körpers enthält im modernen genauso wie im frühneuzeitlichen Kontext eine Hyper-Signifikanz, die scheinbar stets auf eine Störung der sozialen Ordnung hinweist: *„Caliban has been a major sociopolitical emblem throughout the world"*.[74]

"What have we here, a man or a fish?" – Ein Körper, der jeder Beschreibung spottet

Der erste logische Schritt, um sich mit der besonderen Körperlichkeit der Figur Caliban zu beschäftigen, wäre, diese Körperlichkeit zunächst zu definieren. Genau hier liegt aber das Problem von Calibans Körper: Außergewöhnlich ist er, daran lässt der Text keinen Zweifel, nur wie er eigentlich genau aussieht, darüber ist man sich auch nach fast vier Jahrhunderten Bühnengeschichte immer noch nicht einig.

Interpretations- und Bühnengeschichte

Scheinbar absichtlich hat Shakespeare es Schauspielern, Regisseuren und Lesern selbst überlassen, wie sie sich dieses „Monster" vorzustellen haben. Diese Vorstellungen waren über die Zeit natürlich eng mit den jeweils vorherrschenden historischen und kulturellen Konzepten von körperlicher Andersartigkeit und exotischen Ethnien verbunden – und so hat Caliban seit seinem ersten Bühnenauftritt zahlreiche bemerkenswerte Metamorphosen durchlaufen.

The Tempest wurde wahrscheinlich im Jahr 1611 von den *King's Men* als Teil der Hochzeitsfeierlichkeiten von König James' Tochter Elisabeth bei Hofe erstaufgeführt. Leider sind uns keine Augenzeugenberichte von dieser oder den anderen Aufführungen unter Shakespeares eigenen Bühnenanweisungen erhalten, so dass sich nicht mehr rekonstruieren lässt, welche Vorstellungen der Dramaturge selbst für Calibans Darstellung hatte.

Bis ins 19. Jahrhundert erfreute sich das Stück großer Popularität in einer vom Dichter und Dramatiker William Davenant teilweise deutlich veränderten Form.

---

[74] Vaughan, Alden T. & Virginia Mason Vaughan, *Shakespeare's Caliban: A Cultural History*. Cambridge, 1991, S. XIV.

Seine Adaption „The Tempest, or The Enchanted Island", 1767 uraufgeführt und einige Jahre später zu einer Operette umgewandelt, zeigt Caliban als einen lüsternen, ewig betrunkenen Bösewicht. Als *„the epitome of monstrousness, a non-human symbol of human iniquity"*, so Virginia MASON VAUGHAN in ihrem Aufsatz über Calibans Bühnengeschichte[75], verliert der Caliban dieser Zeit jegliche Menschlichkeit, die in Shakespeares Original doch immer wieder deutlich durchschimmert. Hier ist er kein menschliches Wesen im Naturzustand, sondern ein unzähmbares Monster, das letztendlich die Ängste der Europäer vor der außereuropäischen Welt widerspiegelt:

> Since he represented bestial desires without the control of right reason, he could never be considered sympathetically as a human being.[76]

In den Aufführungen des frühen 18. Jahrhunderts wurde der Figur Caliban nur eine sehr kleine Rolle zugedacht, bevor sie sich mit William Macreadys erfolgreicher Aufführung von 1838 größtenteils dem Original-Text wieder annäherten. Mit seinem grotesken Äußeren und seinem tierhaften, primitiven Verhalten wollte er einfach nicht zu den zeitgenössischen Vorstellungen der Komödie passen.[77]

Zum Bild des „noble savage", wie es in der Romantik vorherrschte, passte er dagegen sehr gut, denn hier war nicht Rationalität, sondern Emotionalität und intuitives Verhalten gefragt, daher erfuhr die Rezeption der Figur Caliban im 19. Jahrhundert eine drastische Veränderung und wurde sogar zu einer begehrten Rolle, die Raum für schauspielerische Interpretationen ließ. Elemente Calibans, die zuvor vernachlässigt oder übersehen worden waren, wie zum Beispiel sein poetisches Gespür, seine Tragik und Groteskheit, waren nun fester Bestandteil der Aufführungen und kreative Herausforderung an die Darsteller, von denen besonders George Bennett Maßstäbe für alle späteren Darstellungen setzte. Zwar immer noch vor allem eine tierartige Kreatur, seit der Mitte des 19. Jahrhunderts meist mit amphibischen Attributen dargestellt, war Caliban doch nicht mehr ganz Monster, sondern im Kern ein menschliches Wesen, zugleich komisch und tragisch – und zum ersten Mal erschien er als Opfer von Prosperos Tyrannei.

Ende des 19. Jahrhunderts durchlief der Bühnen-Caliban abermals einen wichtigen Wandel. Unter dem enormen Eindruck der darwinistischen Evolutionstheorie

---

[75] Mason Vaughan, Virginia, "'Something Rich and Strange': Caliban's Theatrical Metamorphoses", *Shakespeare Quarterly* 36, No. 4 (1985), S. 392.

[76] Ebd., S. 395.

[77] Vaughan & Mason Vaughan, S. 178.

stellte der Geschichts- und Literaturprofessor Daniel Wilson 1873 in seiner Abhandlung „*Caliban: The Missing Link*" eine Verbindung zwischen Shakespeares Bühnencharakter und Darwins These von einem unbekannten Zwischenglied in der Evolutionsgeschichte des Menschen her, eine Theorie, aus der sich eine neue Darstellungsweise dieser Figur als affenähnliche Kreatur mit Fell und Krallen, aber aufrecht gehend, entwickelte: Caliban als eine frühe Entwicklungsstufe des modernen Menschen. Zu Beginn nicht viel mehr als ein primitives Tier mit Ansätzen zu menschlichem Verstand, lernt dieser neue Caliban im Laufe des Stückes, Lust und Gewalt zu zügeln und echte menschliche Liebe zu empfinden.

Dieses darwinistische Verständnis von Caliban als prähistorischem Wesen mit der Fähigkeit zur Mensch-Werdung hielt sich bis weit ins 20. Jahrhundert, bis in 1950er Jahre, als die im Grunde bis heute anhaltende Politisierung Calibans einsetzte. Die Literaturkritiker dieser Zeit betrachteten *The Tempest* zunehmend als eine Studie der Kolonisierung der außereuropäischen Welt, zunächst vor allem Amerikas, dann auch der Dritten Welt. So wie Caliban waren die indigenen Bewohner der Kolonien enteignet, unterworfen und ausgebeutet worden. Wie er waren sie gezwungen, die Sprache und Kultur der Eroberer anzunehmen, hatten Versklavung und Diskriminierung ertragen müssen und sich am Ende dagegen aufgelehnt.[78]

In den späten 1960er Jahren wurde Caliban so zu einer Paraderolle für schwarze Schauspieler, vom „Monster" wurde er zu einem Symbol der schwarzen Anti-Rassismusbewegung: „*Caliban was now a black militant, angry and recalcitrant.*"[79] Calibans politische Einspannung erreichte in den frühen 80er Jahren ihren Höhepunkt. In einer Vielzahl von unterschiedlichen Interpretationen auf der ganzen Welt verkörperte er nun vom schwarzen Sklaven bis zum Punk-Rocker jede von der Gesellschaft marginalisierte Minderheit.[80]

In der kritischen Diskussion und in den Aufführungen des Stückes hat auch heute noch die kolonialistische Interpretation einen großen, wenn auch schwindenden Einfluss. Insgesamt hält sich die Auffassung, dass *The Tempest* ein System der politischen Unterdrückung skizziert, in dem Prospero als imperialistischer Herrscher und Caliban als indigener Bewohner der Insel fungieren. Calibans Rebellion gehen dabei sprachliche Umerziehung, Versklavung und territoriale Enteignung

---

[78] Mason Vaughan, S. 402.

[79] Ebd., S. 403.

[80] Vaughan & Mason Vaughan, S. 194 f.

voraus. Der Schauplatz ist dabei mal eine karibische Insel, mal eine Kolonie in der Dritten Welt, in der schauspielerischen Darstellung wird die körperliche „Monstrosität" Calibans mal betont, mal ganz ausgeklammert.

Die in den letzten Jahrzehnten erfolgte Inszenierung der kolonialen Symbolik des Stückes hat seine kreativen und innovativen Grenzen scheinbar langsam erreicht, und auch in der Literaturwissenschaft wird dem Stück zunehmend eine alternative Verortung zugestanden, weg von einer neuweltlichen Verortung hin zum Beispiel nach Irland oder in europäische dynastische, politische und seeräuberische Konflikte.[81] Zu dieser Rückorientierung auf den europäischen geographischen und kulturellen Raum gehört auch eine Interpretation von Caliban auf Grundlage des frühneuzeitlichen „Monster"-Diskurses.

In diesem Interpretationszusammenhang erscheint Caliban nicht als „Exot", als Bewohner der *terra incognita,* sondern als Vertreter einer „Monstrosität", die nicht so sehr als Teil der Neuen Welt, sondern vielmehr in altbekannten lokalen Konstruktionen von *monstrous births* und *fairgrounds* dargestellt wird, also in typisch englischen Kontexten.

Elemente des Stückes, die als Hinweise für die Verortung von Handlung und Problematik in einen kolonialen Zusammenhang gegolten haben, werden dadurch in ihrer Bedeutung sehr viel niedriger eingestuft. Gegen eine koloniale Lesart spricht zum Beispiel, dass Prospero aufgrund der Vorgeschichte kein „Entdecker", sondern selbst ein Flüchtling ist, wenn er sich auch wie ein Kolonialherr die Insel Untertan machen will, und Caliban keinesfalls ein „Eingeborener" ist, sondern mit seiner Mutter Sycorax als Exilant auf die Insel kam. Nirgendwo im Stück ist außerdem Calibans körperliche Andersartigkeit mit der Zugehörigkeit zu einer exotischen „Rasse" erklärt, sondern seine „Monstrosität" wird, weit entfernt von irgendwelchen kolonialen Geschichten von Kannibalen und Meeresungeheuern, innerhalb des mythologischen Bezugsrahmen der „unnatural births" gedeutet, denn seine Mutter soll eine Hexe und er das Produkt ihrer Vereinigung mit dem Teufel gewesen sein.

Besonders durch Prosperos unterdrückerische Behandlung von Caliban und der daraus ersichtlichen Diskriminierung des Inselbewohners als „Monster", als minderwertiges Geschöpf, erlaubt und rechtfertigt das Stück, ob nun ursprünglich ge-

---

[81] Mark Thornton Burnett, *Constructing "monsters" in Shakespearean drama and early modern culture.* Basingstoke, 2002, S. 125 f.

wollt oder nicht, eine Interpretation auf der Grundlage des Kolonialismus-Diskurses. Sie ist aber nicht die einzige und vermutlich auch nicht die ursprüngliche Möglichkeit, *The Tempest* zu verstehen, wie Frank KERMODE 1954 bemerkte:

> ...there is nothing in The Tempest which could not have existed had America remained undiscovered, and the Bermuda voyage never taken place. The New World stimulated interest in the great and perennial problem of the nature of Nature; but the fact that Shakespeare is at pains to establish his island in the Old World may be taken to indicate his rejection of the merely topical.[82]

Um sich nun von der bewegten Bühnen- und Interpretationsgeschichte der Figur Caliban weg zu einer Betrachtung der Figur und ihrer besonderen, auch durch ihre *disabilities* bedingten Signifikanz zuzuwenden, sollen zunächst die im Text gegebenen Hinweise auf seine Korporealität und seinen Status untersucht werden.

„Savage" oder „Monster"? – Hinweise auf Calibans Körper im Text

Die Anzahl der möglichen Inspirationsquellen Shakespeares aus antiken Schriften, Romanen, Mythen und Volkssagen, religiösen Schriften und Reiseberichten aus der außereuropäischen Welt ist riesig und lässt höchstens Spekulationen über die Vorbilder und Prototypen für Caliban zu. Am plausibelsten und sinnvollsten auch für die Debatte um die geographische und kulturelle Verortung des Stückes ist daher die Erklärung, dass Shakespeare seinen Caliban aus verschiedenen „Bausteinen" zusammengesetzt hat.

Ein gerade im Zuge der „Re-Europäisierung" wieder häufig herangezogener „Baustein" ist sicherlich der „wild man", oder „wodewose", eine uralte Figur des englischen Volksglaubens, der sowohl die Wälder und Einöden der Heimat als auch die fernen, unerforschten Länder außerhalb Europas bewohnte, und mit seinen zahlreichen Versionen *„from fully human to almost animal, from essentially moral to hopelessly corrupt, from gentle to ferocious"*[83] genau die Bandbreite von Calibans Rezeptionsgeschichte widerspiegelt. Der „wild man" der letzteren Kategorie erscheint wiederholt in Edmund SPENSERS Werken, von denen besonders die „Faerie Queene" häufig als wichtige Inspirationsquelle für Shakespeare vermutet

---

[82] Frank Kermode (Hrsg.), *William Shakespeare: The Tempest. (New Arden Edition)*. London, 1954, S. 26.

[83] Vaughan & Mason Vaughan, S. 274.

wird. In Buch drei, Canto sieben taucht ein Monster auf, dass Vorbild für den von Prospero als „*freckled whelp*" bezeichneten Caliban sein könnte[84]:

> An hideous beast of horrible aspect,
> That could the stoutest courage have appald;
> Monstrous misshapt, and all his back was spect
> With thousand spots of colours queint elect. (FQ III.7.22.2-5)[85]

Es ist durchaus möglich, dass diese Mythenfigur eines der Vorbilder für Caliban war, allerdings, so Barry GAINES, gibt es im Stück selbst keinerlei Hinweise auf das typische Aussehen des „wild man", den man sich als mit einem dichten Pelz bewachsen und mit einem Lendenschurz aus Efeu bekleidet vorstellte, unübersehbare Attribute, die sicherlich irgendwo im Stück Erwähnung gefunden hätten.[86]

Auf der anderen Seite scheint Caliban auch vom frühneuzeitlichen Bild der Bewohner der „Neuen Welt" beeinflusst, denn seine Tierhaftigkeit, seine Anfälligkeit für die Verführungen des Alkohols und sein sexueller Appetit decken sich mit den Augenzeugenberichten von Amerika-Reisenden dieser Zeit.[87]

Aufgrund von zwei vagen Andeutungen im Text – einmal spricht Trinculo im Zusammenhang mit englischen „Monster"-Ausstellungen von einem „*dead Indian*" (II.2.32-34) und Stephano vermutet, als er auf Trinculo und Caliban trifft, einen Streich „*with savages and men of Ind*" (II.2.57) – wurde Caliban häufig als Vertreter der amerikanischen Ureinwohner gedeutet und politisiert.

Was allerdings, wie VAUGHAN & VAUGHAN bemerken, deutlich nicht in das viel bemühte Bild von Caliban als „Indianer" passt, ist sein äußeres Erscheinungsbild. Trotz aller Verachtung und Abscheu der europäischen „Eroberer" der Neuen Welt gegenüber den „Indianern" wurden diese von allen Berichterstattern doch immer als wohlgestalt, sogar attraktiv beschrieben.[88] Außerdem besitzt Caliban, soweit

---

[84] Barry Gaines, "What Did Caliban Look Like?" *Shakespeare Yearbook* 1 (1990), S. 51.

[85] R.S. Bear, (Hrsg.) *The Complete Works in Verse and Prose of Edmund Spenser*, London, 1882. Online zur Verfügung gestellt durch das *Renascence Editions*-Projekt der University of Oregon unter http://darkwing.uoregon.edu/%7Erbear/queene3.html#Cant.%20XII.

[86] Gaines, S. 52.

[87] Vaughan & Mason Vaughan, S. 17.

[88] Ebd., S. 19.

wir durch seine Mit-Figuren im Stück selber und durch Augenzeugen der frühesten Aufführungen informiert werden, keine der schon damals stereotypisch „indianischen" Attribute wie Körperbemalung, Pfeil und Bogen und Federschmuck.

Auch einige Andeutungen über seine *disabilities* scheinen verschiedenen *travel books*, von denen Shakespeare mit Sicherheit Kenntnis besaß, entnommen: Die Bemerkung, er sei „*puppy-headed*" (II.2.148) erinnert an Berichte über die so genannten *Cynocephali*, hundeköpfige Eingeborenenstämme, die man in Ethiopien and Indien entdeckt haben wollte. Eine Besonderheit seiner Augen, über die gesagt wird, sie seien „*not set in his head*" (III.2.8), wird häufig mit den *Anthropophagi* in Verbindung gebracht, seltsamen Fabelwesen ohne Köpfe, deren Mund auf Höhe der Brust und deren Augen an den Schultern saßen.[89] *Anthropophagi* kamen in Reiseberichten aus Afrika und Amerika vor. Diese Geschöpfe finden sich aber auch schon in der englischen Folklore und werden von Shakespeare schon in *The Merry Wives of Windsor* erwähnt; sie müssen also nicht unbedingt auf eine exotische Herkunft Calibans hindeuten.

Überhaupt sind die häufigen Tier-Analogien, mit denen Caliban von seinen Mitmenschen bedacht wird, eher Teil des einheimischen frühneuzeitlichen „Monster"-Diskurses. Keith THOMAS beschreibt in *Man and the Natural World* die zu dieser Zeit äußerst sensible Grenze zwischen Mensch und Tier.[90] Schon das frühe Christentum habe, so THOMAS, eine feindliche Einstellung gegenüber den animistischen Vorstellungen der heidnischen Kulturen angenommen und in diesem Zuge eine entschieden antimythische Doktrin entwickelt, in der die Trennung von Mensch und Natur durch die Ausstoßung von Adam und Eva aus dem Paradies symbolisiert wurde. Daraus resultierte in der Frühen Neuzeit eine unterschwellige Angst vor jeder Form von Verhalten, dass die zerbrechliche Grenze zwischen Mensch und Tier zu überschreiten drohte. Durch seine Tierhaftigkeit deutet Caliban, das „Monster", auf eine solche Grenzüberschreitung, auf ein Chaos in der göttlichen Ordnung der Welt hin.

Dass Trinculo ihn bei der ersten Begegnung als „fish" bezeichnet, wurde in Calibans wechselhafter Rezeptionsgeschichte oft zum Anlass genommen, ihn als fischähnliche Kreatur darzustellen. Tatsächlich erinnert Trinculos Reaktion beim Anblick von Caliban an Seemannsgeschichten von halb menschlichen Meeresbewohnern wie Meerjungfrauen und Wassernixen, und die Worte, die Shakespeare

---

[89] Thornton Burnett, S. 133.

[90] Keith Thomas, *Man and the Natural World*, London 1983.

Trinculo bei Calibans Anblick in den Mund legte, erinnern an eine konkrete
Quelle, nämlich die Schilderungen des reisenden Mönches Joanno dos Sanctos
von 1597:

> Here I may mention also a Sea monster...He was ten spans long, thicker
> than a man; his tayle thick, a span long, eares of a Dog, armes like a
> Man without haire, and at the elbows great Finnes like a fish[91]

Für Trinculos Anspielungen auf eine besondere „Fischigkeit" von Caliban gibt es,
so VAUGHAN & VAUGHAN eine Erklärung, die Caliban noch mehr von seiner tierhaften Monstrosität weg und hin zu einem menschlicheren Körper rückt: Tatsächlich beziehe sich Trinculos Ausruf „*What have we here – a man or a fish?*" ganz
offenbar auf Calibans Geruch, denn er fährt fort: „*he smells like a fish; a very
ancient and fish-like smell*"[92] (II.2.24-26), Seine weitere Beobachtung „*Legged
like a man, and his fins like arms!*" (II.2.33-34) bestätigt, dass das, was er wegen
des Geruchs zunächst für einen Fisch gehalten hatte, offensichtlich doch menschliche Formen hat.

Bezeichnungen wie „*this thing of darkness*" (V.1.276) und „*thou earth*" (I.2.314)
sind regelmäßig als Hinweis auf eine dunkle Hautfarbe Calibans gedeutet worden,
können aber auch Calibans „düsteres", primitives Wesen bezeichnen. Beides
schließt sich nicht aus und würde sich aus der kolonialistischen Perspektive für
die zeitgenössische Vorstellung von den „salvages" und „blackamoores" der außereuropäischen Welt sogar bedingen. Dennoch sind auch diese zweideutigen Attribute nicht als sicherer Hinweis auf Calibans Äußeres verwertbar.

Wenn man alle diffusen und wenig hilfreichen Hinweise auf Calibans vermeintliche *disabilities* beiseite schiebt, bleibt am Ende eine Gewissheit: Er ist als
„Monster" nicht in erster Linie durch sein am Ende vielleicht gar nicht so „monströses" Aussehen definiert, sondern, ebenso wie Richard, wegen der Umstände
seiner Geburt.

Was nämlich, im Gegensatz zu den sich zu dieser Zeit gerade erst herauskristallisierenden Stereotypen der Bewohner der Karibik, in den Köpfen aller Zuschauer

---

[91] William Stansby, *Purchas His Pilgrimes*, London 1625, zitiert in Gaines, S. 50.

[92] Vaughan & Mason Vaughan, S.12. In der Medizin wird Caliban übrigens als eine der frühesten Erwähnungen der seltenen Stoffwechselkrankheit *Trimethylaminurie* oder „Fish Odour Syndrome", gedeutet, die einen starken, fischähnlichen Körpergeruch hervorruft. (www.sciencenews.org/sn_arc99/5_15_99/bob2.htm [13.01.2007]).

der ersten Aufführungen des Dramas präsent war, ist der zuvor ausgeführten Diskurs der „unnatural births".

Schon bevor das „Monster" zum ersten mal auf der Bühne erscheint, erfährt das Publikum von Prospero, wer Calibans Mutter war („*The foul witch Sycorax, who with age and envy / Was grown into a hoop*" (I.2.258-9)) und von der „*unnatural birth*", dessen Produkt er ist: „*the son that she did litter here, / A freckl'd whelp, hag-born – not honour'd with / A human shape*" (II.2.28284).

Unter dem Eindruck der zahlreichen anschaulich illustrierten Pamphlete und *broadside ballads* über *monstrous births* müssen diese ersten Hinweise auf das „Monster", das sie bald zu sehen bekommen würden, beim Publikum Assoziationen hervorgerufen haben, die mit späteren literaturwissenschaftlichen Konstruktionen zur geographischen oder etymologischen Herkunft der Figur zunächst nichts zu tun haben.

Ideen von „Indianern", „Kannibalen" und Imperialismus sind später auf Caliban projiziert worden, und sie alle haben ihre Berechtigung und lassen sich im Text nachweisen. Dass er aber ein „Monster" ist, wird von Shakespeare zunächst allein durch seine Entstehung begründet. Immer wieder wird darauf hingewiesen, dass die Hexe Sycorax ihn durch sexuellen Verkehr mit einem Teufel oder Inkubus empfangen hatte, eine in Mittelalter und Früher Neuzeit üblicherweise herangezogene Erklärung für Geburtsfehler, die König James I. selbst in seiner *Daemonology* aufgriff.[93]

Auch Trinculos Überlegungen zum wirtschaftlichen Wert dieses „*strange fish*" als Jahrmarkt-Attraktion verstärken eher den Eindruck von Caliban als klassischem Monster:

> Were I in England now, as once I was, and had but this fish / painted, not a holiday fool there but would give a piece of silver. There would this monster make a man, any strange beast there makes a man; when they will not give a droit to reliv a lame beggar, they will lay out ten to see a dead Indian (II.2.27-33)

Die Erwähnung des „*dead Indian*" im Gegensatz zu „*this monster*" verdeutlicht, dass Caliban auf Trinculo nicht wie ein „indianischer" oder karibischer Exot wirkt. Und dass er wenig später konstatiert, es handelt sich hier doch nicht um

---

[93] Gaines, S. 53.

einen Fisch, sondern um einen „*islander, that hath lately suffered a thunderbolt*"(II.2.36), ist noch einmal ein Hinweis darauf, dass Caliban zwar essentiell menschlich, aber körperlich „anders", eventuell sogar durch äußere Einwirkung entstellt ist.

Auch die zahlreichen Versuche, die Etymologie seines Namens zu rekonstruieren, um seine ethnische Zugehörigkeit zu klären, ob als Anagramm von „canibal"[94] oder als Ableitung des Roma-Wortes „cauliban"[95] für „schwarz, dunkel", haben noch zu keinem eindeutigen Hinweis auf die Herkunft und das Wesen Calibans geführt.

Es scheint, dass das vormoderne Streben, das „Monströse" zu erklären, zu kategorisieren und entmystifizieren, sich auch in unserer Zeit für die Figur Caliban fortsetzt. Es stellt sich allerdings die Frage, ob die Diskussion um die „richtige" geographische und kulturelle Herkunft dieser Figur für das Verständnis und ihren Beitrag für das Stück wirklich so grundlegend ist. Gerade durch seine Undefinierbarkeit und Offenheit für unzählige Adaptionen und Ausgestaltungen hat Caliban die Jahrhunderte überdauert, zwar mit einem „monströsen", aber dafür immer wieder erneuerten Körper.

Nach der Beschäftigung mit der Frage nach dem eigentlichen Aussehen von Caliban wird im nun folgenden Schritt auf die sexuelle Signifikanz seines außergewöhnlichen Körpers eingegangen, und zwar mit dem Fokus auf den männlichen Angstphantasien, die Prospero als Vertreter des Patriarchats und als Vater einer Tochter auf diesen Körper projiziert.

Calibans sexuelle Identität(en)

Nicht nur in seiner Bühnengeschichte, sondern auch in der Analyse des Stückes selbst nimmt Caliban die unterschiedlichsten Formen und Bedeutungen an. Sein für uns nie klar erkennbarer Körper gewinnt gerade durch seine Undefinierbarkeit an Signifikanz, er ist „*a blank page (...) onto which are projected conflicting anxieties and ambitions*".[96]

---

[94] John E. Hankins sieht sogar den einzigen Schlüssel zur Aufdeckung von Calibans Herkunft „*in his* [Shakespeares] *choice of Caliban's name."* (John E. Hankins, "Caliban the Bestial Man", *PMLA* 62, No. 3 (1947), S. 801.).

[95] Vaughan & Mason Vaughan, diesen und weitere Vorschläge zur Namensherkunft auf S. 2636.

[96] Thornton Burnett, S. 134.

So ist der sexuelle Caliban, den es nun zu untersuchen gilt, in seiner bedrohlichen, hypersignifikanten Andersartigkeit auch eine Projektionsfläche für den Vater und Patriarchen Prospero, auf der sich dessen eigene Befindlichkeiten und Ängste widerspiegeln. Caliban scheint bisweilen ebenso wenig wie Ariel einen materiellen Körper zu besitzen, das „Monster" erscheint immer nur als das, was seine Umwelt in ihm sehen *will*: Vielleicht ist das auch die Erklärung für Calibans seltsame Undefinierbarkeit, und das in einem kulturellen „Monster"-Diskurs, der die Klassifizierung, Katalogisierung und Deutung des außergewöhnlichen Körpers zu seiner wichtigsten Aufgabe gemacht hat.

In der folgenden Darstellung von Calibans sexueller „Monstrosität" soll auf drei verschiedene Varianten seiner sexuellen Signifikanz eingegangen werden. Der erste Caliban steht für die Bedrohung der Ordnung durch ungezügelte männliche Sexualität, der zweite für die dämonisierte weibliche Sexualität und mütterliche Macht im Stück. Der dritte Caliban verkörpert schließlich Prosperos Angst vor seinem eigenen Verlangen gegenüber seiner Tochter.

Der erste Caliban: Die Bedrohung der Ordnung durch ungezügelte Sexualität

Im Gegensatz zu seiner körperlichen Beschaffenheit sind Calibans kultureller und daraus resultierend sozialer Status klar definiert: In der Personenliste der Folio-Edition von 1623 wird Caliban als „*a salvage and deformed slave*" beschrieben.[97] Er ist also ein „Wilder", ein aus eurozentrischer Sicht kulturell minderbemittelter Mensch ohne Religion, Schrift, Bildung und Manieren.

Mit dem Etikett „sa(l)vage" wurde im England der Frühen Neuzeit recht großzügig umgegangen. So bezeichnete es die Iren ebenso wie die weit entfernten Völker Afrikas und Asiens und natürlich die gerade erst „entdeckte" indigene Bevölkerung der „Neuen Welt", aber auch Randgesellschaften im eigenen Land wie Bettler, Obdachlose und Zigeuner.[98]

Die Bezeichnung „salvage" sagt also zunächst nichts über die geographische Herkunft Calibans aus, sondern nur über seinen kulturellen Entwicklungsstand – auch wenn sie von Vertretern der kolonialistischen Interpretationsrichtung als Argument für seine Verortung in diesem Diskurs herangezogen wird.

---

[97] Vaughan & Mason Vaughan, S. 18.
[98] Thornton Burnett, S. 8f.

Auf der sozialen Leiter befindet Caliban sich also ganz unten. Er ist ein Sklave und wird auch von Prospero, seinem Herren, schon in der ersten Szene seines Erscheinens immer wieder als solcher angesprochen: „*Caliban, my slave*" (I.2.308), „*What ho, slave*" (I.2.313), „*poisonous slave*" (I.2.320), „*most lying slave*" (I.2.345). Als Sklave muss er, ebenso wie Ariel, Prosperos Befehle ausführen. Seinen Status als Prosperos Leibeigener wird Caliban erst nach der letzten Szene des Stückes verlieren, aber dann ist er allein auf „seiner" Insel; es bleibt unklar, ob die „Herrschaft" über eine menschenleere Insel für ihn ein glückliches Ende ist.

Trotz seines rätselhaften, als „monströs" empfundenen Äußeren scheint Caliban doch auch ein Mensch zu sein, denn für Miranda und Prospero gehört er offenbar zur menschlichen Bevölkerung der Insel. Immerhin zählt Miranda ihn mit zu den Männern in ihrem Leben, wenn sie bei Ferdinands Anblick schwärmt: „*This / Is the third man that e'er I saw, the first / That e'er I sigh'd for*" (I.2.445-7). Sie scheint sich später zwar selbst zu widersprechen, wenn sie zu Ferdinand sagt: „*...nor have I seen / More than I may call men than you, good friend, / And my dear father*" (III.i.50-52), aber es ist anzunehmen, dass die in Liebe entbrannte junge Frau den monströsen Caliban einfach nicht zu den „echten" Männern, wohl aber zu den Menschen auf der Insel zählt. Ungeachtet seiner offensichtlich als legitim angesehen Versklavung durch Prospero und Miranda haben die beiden, wenn ihrer Meinung nach auch vergeblich, zudem ein ganz humanistisches Bemühen an den Tag gelegt, dem „Wilden" etwas Bildung und Erziehung zukommen zu lassen (siehe z.B. I.2.351-361). Dies ist nicht zuletzt ein weiterer Hinweis auf seine zumindest in Ansätzen veranlagte Menschlichkeit.

Als Teil seines – wenn auch noch so rudimentären – menschlichen Wesens, besitzt Caliban auch eine sexuelle Identität. Bei aller Tierhaftigkeit ist er auf sexueller Ebene doch ein Mann und offenbar durchaus fähig und willens, sich Miranda sexuell zu nähern. Ebenso wie bei Richard III. entspringt dieser Übergriff nicht allein einem primitiven Sexualtrieb, sondern dem Wunsch, sich zu vermehren:

> O ho, O ho! Would't had beend one. Thou didst Prevent me; I had Peopl'd else this isle with Calibans (I.2.350-51)

Das Thema Fortpflanzung ist während des ganzen Stückes ohnehin ein problematisches Gebiet. Wie Mark THORNTON BURNETT bemerkt, scheint keine der tatsächlichen oder nur imaginierten Geburten, die im Stück erwähnt werden, ohne Komplikationen ablaufen zu können. Sexuelle Kontakte zwischen Mann und Frau werden gefürchtet wegen ihrer möglichen Konsequenzen: „*Good wombs have borne bad sons*" (I.2.119), sagt ausgerechnet das einzige sexuelle Objekt des Stückes, Miranda[99].

Besonders Prospero, der besorgte Vater, beschäftigt sich mit den möglicherweise „monströsen" Folgen von *„that which breeds"* (III.1.76) zwischen seiner Tochter und Ferdinand. Obwohl es stets recht konstruiert erscheint, bei der Interpretation von Shakespeares Werken Bezüge zu seiner damaligen Lebenslage zu ziehen, ist es vielleicht kein Zufall, dass der Autor sich zur Zeit der Entstehung von *The Tempest* offenbar gerade selbst mit der Verheiratung seiner Töchter befassen musste.[100] Dabei entspringt Prosperos Besorgtheit um die Unberührtheit seiner Tochter wahrscheinlich noch am wenigsten seinen väterlichen Gefühlen, denn wie für jeden adeligen Vater bedeutet auch für ihn eine heiratsfähige Tochter vor allem ein wertvolles politisches Unterpfand. Der Prestige- und Machtgewinn für den entmachteten Prospero durch die Vermählung seiner Tochter mit dem Sohn des Königs von Neapel wäre beträchtlich, aber nur bei einer legitimen Vereinigung, das heißt, wenn Miranda jungfräulich in die Ehe ginge. Mit recht drastischen Worten warnt Prospero seinen zukünftigen Schwiegersohn deshalb vor der Sünde des vorehelichen Geschlechtsverkehrs (IV.1.15-21): Aus einer solchen Zügellosigkeit könne nicht Gutes entstehen, ermahnt er den Prinzen, entweder würden sie unfruchtbar und ohne Liebe bleiben („*barren hate*") oder unter einer Folge zu leiden haben, die so schändlich ist, dass sie unter „*weeds*" verborgen werden müsste – hier droht das Schreckgespenst einer *monstrous birth* als Folge der verbotenen Vereinigung.

Mirandas Unschuld ist also von zwei Seiten gefährdet – einmal durch die ungezügelte, tierische Sexualität des „Monsters" Caliban, der sich bereits auf sie gestürzt hat mit dem Wunsch, „*to people this island with Calibans*" (I.2.350), und durch Ferdinand, der dem Schwiegervater in spe zwar prinzliche Zurückhaltung gelobt hat, aber in Prosperos Augen dieselbe animalische Gefährdung der Unschuld seiner Tochter bedeutet, einem kostbaren Besitz, den er dem jungen Mann nicht zu leicht übergeben will: „*...lest too light winning / Makes the prize light*" (I.2.450-51).

Aber Ferdinand, der gebildete und wohlerzogene Prinz, absolutes Gegenteil seines sexuellen „Nebenbuhlers" Caliban, hofft – den politischen Anforderungen des Adels gemäß – vor allem auf geeignete Nachkommen, auf „fair issue" (IV.1.24)

---

[99] Thornton Burnett, S. 140f.

[100] Vaughan & Mason Vaughan, S. 5.

und weiß seine Triebe unter Kontrolle zu halten, so dass das junge Glück sich höchstens mit Schachspielen beschäftigt.

Caliban als Verkörperung ungezügelter Männlichkeit, gegen die der edle Prinz sich als immun erweist, „befällt" auch die beiden clownesken Figuren Stephano und Trinculo. Caliban stachelt die beiden zu einem Aufstand an, indem er nicht zuletzt Stephano Miranda als sexuelles Objekt verspricht: „...*she will become thy bed, I warrant, / And bring thee forth brave brood.*" (III.2.100-101). Die beiden werden selbst zu „Monstern", indem sie sich durch ihren – freilich eher komischen – Usurpationsversuch und die Vereinigung mit Miranda eine ihnen nicht zustehende Position anmaßen wollen. Dies wird besonders deutlich in Akt V, Szene 1, als die Dreiergruppe in Prosperos Zelle eindringen will, die beiden Männer aber von dem „*glistering apparel*" (IV.1.193) auf einer Wäscheleine abgelenkt werden. Indem sie sich, entgegen Calibans Warnung, die kostbare Kleidung anziehen, begehen sie eine Überschreitung der sozialen Grenzen, die in der vormodernen Gesellschaftsordnung als Verbrechen geahndet wurde. „Transgressive dressing", ob nun *gender-* oder standesübergreifend, war eine sündhafte Praxis, die von den protestantischen Reformatoren dieser Zeit im Übrigen auch den Schauspielern vorgeworfen wurde und in der rigiden sozialen und moralischen Ordnung als „monströs" galt.[101]

Im Gegensatz zu diesem lächerlichen Rebellionsversuch, über den er die ganze Zeit bestens informiert ist, stellt die Gefahr einer ungezügelten sexuellen Leidenschaft zwischen Miranda und Ferdinand für Prospero, den spirituellen Kontroll-Freak, ein Problem dar, das seine Pläne durchkreuzen könnte. Seine wiederholte Ermahnung Ferdinands formuliert er in einer unnötig drastischen Weise, die ihn fast schon hysterisch wirken lässt, so sehr fürchtet er die chaotische Kraft der Sexualität der beiden jungen Leute.

Auch das Maskenspiel, das „Stück im Stück" in *The Tempest*, ist Ausdruck von Prosperos Bedürfnis, die unberechenbare Variable der körperlichen Lust aus seiner genau berechneten Welt zu entfernen, denn es wird ausdrücklich erwähnt, dass Venus und ihr „*waspish-headed son*" (IV, 1.99) Cupido aus der Aufführung entfernt wurden. Was bleibt, ist die Illusion einer asexuellen, geordneten, ewig sommerlichen Welt, in der die Tochter, im Spiel verkörpert durch Persephone, vor den Bedrohungen der Sexualität sicher ist.

---

[101] Thornton Burnett, S. 148f.

Bezeichnenderweise wird Prosperos Vorführung jäh durch Calibans Verschwörung unterbrochen, der der Magier sich zuwenden muss. In seiner Fantasie mag es ihm also gelingen, die primitive, dunkle Macht, die der Sex für ihn darstellt, auszuschließen. In der Realität holt sie ihn, verkörpert durch Caliban und implizit ihm Heranreifen seiner Tochter, immer wieder ein. Das einzige, was ihm zu tun bleibt, ist, Miranda vor dieser Bedrohung, die sie selber in sich trägt, zu bewahren, indem er sie in die kontrollierte Sphäre des Ehebettes manövriert, mit einem Mann, dessen Selbstbeherrschung er zuvor selbst geprüft hat.

Der zweite Caliban: Weibliche Sexualität und tote Mütter

Die zweite Bedeutungsebene von Calibans sexueller Signifikanz bezieht sich auf die unheimliche schöpferische Kraft der Mutter. Als Produkt einer „monstrous birth", als Sohne der Hexe Sycorax, ist er selbst das lebende Symbol für diese Macht des Weiblichen, die der Patriarch Prospero von seiner Insel zu verbannen versucht.

Obwohl das Thema der Fortpflanzung, im erstrebenswerten oder im monströsen Sinne, im Stück einen so wichtigen Platz einnimmt, fehlen in der Welt von *The Tempest* die Mütter – so sehr, dass die Männer selbst den Part des Gebärens übernehmen:

> In The Tempest, men are envisaged as agitating to give birth without the agency or intervention of female influence.[102]

So besteht das Aufeinandertreffen von Caliban, Trinculo und Stephhano aus einer slapstickhaften, analen „Geburtsszene", in der Stephano Trinculo aus Calibans Umhang zieht: *„How cam'st thou be the siege of this mooncalf? Can he vent Trinculos?"* (II.2.105-106).

Von zwei tatsächlichen Müttern ist im Stück explizit die Rede, beide sind tot. Eine ist Mirandas Mutter, an die das Mädchen keinerlei Erinnerung hat und die nur in einem einzigen Satz erwähnt wird, die andere ist die Hexe Sycorax, die, aus ihrer Heimat Algier verbannt, das „Monster" Caliban auf der Insel zur Welt gebracht hat. Trotz der Tatsache, dass beide Frauen nicht mehr leben, können sie doch als zwei Endpunkte auf der Skala der männlichen Konzepte von Weiblichkeit gesehen werden. Auf der einen Seite die untergeordnete, stille, sich gänzlich im Hintergrund der männlichen Lebensgestaltung befindende Ehefrau, die zwar nicht den optimalen männlichen, aber doch einen gelungenen Nachwuchs geboren hat;

---

[102] Thornton Burnett, S. 142.

auf der anderen Seite die „Hexe", die unverheiratete, unabhängige, machthungrige, sexuell ungezügelte Frau. Das überwiegende Fehlen von Mutterfiguren bei Shakespeare hat Janet ADELMANN in „Suffocating Mothers" ausführlich untersucht und auch in The Tempest wurde der bedrohliche mütterliche Körper systematisch entfernt, denn nicht zuletzt geht es in dieser Romanze um eine Widerherstellung der „paternal authority with a vengeance"[103].

Sycorax

Obwohl Sycorax lange tot und deshalb im Stück genauso wenig physisch anwesend ist wie Mirandas Mutter oder die Prinzessin Claribel, ist sie im Gedächtnis der Inselbewohner auf unheimliche Weise lebendig.

Besonders Prospero benutzt die Erinnerung an Calibans Mutter häufig für seine Zwecke. Im Grunde wird alles, was die Zuschauer über Sycorax erfahren, aus Prosperos Perspektive erzählt, und als ein geübter Manipulator von Menschen nutzt er diese „*power of the storyteller to narrate the past in ways that justify the present and shape the future*"[104].

Schon bei der ersten Erwähnung der „*damn'd witch*" (I.2.263) wird dies deutlich. Als Ariel den Magier an sein Versprechen erinnert, ihm nach einem Jahr seine Freiheit zu schenken, fragt Prospero ihn: „*Dost thou forget / From what a torment I did free thee?*" (I.2.250-51). Er erinnert den Luftgeist so an seine von Sycorax über ihn verhängte qualvolle Gefangenschaft in einer gespaltenen Kiefer, aus der Prospero ihn nach zwölf Jahren endlich „befreit" hatte, um ihn zu seinem eigenen Diener zu machen.

Es ist interessant, wie Prospero die tote Sycorax einerseits als bedrohliche Beschwörerin von „*mischiefs manifold and sorceries terrible*" (I.2.264) und als mächtige Hexe „*that could control the moon, make flows and ebbs, / and deal in her command without her power*" (V.1.271-72) darstellt, auf der anderen Seite aber auch wiederholt die Unterlegenheit ihrer magischen Fähigkeiten betont: Nur mithilfe ihrer „*more potent ministers*" (I.2.275) sei es ihr überhaupt gelungen, Ariel in dem Baum einzusperren.

---

[103] Adelmann, S. 237.

[104] Irene Lara, "Beyond Caliban's Curses: The Decolonial Feminist Literacy of Sycorax", in: Journal of International Women's Studies 9 (2007), S. 83.

Sycorax' matriarchalische Kraft stellt auch über ihren Tod hinaus durch ihren Erben Caliban eine Gefährdung von Prosperos Machtanspruch dar, die er zerschlagen muss, denn „*witchcraft exposed the yawning possibility that an individual might attack paternal authority, and, with it, society.*"[105]

Zusätzlich konstruiert Prospero einen Zusammenhang zwischen Sycorax moralischer Verdorbenheit und ihrer körperlichen Devianz. Wie auch Richard III. wird diese bösartige Kreatur als bucklig beschrieben, als ob ihr Körper sich unter der Last ihrer „*mischiefs manifold*" beugen würde: „*The foul witch Sycorax, who with age and envy / Was grown into a hoop*" (I.2.257-8). Wie ihr Sohn Caliban wird auch Sycorax dem Element Erde zugeschrieben, mit den Assoziationen von Schmutz, Primitivität, Derbheit, im Gegensatz zu Miranda und Ariel, die Geschöpfe des Elementes Luft sind, also rein, unschuldig, „*delicate*" (I.2.272).

In enger Verbindung zu ihren bösen Machenschaften wird Sycorax, ganz dem mittelalterlichen und frühneuzeitlichen Hexenglauben entsprechend, auch eine perverse Sexualität unterstellt. Der Hexenglaube wurde gerade im Moralismus der Jahre der Reformation und Gegenreformation durch die theologisch begründete Diskriminierung der weiblichen Sexualität angefacht. Katholiken und Protestanten propagierten einen strengen Sexualcode, der Prostitution und Ehebruch, vorehelichen Geschlechtsverkehr und den lustvollen, nicht allein der Zeugung dienenden Akt auch im Ehebett verbot.[106] Als Verursacherin dieser Überschreitungen der christlichen Moral galt die Frau mit ihrer unheimlichen, zügellosen Sexualität, Nachfahrin der Sünderin Eva, die ja erst durch ihre Verführungskünste den Niedergang der Menschheit verursacht hatte.

Die tote Mutter Sycorax verkörpert im Kern also die männlichen Ängste vor den vermeintlich übermächtigen sexuellen Energien und den geheimnisvollen Fähigkeiten der Frau bei der Fortpflanzung, von denen der Mann völlig ausgeschlossen ist und die deshalb im sexuellen Diskurs der Frühen Neuzeit nur als „monströs" angesehen werden konnten.

Was Prosperos Diskriminierung von Sycorax besonders pikant macht, sind die offensichtlichen Parallelen zwischen den beiden Machtmenschen: Beide wurden aus ihren Reichen verbannt, weil sie sich mit Magie beschäftigt hatten, beide machten sich mithilfe dieser Magie die Insel Untertan, beide brachten ein Kind

---

[105] Lyndal Roper, *Oedipus and the Devil. Witchcraft, sexuality and religion in early modern Europe*. London/New York, 1994, S. 239.

[106] Tilmann Walter, *Unkeuschheit und Werk der Liebe*, Berlin 1998, S. 154f.

mit, das ihr einziger Erbe ist. Diese Ähnlichkeiten manifestieren sich zum Beispiel in Prosperos Umgang mit Ariel, den er erst an die schrecklichen Qualen erinnert, die Sycorax ihm mit der Verbannung in den gespaltenen Baum zugefügt hatte, um ihm im selben Atemzug dieselbe Folter anzudrohen (I.2.294-95).

Mirandas Mutter

Anders als die vor allem durch Prospero für seine eigenen Zwecke lebendig gehaltene Erinnerung an Sycorax ist das Andenken an seine eigene Frau fast gänzlich verschwunden. Seltsamerweise gewährt er seiner Tochter keine nähere Beschreibung, keine liebevolle Erinnerung an ihre Mutter. Während er selbst gezielt ein negatives Gedächtnis an die Hexe Sycorax erschaffen hat, eine Frau, die er selbst niemals getroffen hat, scheint es, als wolle er die Erinnerung an seine tote Frau absichtlich auslöschen.

Wir erfahren nichts über ihren Verbleib und die eigentlichen Gründe ihrer Abwesenheit. Die Ursache ihres Todes ist, wie bei Sycorax auch (obwohl diese laut Prospero zumindest schon alt war), unklar. Starb sie lange vor der Entmachtung des Herzogs oder vielleicht während dieser schicksalhaften Ereignisse? Oder ist sie vielleicht gar nicht tot, sondern wurde in Mailand zurückgelassen? Nichts davon wird erwähnt und von Trauer über ihren Verlust oder irgendwelchen liebevollen Gefühlen für die Mutter seiner Tochter ist bei Prospero jedenfalls nichts zu spüren. Nur ein einziges Mal im ganzen Stück erwähnt er sie überhaupt:

> Miranda: Sir, are you not my father?
>
> Prospero: Thy mother was a piece of virtue, and
> She said thou wast my daugter. (I.2.52-58)

Mit dieser Antwort auf Mirandas seltsame Frage gibt er zwar die einzige Beschreibung seiner Frau, stellt aber die ihr attestierte „virtue" gleichzeitig in Frage: Er muss sich ganz auf ihr Wort verlassen, was seine Vaterschaft angeht, und offenbar hatte er es damals für nötig gehalten, sich überhaupt ihr Wort darauf geben zu lassen. Hier kommt erneut die männliche Angst vor den geheimnisvollen Reproduktions-Fähigkeiten der Frau zutage, von denen der Mann abhängig ist. Wegen der potentiell immer untreuen Ehefrau läuft ein Mann stets Gefahr, einen Bastard untergeschoben zu bekommen. Diese männliche Ur-Angst ist für den Adligen Prospero, für den eine reine Blutlinie und ein legitimer Erbe unerlässlich sind, natürlich besonders quälend.

Die ewige Ungewissheit der Vaterschaft sowie der bereits thematisierte Einfluss, den die schwangere Frau auf das ungeborene Kind nehmen kann, bedeuten ebenso eine Gefahr für Prosperos patriarchalische Macht wie die durch Sycorax verkörperte weibliche Sexualität. Um diese mütterliche Machtsphäre zu verdrängen, hat er die Mutter völlig aus Mirandas Kindheit, ja sogar aus ihrer Geburt ausgeklammert, bis hin zu einer AutogamieVorstellung, die sich in einer Sprache niederschlägt, die Assoziationen von Schwangerschaft und Geburt hervorruft:[107]

> Thou didst smile
> Infused with a fortitude from heaven
> When I have decked the sea with drops full salt
> Under my burden groaned; which raised in me
> An undergoing stomach, to bear up
> Against what should ensue. (I.2.153-58)

Mit der Ankunft auf der Insel wurde Miranda also gleichsam neu „geboren", mit Prospero als Vater und Mutter zugleich. Für ihre eigentliche Mutter gibt es keinerlei Verwendung in Prosperos Absichten, seine Tochter zu formen. Ohne ihre Anwesenheit ist er ihr einziger Versorger und Bezugspunkt, ihre ganze kindliche Zuneigung gehört ungeteilt ihm und keine Erinnerung an eine „echte" Frau kann bei Miranda Zweifel oder Widerspruch gegenüber den Vorstellungen erwecken, nach denen Prospero ihre Weiblichkeit gestalten und am Ende gewinnbringend einsetzten will. Es scheint, als habe er sich nicht nur mit väterlicher Liebe, sondern auch mit strategischem Kalkül um seine Tochter gekümmert und sie, ganz den Verheiratungsstrategien des frühneuzeitlichen Adels entsprechend, zu einer angemessenen Ehefrau herangezogen:

> ...here / Have I, thy schoolmaster, made thee more profit / Than other princess' can, that have more time / For vainer hours, and tutors not so careful. (I.2.171-74)

Sie ist ein wichtiger Teil, des „*present business / wich now's upon's*" (I.2.135), des Planes, den er durch den magischen Sturm in Gang gesetzt hat und der ihm die Gelegenheit bietet, sein Herzogtum und damit das Repräsentationsfeld seiner männlichen Potenz zurück zu erlangen.

Durch ihr Exil auf der Insel ist Miranda ist in einer Welt ganz ohne Frauen aufgewachsen:

---

[107] Aarthi Vadde, "On the Absent Presence of Mothers in The Tempest", online verfügbar unter *The Association of Young Journalists and Writers (AYJW)*, http://ayjw.org/articles.php?id=605901 [20.01.2007].

> I do not know
> One of my sex; no woman's face rememeber,
> Save, from my glas, mine own (III.1.49-51)

Sie hat nie eine echte Mutter kennen gelernt, sondern nur die zwei Konzepte, die ihr Vater ihr vermittelt hat: Zum einen die ihr unbekannte, gesichts- und namenlose Frau, die sie zur Welt gebracht hat, ein „*piece of virtue*", die aber ansonsten ganz ohne Bedeutung für ihr Leben ist, das vollkommen durch den Vater bestimmt wird. Zum anderen Sycorax, die abscheuliche Hexe, dunkles Gegenstück zur tugendhaften, substanzlosen Mailänderin. Beide Mütter sind tot, als hätten sie ihre Aufgabe schon erfüllt, indem sie ihre Kinder zur Welt brachten. Die liebevolle Versorgung und Erziehung geschieht allein durch den Vater, und wenn dieser wie bei Caliban ebenfalls nicht da ist, wächst das Kind zu einem „Monster" heran, ohne Bildung, Moral, ja ohne Sprache.

Die junge Frau, zu der Miranda auf der Insel herangereift ist, „*so perfect and so peerless*" (III.1.47) in Ferdinands Augen, ist, wenn man von den modernen Vorstellungen eines durch Sozialisierung geformten *Gender*-Verhaltens ausgeht, ganz und gar eine Schöpfung ihres Vaters; und es ist kein Wunder, das sie dadurch auch Ferdinands Ansprüchen an eine perfekte Ehefrau entspricht.

Ein Faktor, der in der Untersuchung der sexuellen Unterströmungen in *The Tempest* nur sehr selten beachtet wird, ist aber Mirandas eigenen Sexualität. Meist nur als Objekt der Begierde aller männlichen Figuren gesehen, geht es in der dem Stück zugrunde liegenden Vater-Tochter-Beziehung doch auch um Mirandas Erwachsenwerden und die Entwicklung ihrer weiblichen Lust, und damit dem Erwachen einer Macht, die schon im Zusammenhang mit den toten Müttern als zerstörerisch für die patriarachalen Strukturen von Prosperos Herrschaft dargestellt wird.

Miranda

Die verschiedenen Vater-Tochter-Beziehungen in Shakespeares Dramen untersucht Diane Elizabeth DREHER in *Domination and Defiance*. Für die Romanzen hat sie dabei eine Besonderheit dieser Beziehung konstatiert: Im Gegensatz zu den Komödien, in denen es um androgyne Heldinnen und deren Befreiung aus der väterlichen Dominanz gehe, betonen Shakespeares Romanzen das Bedürfnis des

Vaters nach seelischem Gleichgewicht und innerer Vollständigkeit, dass er nur mithilfe der Tochter am Ende erfüllen könne.[108]

In sämtlichen Dramen aller Genres, in denen das Vater-Tochter-Verhältnis eine wesentliche Rolle spielt, treffen wir Vater und Tochter in der selben Situation an: Die Tochter, die den Kinderschuhen entwachsen und zur Frau geworden ist, und der Vater, der sich schwer damit tut, sie in die Erwachsenenwelt zu entlassen und damit letztlich auch seinem eigenen Verfall ins Gesicht zu sehen. In einer fiktiven Welt, in der Mütter entweder nicht existieren oder sich ihren Kindern entfremdet haben, nimmt das Verhältnis zwischen Vater und Tochter eine wichtige Funktion bei der Abhandlung von männlichen und weiblichen Rollenkonflikten, moralischen Fragen und der Überschreitung oder Einhaltung von sozialen Normen ein. Immer ist diese Beziehung, gemäß der Konventionen der Frühen Neuzeit, auch ein Machtverhältnis. Die Tochter ist Besitz des Vaters und kann ihm politischen und sozialen Gewinn einbringen, gleichzeitig ist sie formbar: Er kann sie zu dem machen, was ihre abwesende Mutter nicht sein konnte: *„For him, a daughter is, at last, a controllable female, one he can mold to his image of the ideal woman."*[109] Die erwachende sexuelle Kraft der Tochter wird schließlich jedoch zu einem starken Gegenspieler für die väterlichen Idealvorstellungen, die seine Illusionen über seine eigene männliche Potenz und Kontrolle herausfordert.

Weil die dramatische Perspektive hier die des Vater ist, hat die Tochter nur eine symbolische Funktion: Jung, unschuldig, ganz und gar unverdorben verkörpert sie die perfekte Weiblichkeit und die Väter sonnen sich im Glanz dieses von ihnen erschaffenen Geschöpfes. Sie sind der erste Mann im Leben dieser jungen Frau und wollen am liebsten auch der einzige bleiben. Wenn DREHER diese Töchter der Romanzen jedoch als *„shimmering emblems of purity who (...) chasten men's lust with a transcendent, spiritual power"*[110] bezeichnet, scheint sie diesen keine eigene sexuelle Energie zuzugestehen. Genau hier liegt aber, wie auch in *The Tempest*, das größte Konfliktpotential in der Vater-Tochter-Beziehung, denn mit den ersten Anzeichen der Pubertät muss der Vater entdecken, dass das „unschuldige Kind" zur Frau wird. Die Tochter trägt in sich den Keim für die von ihm gemäß des Sexualitäts-Diskurses der Vormoderne gefürchtete weibliche Lust, die seine

---

[108] Diane Elizabeth Dreher, *Domination and Defiance: Fathers and Daughters in Shakespeare*. Lexington (Kentucky), 1986, S. 143.

[109] Michael E. Lamb (u.a.), "The Father-Daughter Relationship", in: Kopp, Claire B. & Martha Kirkpatrick (Hrsg.), *Becoming Female*. New York 1979, S. 89.

[110] Dreher, S. 143.

väterliche Kontrolle zu sprengen droht. Die zur Frau werdende Miranda ist nicht mehr nur das schutzbedürftige Opfer männlicher Lust, sondern wird schon bald selbst sexuell aktiv werden.

Leslie FIEDLER sieht in Ariel und Caliban spirituelle Spiegelungen von Prospero und Miranda:

> Corresponding to each, there is an otherworldly double, an elemental: the gross shadow of the father, compounded of earth and water in Caliban; the etheral anima of the daughter, compounded of fire and air in Ariel[111]

Betrachtet man die Signifikanz dieser beiden Manifestationen von Prosperos inneren Konflikten aber unter den oben genannten Gesichtspunkten, könnten sie auch die zwei Seiten von Miranda in der Vorstellung ihres Vaters verkörpern. Dann stünde der Luftgeist Ariel mit seiner verspielten Unbekümmertheit für das junge Mädchen Miranda, das unschuldige Kind, für das der Vater die Phantasiewelt der Insel geschaffen hat, und Caliban ist die düstere Bedrohung der potentiell „monströsen" Sexualität der erwachsenen Tochter, die in der Isolation der Insel zu etwas Ungeheuerlichem, vielleicht sogar zu einem inzestuösen Verhältnis zum eigenen Vater führen könnte.

Der dritte Caliban: Die Versuchung des Vaters

Wenn der Vater sich wegen der aufblühenden Sexualität der Tochter Sorgen macht, muss er sich auch über seine eigenen sexuellen Regungen klar werden. Dazu gehört womöglich, dass er sich eingestehen muss, dass seine Tochter für ihn eine attraktive Frau ist: „*Incest is an undeniable element in this emotional bond.*"[112] In seinen verzweifelten Anstrengungen, die Tochter vor den Bedrohungen sowohl durch die sie umgebende männliche als auch ihrer eigenen Sexualität zu schützen, zeigt sich auch die Angst vor einem Kontrollverlust über die eigenen Triebe. Es ist auffällig, dass Sex in *The Tempest*, im Gegensatz zu anderen Dramen Shakespeares, in der Realität nicht ein einziges Mal passiert. Sämtliche sexuelle Handlungen spielen sich nur in Prosperos Kopf ab, so auch Calibans missglückter Übergriff auf Miranda, der diese im Übrigen in ihrer Beziehung zu Männern nicht besonders erschüttert haben kann, wenn man die Neugier und Unbe-

---

[111] Leslie A. Fiedler, *The Stranger in Shakespeare*. London, 1973., S. 223.
[112] Dreher, S. 58.

kümmertheit sieht, mit der sie sich dem Fremden Ferdinand nähert. Das Misstrauen, mit dem der Vater – und nicht etwa die beinahe vergewaltigte Tochter – seinem zukünftigen Schwiegersohn begegnet, deutet auf sein eigenes sexuelles Verlangen hin, dass er auch allen anderen Männern unterstellt, lässt ihn aber gleichzeitig selbst wie einen eifersüchtigen Liebhaber erscheinen.

Die Problematisierung der eigenen Sexualität gerade bei Männern mittleren Alters erklärt DREHER mit einer fehlenden Integration ihrer männlichen und weiblichen Anteile. Zu einem ausbalancierten Seelenleben gehöre nach der Jungschen Psychologie die Integration der eigenen Anteile des jeweils anderen Geschlechts und in den Romanzen müssten die Väter gewissermaßen ihre *anima*, ihre weibliche Seite in sich entdecken und akzeptieren, um ihr inneres Gleichgewicht wieder zu finden. Die Integration der *anima* – und damit die Wiederherstellung der emotionalen Intaktheit des Vaters – sei die Aufgabe der Töchter in Shakespeares Romanzen.[113]

DREHER ist der Meinung, dass Prospero zum Zeitpunkt der Handlung von „The Tempest" diese Integration während der zwölf Jahre auf der Insel bereits erreicht habe:

> While educating Miranda, he has eductaed his own emotional nature, developing the anima, which has made him a great magus.[114]

Was sein Verantwortungs- und Pflichtbewusstsein angeht, so hat ihm die Zeit im Exil als „Alleinerziehender" einer kleinen Tochter sicher gut getan. Zuvor hatte er sich, wie er selber zugibt, von der Welt und seinen Aufgaben als Fürst und Vater zurückgezogen: „*The government I cast upon my brother / And to my state grew stranger, being transported / And rapt in secret studies*" (I.2.75-77). Auf der Insel war er endlich gezwungen, aus der Welt der Bücher in die ganz profane Welt des täglichen Überlebens zurückzukehren. Die Entdeckung seiner Vatergefühle für Miranda hat ihm geholfen, seine Wut und Verbitterung über den Verrat seines Bruders zu überwinden oder zumindest zur Seite zu schieben: „*O, a cherubin / Thou wast that did preserve me!*" (I.2.152-53).

Seine sexuelle Identität, die Integration seiner *anima*, ist jedoch, anders als DREHER argumentiert, ganz und gar nicht im Gleichgewicht und befindet sich sogar bei Einsetzen der Handlung in einem großen Chaos. Weit davon entfernt, mit dem

---

[113] Dreher, S. 144f.

[114] Ebd., S. 158.

„Weiblichen" im Reinen zu sein, sieht er es als Gefahr für die von ihm etablierte Ordnung auf der Insel und die Herrschaft über seine Tochter. Zusätzlich ist davon auszugehen, dass er seine eigene Sexualität in all den Jahren auf seiner vollkommen frauenlosen Insel nur schwerlich ausleben konnte.

Das Misstrauen gegenüber dem eigenen sexuellen Verlangen, das einen Mann verwundbar macht und mit moralischen Verstößen wie Inzest oder Ehebruch bedroht, war in Mittelalter und Früher Neuzeit das Motiv zur Verteufelung und Mystifizierung der Frau und der weiblichen Sexualität. Genau so verhält sich auch Prospero, indem er sein eigenes unterdrücktes Verlangen auf seine Umwelt überträgt. Um sich und seine Tochter vor einem inzestuösen Verhältnis, einer sexuellen Ausnutzung seiner Macht über die eigene Tochter zu schützen, muss er sich von seinem eigenen „Caliban" befreien und Miranda einem anderen Mann, Ferdinand, übergeben.

Caliban ist im vielfachem Sinne eine Verkörperung der väterlichen Ängste Prosperos: Als „mooncalf" führt er ihm stets die monströsen Folgen eines illegitimen, auch eines inzestuösen Geschlechtsverkehrs vor Augen. Andererseits steht er auch für die erwachende weibliche Sexualität seiner zur Frau herangewachsenen Tochter, die er schon bald nicht mehr in der unschuldigen Fantasiewelt der Insel wird halten können. Er weiß, dass auch er einen „Caliban" in sich trägt: *„This thing of darkness I / acknowledge mine"* (V.1.275-6). Auch die größte humanistisch-spirituelle Anstrengung kann das chaotische Element der körperlichen Lust am Ende nicht unter Kontrolle bringen, denn dieses „Monster" ist Teil der menschlichen Natur:

> Prospero comes to identify his own ‚monstrositiy' and, through conjuring Caliban, begins to appreciate the impossibility of ever adequately separating out ‚monster' and 'man'[115]

Die Anerkennung des „Monströsen" im Menschen bedeutet zugleich auch die Erkenntnis des Menschlichen in Caliban, eine Entwicklung, die dieser selbst auch wahrnimmt: *„I will be wise hereafter/ And seek for grace"* (V.1.294-5). „Grace", als „Anmut" verstanden, würde zugleich bedeuten, dass mit Calibans quasi-evolutionärer Entwicklung sich auch sein Körper vom Monströsen zum Menschlichen hin verändern würde.

---

[115] Fiedler, S.148.

Und so wie Prospero am Ende Ariel, den väterlichen Traum von der ewigen Unschuld der Tochter, loslässt, bleibt auch Caliban, die vormals gestaltlose Bedrohung durch ungezügelte männliche sowie weibliche Sexualität, auf der Insel zurück. Befreit von den Projektionen des ängstlichen Magier-Vaters ist er dem Menschsein einen Schritt näher, aber allein.

Falstaff – Die Weiblichkeit des fetten Mannes

> I am not only witty in myself, but the cause that wit is in other men(2HIV, I.2.8-9)

Der letzte hier zu untersuchende Charakter ist Sir John Falstaff, eine der bekanntesten und beliebtesten Figuren Shakespeares und der einzige, der nicht nur in mehreren Stücken, sondern auch in zwei verschiedenen Genres auftaucht. Die folgenden Ausführungen werden sich allerdings auf den Ritter aus der Henriade konzentrieren. Der Falstaff in *The Merry Wives of Windsor*, den Shakespeare wohl aufgrund seiner Beliebtheit beim Publikum hat „wieder auferstehen" lassen, soll hier größtenteils beiseite gelassen werden, weil er sich dort als eine vollkommen andere Figur darstellt, deren spezielle Korporealität eine andere Signifikanz hat als noch in den Henry IV-Dramen und eher die Komik des alternden Möchtegern-Weiberhelden unterstützen soll.

Was aber ist Falstaff? Seine über seine körperliche Andersartigkeit transportierte Bedeutung scheint ebenso vielschichtig und schillernd zu sein wie die Calibans, obwohl im Gegensatz zu diesem Falstaffs „disability" eindeutig greifbar ist. Seine legendäre Fettleibigkeit als „disability" zu bezeichnen, entspricht dabei durchaus der anfangs zitierten Definition dieses Begriffes.[116] Falstaffs Übergewicht bedeutet für ihn zum einen eine ganz unmittelbare „Behinderung". Zwar nimmt er als Ritter an der Schlacht teil und scheint auch für eine schnelle Flucht durchaus beweglich genug zu sein, mehrfach ist aber von seiner Unbeweglichkeit und Schwerfälligkeit die Rede: „*Falstaff sweats to death / And lards the lean earth as he walks along. / Were't not for laughing, I should pity him.*" (1HIV, 2.101-104). Aussagen wie diese von Prinz Hal zeigen den anderen, gesellschaftlichen Aspekt seines außergewöhnlichen Körpers. Es sind, wie auch bei Caliban, der sich seiner eigenen Andersartigkeit und damit „Minderwertigkeit" vermutlich ursprünglich gar nicht bewusst war, seine „normalen" Mitmenschen, die ihn als nicht den Normen entsprechend, als Außenseiter, brandmarken.

Die Frage, warum Shakespeare, abgesehen von seiner komödiantischen Wirkung, seinem Ritter einen solch außergewöhnlichen Körper zugedacht hat, hat die Literaturwissenschaft zu zahlreichen, sich teils widersprechenden, teils überlappenden Erklärungsmodellen geführt. Es können hier nur einige wenige Interpretatio-

---

[116] Mitchell/Snyder (S. 6): "*cognitive and physical conditions that deviate from normative ideas of mental ability and physiological function*"

nen von Falstaffs „gehaltvollem" Körper berücksichtigt werden, denn das Hauptaugenmerk soll ja auf seiner speziellen *disability* in ihrer Bedeutung für seine „Männlichkeit", seiner sexuellen und sozialen Signifikanz liegen. Hierfür sollen zunächst die in der Vormoderne gültigen biologischen und sexuellen/genderbezogenen Bedeutungszuschreibungen von Fettleibigkeit in ihren Hauptzügen dargelegt werden.

Fettleibigkeit im Licht der vormodernen Medizin

Schon im frühesten westlichen Medizin-Diskurs war Fettleibigkeit eine pathologische Kategorie.[117] Nach der Vier-Säfte-Theorie des Hippokrates galt ein Überfluss an Phlegma als Ursache für Übergewicht. Das Temperament des Phlegmatikers war durch Eigenschaften wie Faulheit, Trägheit und vor allem geistiger Langsamkeit geprägt. Noch heute wird Fettleibigkeit an erster Stelle mit „Dummheit" assoziiert. Die Unausgeglichenheit der Körpersäfte konnte im günstigsten Fall durch eine spezielle Diät behoben werden, konnte aber auch ein permanenter Zustand sein. Verbunden mit dem phlegmatischen Temperament war „polysarkia", „zu viel Fleisch", denn in seinem Zustand körperlicher und geistiger Trägheit neigte der Phlegmatiker dazu, zu viel zu essen. Dabei wurde durchaus ein Unterschied zwischen „gesundem" Fett, das die Wärme im Körper hielt und deshalb das Leben verlängerte, und krankhaftem Fett gemacht. Excessive Fettheit war also – und das gilt bis heute – ein Zeichen mangelnder Disziplin, ein Kontroll- und damit Machtverlust, den der Kranken als „unmännlich" kennzeichnete.

Im Zusammenhang damit steht auch die dem weiblichen Körper zugeschriebene „Rundlichkeit". Schon im Altgriechischen bestand ein linguistischer Zusammenhang zwischen dem Bauch eines dicken Mannes und dem einer schwangeren Frau. Fettleibigkeit hat bei Frauen und Männern unterschiedliche Konnotationen. Während die ausladende Weiblichkeit einer übergewichtigen Frau in vergangenen Kulturen die sexuelle Attraktivität und das Ansehen der Frau verstärkte, bedeutet

---

[117] Die Geschichte und Kultur des übergewichtigen Körpers hat vor allem für das männliche Geschlecht bis heute in der humanwissenschaftlichen Forschung nur wenig Beachtung gefunden und unterliegt ähnlichen Mechanismen und Beschränkungen, wie sie eingangs für die Disability Studies formuliert wurden. Die folgende kurze Ausführung zur Kulturgeschichte der (männlichen) Fettleibigkeit sind Gilman Sanders „Fat Boys. A Slim Book." (Lincoln (Nebraska), 2004) entnommen. Eine innovative Studie von Elena LEVY-NAVARRO zu diesem Thema ist zum gegenwärtigen Zeitpunkt noch nicht veröffentlicht. (Elena Levy-Navarro, The Culture of Obesity in Early and Late Modernity: Body Image in Shakespeare, Jonson, Middleton, and Skelton. Voraussichtlich Juli 2008)

für den Mann in allen Kulturen eine Zunahme an Körperfett zugleich eine Entfernung von seiner „Männlichkeit" im Sinne seiner Sexualität und seiner gesellschaftlichen Rolle als Mann. Ein Körperumfang wie der Falstaffs widersprach zutiefst dem zumindest anfänglich an die griechische Antike angelehntem männlichen Körperideal der Renaissance und war mit einer gewissen Entsexualisierung der betroffenen Person verbunden, die auch in der modernen Gesellschaft greift. Ein dicker Mann, so AUDEN, „*looks like the cross between a very young child and a pregnant mother*"[118], ist also entweder ein unreifes, unsexuelles Wesen oder besitzt eine mütterliche Weiblichkeit, keinesfalls jedoch ist er ein potentieller Teilnehmer an heteronormativer Sexualität. Nicolas Abraham DE LA FRAMBOISIÈRE, französischer Chemiker und Arzt, beschrieb den Phlegmatiker Mitte des 17. Jahrhunderts so: „*They are of a dull wit…they are fearfull, covetous, and given to heape up riches, and are weake in the act of venerie.*"[119] Einige dieser Eigenschaften treffen ganz sicher auf den pathologisch fetten Falstaff zu, von „dullness" kann bei ihm jedoch keine Rede sein. Im Gegenteil ist sein wichtigstes Charakteristikum seine hellwache, vor Geist sprühende Intelligenz, die sich in einer humorvollen, schlagfertigen Redegewandtheit äußert – ein äußerst beweglicher Geist gefangen in einem trägen, grotesk aufgeblähten Körper? Wie auch bei Richard und Caliban werden die Beweggründe für Shakespeare, seiner Figur genau diesen Körper zu kreieren, zunächst in der Quellenforschung und in ideologisch-kulturellen Strömungen zur Zeit seiner Entstehung gesucht.

Historisches Vorbild und traditionelle Interpretationen

Wie auch Richard III. ist die Figur Falstaff an ein historisches Vorbild angelehnt. In der ursprünglichen Bühnenfassung trug Falstaff noch den Namen seiner Vorlage, Sir John Oldcastle, einem der Anführer der Lollardenbewegung des frühen 15. Jahrhunderts, der 1517 in London hingerichtet und von den Protestanten fortan als Martyrer verehrt wurde. Auf Drängen des empörten Nachfahren Oldcastles, Baron Cobham, zu dieser Zeit Lord Chamberlain, musste Shakespeare nach der Fertigstellung von *Henry IV., Part 1* seine Figur umbenennen. Dem elisabethanischen Publikum war die historische Figur Oldcastle aus Geschichtsbüchern und Theaterstücken wohlbekannt, Shakespeares „Neuinterpretation" wird deshalb

---

[118] W.H. Auden, "The Pince's Dog" (1959), in: G.K. Hunter (Hrsg.), *Shakespeare: Henry IV Parts I and II*. London, 1970, S. 200.

[119] Nicolas Abraham de La Framboisière, *An Easy Method to Know the Causes and Signs of the Humour Most Ruled in the Body*. London (?) 1640, zitiert bei Alexandra Shepard, *Meanings of manhood in early modern England*. Oxford, 2003, S. 61.

wohl einiges Aufsehen erregt haben. Warum er sich überhaupt dafür entschieden hatte, den protestantischen Märtyrer auf diese Art in seiner Henriade zu verarbeiten, ist umstritten. Während Richards *disabilities* zumindest in der Propaganda der Gegenseite überliefert sind, ist Oldcastles/Falstaffs überdimensionaler Körper ganz Shakespeares Kreativität zuzuschreiben – in den historischen Quellen zu Oldcastle gibt es jedenfalls keinerlei Hinweise auf eine besondere Korpulenz des Ritters. Neben Spekulationen, dass Shakespeare aufgrund persönlicher Animositäten die Cobham-Familie verspotten wollte, wird eine weitere Erklärung im religiösen Bereich, auf der Basis von Shakespeares eigener katholischer Orientierung, gesucht. So sieht David WOMERSLEY die Gestaltung der Bühnenrolle auf der Basis des Märtyrers Sir John Oldcastle in einem größeren Zusammenhang, nämlich als Shakespeares Reaktion auf die protestantischen Bestrebungen seit dem frühen 16. Jahrhundert, die englische Geschichte nach ihren eigenen Vorstellungen und zu religionspolitischen Zwecken umzuschreiben.[120]

Bernard SPIVACK ist ein Vertreter einer anderen Lesart von Falstaffs spezieller körperlicher Beschaffenheit. Falstaff ist demnach nicht auf einer historischen Person aufgebaut, er ist tatsächlich überhaupt keine Person, sondern eine Personifikation der „Untugenden" aus dem mittelalterlichen allegorischen Bühnenspiel, *„the composite image of Gluttony, Lechery, and all the rest of the fleshly sins"*. Obwohl die moderne Interpretation ihn im Allgemeinen für eines von Shakespeares gelungensten Portraits des menschlichen Wesens an sich hält, gehöre seine Rolle zu einer Bühnentradition, die ganz und gar nicht naturalistisch sei.[121]

Dass Fettleibigkeit mit menschlichen Schwächen und „fleshly sins" verbunden wurde und wird, ist freilich keine besonders fruchtbare Erkenntnis, um zur Signifikanz von Falstaffs besonderer Körperlichkeit vorzudringen. Diese ist auch hier scheinbar nur eine äußerliche Manifestierung seiner „vices", eine oberflächliche Interpretation, die gern auch auf Caliban und Richard angewendet wird, aber der Ausgestaltung ihrer Charaktere und den Reaktionen ihrer Mitmenschen auf ihre *disabilities* nicht gerecht wird – nicht umsonst wird gerade diesen Charakteren

---

[120] David Womersley, "Why Is Falstaff Fat?", in: *Review of English Studies* 47 (1996), S. 21. Dieser Ansatz beinhaltet allerdings ironischerweise genau das, was Womersley zu Beginn seines Aufsatzes anderen Literaturwissenschaftlern wie Barbara Everett und Dover Wilson vorwirft, nämlich die Vernachlässigung von Falstaffs eigentlichem Charakters „*as they pass on to higher matters"* (S. 1).

[121] Bernhard Spivack, "Falstaff and the Psychomachia", in: *Shakespeare Quarterly 8* (1957), S. 457 und 458.

immer wieder eine besondere Tiefe und Vielschichtigkeit attestiert, die einer bloßen, eindimensionalen „Verkörperung" von Bosheit, Primitivität und Völlerei widerspricht.

Andere Interpretationen sehen Falstaff, diesen „*globe of sinful continents*" (2HIV, II.4.275), in der Tradition des Karnevalesken, als einen Gegenpol zu den machtpolitischen Ideologien des sich entwickelnden modernen Staates:

> Beyond the misdemeanour-like quality of most of Falstaff's failings is the ritualistic, non-rational, wish-fulfilling, and symbolic nature of the carnival discourse that forms such an important part of Falstaff's dramatic function[122]

Im Prozess der Loslösung von traditionellen Weltanschauungen, so GRADY, stelle Falstaff den Entwurf einer neuen, autonomen, autotelischen Subjektivität dar. Falstaffs Karneval beinhalte einerseits die Möglichkeit des Widerstands gegen die unterdrückerischen Vorgaben des Patriarchats, indem sie dessen grausame und ungerechte Praktiken und falsche Moral aufdecke, stellt andererseits aber in ihrer Loslösung sowohl von der sinnvollen zeitlichen Begrenzung als auch von seiner agrargesellschaftlichen Herkunft des Karnevals eine Gefahr dar: „*thus the exploitive side of Falstaff can be seen as enacting one of the dangerous aspects of unfixed subjectivity in the service of unchecked appetite.*"[123]

Sein aus den Fugen und außer Kontrolle geratener Körper ist demnach das äußere Zeichen dieses ungezügelten Appetits, vielleicht Shakespeares satirischer Gegenentwurf zum puritanischen Lebensentwurf der Mäßigung.

Tatsächlich überkommt den Zuschauer schon bald das Gefühl, dass Falstaff in dieser Welt des Heroismus, der Selbstdisziplin und Unterordnung persönlicher Wünsche unter das politische Ziel ein „Fremd-Körper" ist, fremdartiger noch als die Frauen, die zumindest als Objekte politischer Strategien zu gebrauchen sind: „*the world of historical reality which a Chronicle Play claims to imitate is not a world which he can inhabit*".[124]

---

[122] Hugh Grady, "Falstaff: Subjectivity between the Carnival and the Aesthetic", in: *The Modern Language Review*. 96, Nr. 3 (Juli, 2001), S. 613.

[123] Ebd., S. 620.

[124] Auden, S. 188

Szenen, in denen sich der tödliche Ernst der kriegerischen Welt der Historie zeigt, erscheinen als besonders unvereinbar mit Falstaffs Wesen. Hier wirkt sein Verhalten pervers und schwer zu akzeptieren, etwa als er sein Schwert in den Körper des toten Hotspur stößt oder als er den zum Tode verurteilten Colevile mit einer ganz und gar unpassenden Frivolität verspottet. In diesen Momenten zeigt sich, dass er in dieser Welt fremd ist, ihre grausame Realität vielleicht gar nicht zu ihm durchdringt, der das gesamte Leben für einen großen Witz zu halten scheint, den nicht einmal der Tod verderben kann. Er muss den Tod nicht fürchten, denn die Zeit scheint für ihn ohne Bedeutung zu sein. „*What a devil hat thou to do with the time of day?*" (HIV, I.2.6) antwortet Hal ihm auf seine Frage nach der Zeit und tatsächlich scheint Falstaff ein Mensch zu sein, der einzig im Hier und Jetzt lebt. In einem Geschichtsdrama ist er ein Mensch ohne eigene Geschichte, schon „*with a white head and something of a round belly*" (2HIV, I.2.186) auf die Welt gekommen. Es fällt schwer, ihn sich als Kind oder jungen Mann vorzustellen: „*When I was about their years, Hal, I was not an eagle's talent in the waist*" (1HIV, II.4.325-26) – ein junger Falstaff ist ebenso nur als Witz vorstellbar, wie ein dünner.[125]

Falstaff und sein Körper

Obwohl ihm offenbar einige grundlegende menschliche Eigenschaften fehlen, ist Falstaff mehr als eine Allegorie, eine aus dem Ruder gelaufene Figur des mittelalterlichen Karnevals, dessen egozentrische Vergnügungssucht alles um ihn zu verschlingen droht.

Seine Korporealität ist kein bloßes Symbol für karnevalistischen Exzess oder eine liebenswürdige Sinnenfreude, die ihm häufig zugeschrieben wird. Dies mag auf den Falstaff der Komödie zutreffen, in den Historien hat seine Fettleibigkeit ganz konkrete Folgen für sein Leben und seine Persönlichkeit. Unter der Oberfläche der Selbstironie, mit der er mit seiner *disability* umgeht, und sich selbst als „*a goodly portly man, i'faith, and a corpulent, of a cheerful look, a pleasing eye, and a most noble carriage*" (1HIV, II.4.416-18) bezeichnet, leidet er unter dem Spott und den Beleidigungen, mit denen seine Mitmenschen ihm begegnen:

> Men of all sorts take a pride to gird at me. The brain of this foolish-copounded clay, man, is not able to invent anything that intends to

---

[125] Ebd., S. 189

> laughter, more than I invent or is invented on me. I am not only aitty
> in myself, but the cause that there is wit in other men (2HIV, I. 2.6-10)

Falstaff befindet sich nicht im Einklang mit seinem Körper, ein Aspekt, der im Zusammenhang mit der Deutung seines Verhaltens und seines Körpers als dem eines „Genussmenschen" gern übersehen wird. In ihrer überaus positiven Bewertung von Falstaffs „fatness" als Verkörperung seiner Dichte als Figur sieht Barbara EVERETT den Ritter zwar als „*perpetually making a kind of grumbling, smiling peace within himself, between the cumbersome body and the incomparable mind*"[126], übersieht aber, wie er selbst seinen Zustand empfindet und mit welchen Mitteln er sich „Heilung" zu verschaffen sucht. Im zweiten Teil von *King Henry IV.* schildert er, wie sehr er auf den Alkohol angewiesen ist, um trotz seiner *disability* überhaupt zu funktionieren:

> It ascends me into the brain, dries me there all the foolish and dull and crudy vapours which environ it; makes it apprehensive, quick, forgetive, full of nimble, fiery, and delectable shapes: which delivered o'er to the voice, the tongue, which is the birth, becoms excellent wit (2HIV, IV.3.96-101)

Er ist sich seines krankhaften, phlegmatischen Zustandes durchaus bewusst, weiß, dass sein Körper „*the badge of pusillanimity and cowardice*" (2HIV, IV.3.104) ist. Nur durch „*drinking good and good store of fertile sherris*" (2HIV, IV.3.120) ist seine ohnehin schon stark eingeschränkte Teilnahme an der Welt der patriarchalischen Männer überhaupt noch möglich – sogar auf dem Feld trägt er statt eines Schwertes einen Flachmann. Dieses Eingeständnis, dass sein viel gerühmter Wortwitz, sein „Frieden mit sich selbst" nur auf seinem exzessiven Alkoholkonsum beruht, macht ihn, bei aller Sympathie und Lustigkeit, eher zu einem tragischen, als einem komödiantischen Charakter.

Ebenso wie Caliban („*I will be wise hereafter/ And seek for grace*" (V.1.2945)) hat er den Wunsch und die Hoffnung, ein besserer Mensch zu werden, was gleichzeitig bedeutet, einen „normalen" Körper zu besitzen: „*If I do grow great, I'll grow less; for I'll purge, and leave sack, and live cleanly, as a nobleman should do.*" (1HIV, V.4.162-63). Seine Besserung ist für ihn mit dem Aufstieg in eine höhere soziale Position verbunden, wie die anderen männlichen „Monster" auch, muss er dafür auf kriminelle, zutiefst unmoralische Mittel zurückgreifen, indem

---

[126] Barbara Everett, "The Fatness of Falstaff: Shakespeare and Character", in: *Proceedings of the British Academy* 76 (1990), S. 124.

er Hotspurs Leiche schändet und sich dann als seinen Bezwinger ausgibt. Dieser Wunsch nach sozialer und moralischer Besserung, vor allem aber nach der Normalisierung seines „bedeutungsschweren", „monströsen" Körpers, und der abstoßende Weg, den er dafür einschlägt, widerspricht deutlich dem populären Bild vom selbstzufriedenen, unmoralischen aber liebenswerten Bonvivant Falstaff.

Falstaff ist, wie Barbara Everett es ausdrückt „*the whole round world in person*"[127], die Möglichkeiten, ihm und seiner Korporealität Bedeutung zu verleihen, oder seine Bedeutung zu ergründen, sind fast unbegrenzt. Was dabei höchst selten thematisiert wird, ist sein eigenes Verhältnis zu seinem „monströsen" Körper. So sehr wird dieser als Widerspiegelung seines Charakters rezipiert, dass gerne übersehen wird, dass er selbst seinen Körper als krankhaften Zustand empfindet und sein exzessiver Lebensstil sein Weg ist, mit diesem Körper und den Demütigungen, denen er unterworfen wird, zu leben – eine Flucht in den Alkoholismus und eine irreale Parallelwelt. Trotz seiner Redseligkeit erfahren wir allerdings von ihm selbst nicht viel mehr über sein Innenleben und so liegt der Schlüssel zur Entzifferung seines Wesens und der Bedeutung seines Körpers im Sinne der *Gender*-Forschung in seiner vermeintlich engen Beziehung zu Prinz Hal. Hier werden seine Rolle im Patriarchat und Aspekte seiner Sexualität verhandelt und hier liegt auch die Signifikanz, die sein „monströser" Körper beinhaltet, sowohl für den Prinzen, als auch für die Gesellschaft.

Falstaff als Vater

Am Ende von Richard II. erfahren wir, dass der zukünftige König von England in die Gesellschaft einer Bande von „*unrestrained loose companions*" (RII,V.3.7) geraten ist. Wer daraufhin eine jugendliche „Gang" aus kriminellen Schlägertypen und zwielichtigen Unterweltbewohnern erwartet hat, wird eher überrascht sein, im „Boar's Head" auf zwei kleinkriminelle Taugenichtse, eine schlampige Wirtin, eine abgehalfterte Hure und einen fetten, verarmten Ritter lange jenseits der Blüte seiner Mannesjahre zu treffen. Nicht ganz das also, was man von dem „schlechten Umgang" eines vermeintlich auf die schiefe Bahn geratenen Prinzen erwarten würde. Doch Hal hat im „Boar's Head" eine Zuflucht vor dem Einfluss seines Vaters gefunden, Henry Bolingbroke, als Erzieher seines Sohnes ebenso unfähig wie als Herrscher, der die Bürde seiner Illegitimität nicht ablegen kann und dessen Charakterschwächen ihn als guten König disqualifizieren. Er verstößt seinen Sohn auf moralischer und emotionaler Ebene, seine Art zu leben ist völlig

---

[127] Everett, S. 116.

unverständlich für ihn. Hal ist nicht der Erbe, den er sich gewünscht hat, sondern nur ein „*shadow of succession*" ist (1HIV, III.2.99).

Doch in der männerdominierten Welt der Historien braucht ein Junge nicht seine Mutter, sondern einen Vater, um zum Mann heranzureifen, und in Falstaff hat Hal seinen Ersatzvater gefunden, der das glatte Gegenteil seines biologischen Vaters ist. Die Henriade ist eine Studie des Einflusses der Vaterfigur auf die Selbstdefinition eines Mannes. Nicht die Mutter ist hier der Auslöser der Identitätskrise des Heranwachsenden, sondern es ist der Vater, von dem man sich entweder ablösen oder mit dem man sich identifizieren muss, um zum „Mann" zu werden.

Sir John Falstaff ist faul, unmoralisch und feige, aber im Gegensatz zu König Henry macht er auch nie einen Hehl daraus. Die Politik, strategische Erwägungen und Machtspiele sind uninteressant für jemanden, der ganz und gar in der Gegenwart lebt, und deshalb ist ihm auch der männliche Ehrenkodex mit seiner Vorstellung vom „Heldentod" auf dem Schlachtfeld gleichgültig. „*I was now a coward on instinct*" (1HIV, II.4.268-69). Seine „Feigheit" entspringt seinem unbedingten Drang, am Leben zu bleiben, egal durch welches Mittel. Alle Untugenden, die Falstaff im Kosmos seines aufgeblähten Körpers vereinen mag, streben nach der Erhaltung dieses lasterhaften, faulen, selbstzufriedenen Lebens, für eine andere, transzendente Moral hat er keine Verwendung. Er sucht stets nach der Befriedigung seiner lasterhaften Gelüste, ohne auf legale oder moralische Beschränkungen zu achten. Er lebt außerhalb der Gesellschaft und kennt keine Zwänge außer denen, die sein Körper und sein unersättlicher Lebenshunger ihm auferlegen. Das macht ihn zunächst zu einem äußerst fragwürdigen Lehrer. Die Figur des gesellschaftlichen Außenseiters, des „Monsters" als Ziehvater von Helden ist in der Literaturgeschichte nichts Neues. Douglas STEWART sieht eine Parallele zwischen der Beziehung von Falstaff und Hal und der Erziehung der Helden aus den griechischen Sagen durch den Zentauren Chiron.[128] Wie die griechischen Helden habe auch Hal ein gestörtes Verhältnis zu seinem Vater und werde nicht von im erzogen. Ebenso wie Falstaff sei auch Chiron ein gesellschaftlicher Außenseiter, beide seien „*figures of untamed appetite and anti-social vigor*". Gerade das mache sie zu geeigneten Ziehvätern zukünftiger Helden, weil sie den „*wisdom of excess*" besäßen, eine tiefere und intensivere Lebenserfahrung als Normalsterbliche, denn sie hätten „*no limits at all to their inquisitive or their aquisitive tastes*".[129]

---

[128] Douglas J. Stewart, "Falstaff the Centaur", in: Shakespeare Quarterly 28 (1977), S. 5-21.

[129] Ebd., S. 20.

Laut W.H. AUDEN ist das Thema der Trilogie die Frage, welche Qualitäten ein Herrscher mitbringen muss, um eine weltliche Gerechtigkeit zu erschaffen und aufrecht zu erhalten.[130] Hal, der zunächst ein ebenso unwürdiger König zu sein scheint wie sein schwacher und hinterhältiger Vater, beweise im Verlauf des Geschehens, dass er der rechtmäßige und fähige Erbe des englischen Throns sei. Es bestehe kein Zweifel daran, dass es Falstaff mit seiner recht merkwürdigen Pädagogik war, die Hal's menschliche Qualitäten zum Vorschein gebracht haben, dass es nicht die fehlerhaften Gene des biologischen Vaters, sondern die „Erziehung" durch den Ersatzvater war, die Hal zum idealen König gemacht haben. Ob Falstaff dabei bewusst ein „Erziehungsziel" verfolgt hat, ist höchst fraglich, wenn es nach ihm ginge, könnte er den Rest seines Lebens mit Hal unter Kriminellen und Dirnen in Tavernen verbringen und den ein oder anderen Raubüberfall planen.

Falstaff mag zwar der amüsanteste und der „rundeste" Charakter des Dramas sein, er funktioniert aber nur an der Seite von Hal, als sei er gewissermaßen ein ausgelagerter Aspekt der Psyche des Prinzen.

Die psychoanalytische Forschung tendiert dazu, Prinz Hal's Entwicklungsproblem als das Hin-und-Her-Gerissensein zwischen zwei Vätern zu deuten: ein biologischer Vater, Henry IV., der für Überzeugung, Pflicht und Kontrolle steht, aber durch seine illegitime Aneignung der Krone belastet ist; und Falstaff, der Ersatzvater, dessen Hedonismus, Gesetzlosigkeit und Witz eine attraktive, aber nur temporäre Alternative bieten und der ihn durch sein negatives Beispiel am Ende zu einem fähigen Herrscher macht.

Bei genauerer Betrachtung erscheint dies allerdings wenig plausibel, weil nicht der Charakter Henry Bolingbroke eine Anziehungskraft auf Hal ausübt, sondern die Machtposition, die er repräsentiert. Hal ist weniger zwischen zwei „Vätern", als zwischen zwei diametralen Entwürfen von „Männlichkeit" hin- und her gerissen. Auf der einen Seite ist Falstaff, der Feigling und Taugenichts, der abseits der Zwänge von männlichen Prestige- und Ehrvorstellungen ein vermeintlich unbeschwertes Lotterleben führt. Der Vertreter des anderen Extrems von „Männlichkeit" ist Hotspur, der überambitionierte, temperamentvolle Krieger, der sich voll und ganz der Ehre und dem Ruhm des Schlachtfelds verschrieben hat, und der in seiner Eindimensioniertheit wie ein satirisches Abziehbild des „idealen Mannes" wirkt.

---

[130] Auden, S. 191.

Der eine repräsentiert eine selbstsüchtige Moral- und Ehrlosigkeit, der andere selbstgerechte, blinde Tugendhaftigkeit – beide sind in ihrer Extremität Bedrohungen für die Gesellschaft. Als guter Herrscher muss Hal sich irgendwo in der Mitte dieser Skala platzieren – ehrenhaft, aber trotzdem volksnah. Mag Falstaff auch echte Zuneigung für seinen „Ziehsohn" empfinden, der Prinz stellt gleich zu Beginn seine Absicht klar, sich zum passenden Zeitpunkt von ihm und seinen Konsorten loszusagen: *„I know you all, and will awhile uphold/The unyok'd humour of your idleness"* (1HIV.I.2.190-91). Die Zeit fern ab vom Hof in der *„rude society"* des *Boar's Head* soll die Rückkehr des „verlorenen Sohnes" umso effektvoller machen:

> And, like bright metal on a sullen ground, / My reformation, glitt'ring o'er my fault, / Shall show more goodly and attract more eyes / Than that which hath no foil to set it off. (1HIV, I.2.205-208)

Auch angesichts des vorgetäuschten Todes seines Gefährten ist von tiefen Gefühlen nichts zu spüren:

> O, I should have a heavy miss of thee, / If I were much in love with vanity! / Death hath not struck so fat a deer today / Though many dearer, in this bloody fray. (1HI.V.3.105-108.)

Diese kalte Berechnung, die der Beziehung der beiden ungleichen Männer von Hal's Seite aus zugrunde liegt, gibt dem traditionell postulierten Vater-Sohn oder Lehrer-Schüler-Verhältnis einen bitteren Beigeschmack, und spätestens bei der endgültigen Verstoßung Falstaffs, die gleichzeitig seinen Tod zumindest in der Welt der Historie zu bedeuten scheint, empfindet man Mitleid mit diesem unmoralischen, aber nicht arglistigen alten Mann.

Als geborener Herrscher ist Hal allerdings auch ein kühler Stratege und so ist es wenig überraschend, dass er, an seinem politischen Ziel angelangt, Falstaff nicht mehr gebrauchen kann und deshalb effektvoll öffentlich verstößt. Der „männlichste" unter den Machthabern des Patriarchats kann sich keine Sentimentalitäten leisten. Falstaff wurde von der Gesellschaft schon als schlechter Umgang für einen Prinzen betrachtet, für einen König ist er eine absolut inakzeptable Bekanntschaft. Um in der Welt seines leiblichen Vaters anzukommen und die ihm vorbestimmte Rolle einzunehmen, muss er Falstaffs Welt, die Welt des Müßiggangs, der leiblichen Vergnügungen, der ironischhumorvollen Sicht auf die Dinge, die der alte Ritter, dieser „*whoreson round man*", selbst zu verkörpern scheint[131], hinter sich lassen.

Wie der dicke und weißbärtige moderne Weihnachtsmann stellt Falstaff eine Figur aus der Kinderwelt dar, „*the king of childhood and omnipotent wishes*"[132], den Hal in seiner neuen Position in der nüchternen, machtbesessenen und pflichtbeladenen Welt seines Vaters, der Welt des „echten Mannes", nicht dulden kann.

Die politisch notwendige Verstoßung seines ehemaligen Mentors hat jedoch offenbar gravierende Folgen für Hal's Persönlichkeit. STEWARDS recht enthusiastische Schlussfolgerung über die guten Eigenschaften, die der Prinz angeblich durch Falstaff schlechtes Beispiel gelernt haben soll – er sei „*generous, ungrudging, lenient, and amused*"[133] – muss stark in Zweifel gezogen werden, wenn man sich den aus dem „Initiationsritus" der Schlacht hervorgegangenen jungen König anschaut. Indem er Falstaff verstoßen hat, scheint er auch dessen gute Eigenschaften in sich selbst ausgelöscht zu haben. Jeglicher Wortwitz und Humor ist ihm verloren gegangen, er besitzt keine sinnlich-emotionale Seite mehr, seine Sexualität, sein Werben um Katharine von Frankreich scheint sich stets auf dem Schlachtfeld abzuspielen.

Dieser Mangel in Hals Charakter, den Falstaffs Fehlen verursacht, zeigt, dass, obwohl der junge König selbst seine Beziehung zu dem fetten Ritter weniger emotional und eng bewertete, dieser doch einen grundlegenden Aspekt seiner Persönlichkeit ausmachte. Der nächste Abschnitt beschäftigt sich mit diesem Teil von Hal's männlicher Identität, auf den Falstaff als „Monster" verweist – seine sexuelle Identität. Zunächst durch ein auffälliges Desinteresse an Frauen und die Andeutung einer möglichen Homosexualität gekennzeichnet, erlangt der Prinz erst durch den martialischen Initiationsritus der Schlacht und die Inbesitznahme der jungfräulichen Katharine die in seiner Gesellschaft akzeptable männliche Sexualität.

Falstaffs sexuelle Identität(en): Kind, Liebhaber, Mutter

Wie bei Richard und Caliban entzieht sich Falstaffs eigene Sexualität einer eindeutigen Interpretation. Nach Außen inszeniert er sich gern als Weiberheld, dennoch sind seine mehr oder weniger explizit gemachten sexuellen Beziehungen mit

---

[131] Coppélia Kahn, *Man's Estate*. Berkeley/Los Angeles, 1981 Kahn, S. 72f.

[132] Kahn, S. 71.

[133] Stewart, S. 19.

Doll Tearsheet und Mistress Quickly eher amüsant als glaubwürdig, tatsächlich scheinen die beiden weniger leidenschaftliche Gefühle, sondern vielmehr eine Art mitleidige Zuneigung für ihn zu empfinden:

> Thou whoreson little tidy Bartholomew boar pig, when wilt thou leave fighting a days and foining a nights, and begin to patch up thine old body for heaven? (2HIV, II.4.220-223)

Dass seine angeblichen Frauengeschichten nur Teil seines Maulheldentums sind, wäre auch ohne seinen besonderen körperlichen Zustand leicht zu durchschauen: Schon allein wegen seines fortgeschrittenen Alters schließt Poins darauf, dass Falstaff impotent sein muss, auch wenn er noch gerne mit der ebenfalls nicht mehr ganz taufrischen Doll Tearsheet herumtändelt „*Is it not strange that desire should so many years outlive performance?*" (2HIV, 2.4.250).

Falstaff ist also in doppelter Weise von einer aktiven heteronormativen Sexualität ausgeschlossen, oder zumindest darin eingeschränkt, einmal durch sein Alter und durch seinen pathologischen Zustand, denn als Phlegmatiker gilt er ja im medizinischen Diskurs dieser Zeit als „*weake in the act of venerie*".[134]

Es ist daher weniger seine eigene, schwer zu definierende Libido, über die sich Aussagen zu Falstaffs Sexualität machen lassen, sondern seine Beziehung zu dem jungen Prinzen, die durchaus auch implizit homoerotische Züge hat, ein Aspekt, der in der älteren Forschung geflissentlich übersehen wurde[135], sich aber nicht ganz von der Hand weisen lässt, auch wenn es keine eindeutigen Beweise gibt. Warum erfahren wir etwa gleich zu Anfang des Stückes, dass die beiden sich offensichtlich ein Schlafzimmer, vielleicht sogar ein Bett geteilt haben? Was hat Falstaffs Ausspruch „*I would 'twere bed-time, Hal, and all well*" (1HIV, V.1.124.) zu bedeuten? Laut Heather FINDLAY ist Falstaff von einer sodomitischen Aura umgeben, in der Beziehung zu Prinz Hal sei er „*pederast, a pedagogue and finally a ganymede*"[136] Falstaff eine „sodomitische" Sexualität zuzuschreiben würde auch

---

[134] de La Framboisière, zitiert bei Shepard, S. 61.

[135] Beispielsweise thematisiert Stewart, der einen Zusammenhang zwischen der Beziehung von Hal und Falstaff und der Erziehung der antiken Helden durch den Zentauren Chiron konstruiert, nicht, dass die Beziehung zwischen Tutor und Schüler in der griechischen Mythologie traditionell durchaus auch eine erotische sein konnte.

[136] Heather Findlay, "Renaissance Pederasty and Pedagogy: The 'Case' of Shakespeare's Falstaff", in: *Yale Journal of Criticism* 3 (1989), S. 231.

Hal's schlussendlicher Ablehnung des Ritters eine weitere Bedeutungsebene geben: Weil Sodomie zu dieser Zeit ein schweres Verbrechen war, würde er damit zugleich sexuelle und politische Devianz ablehnen.

Wenn es auch nicht möglich ist, Falstaff eindeutig als homosexuell zu interpretieren, ist seine Korporealität doch, wie zuvor angedeutet, ein eindeutiger Hinweis auf sein Abweichen von der normativen „Männlichkeit" und damit auch von der „normalen" Sexualität. Indem ständig auf seinen angeschwollenen Bauch und das, was er in sich hineinstopft und was aus ihm herauskommt, hingedeutet wird, wird sein Körper immer mehr verweiblicht, scheint er im Verlauf vom ersten zum zweiten Teil von *Henry IV.* immer amorpher – und vor allem immer weiblicher – zu werden.

Neil RHODES weist darauf hin, wie der Vergleich von Falstaff mit einem Behälter oder Gefäß ihn zu einer grotesken Figur macht: „*vessels of all sorts, because they can be stuffed with strange matter and thus violate the integrity of things, are a favourite grotesque device.*"[137] Das deutlichste Beispiel für Falstaff als „Behälter" findet sich in diesem verbalen Ausbruch des Prinzen:

> Why dost thou converse with that trunk of humours, that bolting-bunch of beastliness, that swoll'n parcel of dropsies, that huge bombard of sack, that stuff'd cloak-bag of guts, that roasted Manningtree ox with the pudding in his belly (1HIV.II.4.434-8)

Natürlich kann die Groteskheit seines Körpers auch ohne Referenz auf seine weiblichen Funktionen erfolgen. Viele Interpretationen finden darin etwa das Rabelaisische Karnevaleske wieder, aber das Weibliche und besonders das Mütterliche waren in frühmodernen Gesellschaften mit dem Grotesken verbunden. Dies zeigt sich z.B. in bestimmten Verhaltensweisen, was vermeintliche „Verunreinigungen" durch den weiblichen Körper betrifft – so durften menstruierende und kurz nach einer Geburt stehende Frauen keine Kirche betreten.[138]

Aber nicht nur die Vorstellung von Falstaff als einem „gefüllten" Behälter und der ständige Fokus auf seinem angeschwollenen Bauch rufen Assoziationen von Schwangerschaft und Weiblichkeit hervor, sondern auch die Andeutung einer gewissen Durchlässigkeit (1HIV, II.4.219), einer Offenheit seines Körpers, die, wie

---

[137] Neill Rhodes, *Elizabethan Grotesque*. London, 1980, S. 109.

[138] Valerie Traub, "Prince Hal's Falstaff: Positioning Psychoanalysis and the Female Reproductive Body", in: *Shakespeare Quarterly* 40.4 (1989), S. 464.

eingangs erläutert, mit der weiblichen Pathologie verbunden ist. In der frühneuzeitlichen Vorstellung machten die weiblichen Körperfunktionen der Menstruation, Schwangerschaft, Geburt und Milchbildung den Körper der Frau zu einem offenen, hervorquellenden, nie ganz dichten Gebilde.

„*A fat man can look like a pregnant woman, and Falstaff's fatness is fecund: it spawns symbols*"[139], schreibt Coppélia KAHN, und tatsächlich scheint, weniger als die Andeutungen seiner Impotenz oder Homosexualität, besonders diese „Weiblichkeit" von Falstaff seine besondere sexuelle Identität und Funktion in der Beziehung zu Prinz Harry auszumachen. Mehrfach im Stück wird auf Falstaffs „Weiblichkeit" angespielt, er selbst beschreibt sich mehr als einmal in weiblichen, ja sogar mütterlichen Bedeutungszusammenhangen:

> Why, my skin hangs around me like an old lady's loose gown (1HIV, III.1.3-4)
>
> I do here walk before thee like a sow that hath overwhelm'd all her litter but one (2HIV, I.2.8-9)
>
> My womb, my womb, my womb undoes me (2HIV, IV.3.10, 18-22)

Falstaffs sexuelle Identität, die zwischen Impotenz, Homosexualität, und „Weiblichkeit" changiert, könnte im Zusammenhang mit Hal's Entwicklung zu Mann verschiedene Funktionen erfüllen. Zum einen könnte sie Hal's unbewussten Wunsch repräsentieren, sich aus dem sexuellen Wettbewerb zurückzuziehen, „*and by combining mother and child in his own person, to become emotionally self-sufficient*".[140]

Eine ähnliche Interpretation von KAHN besagt, dass Falstaff das Bedürfnis des im Patriarchat heranwachsenden Mannes verkörpere, die Frauen zu meiden, denn für Hal sei Falstaff, wie eine Art Peter Pan, eine Inkorporation seiner eigenen „*rebellion against growing up into a problematic adult identity.*"[141] Beide Lesarten zielen auf eine kindliche Asexualität oder einen mütterlichen Schutzraum, den Falstaff dem jungen Mann als Alternative zu seinem Eintritt in die Erwachsenenwelt bietet, die sein Vater für ihn verkörpert. In ihrer Behandlung der im Stück immer wieder angedeuteten „Weiblichkeit" des Ritters gehen sie aber nicht weit genug.

---

[139] Kahn, S. 72.
[140] Auden, S. 196.
[141] Kahn, S. 72f.

Die Henriade ist, wie alle Historien Shakespeares, nicht zuletzt eine Demonstration des gezielten Ausschlusses des Weiblichen aus allen politischen Vorgängen sowie der sexualisierten Unterdrückung von Frauen, auf denen das Patriarchat sich aufbaut. Wie schon in *The Tempest* herrscht hier eine männliche Angst vor der weiblichen Sexualität, vor der dunklen Macht des fruchtbaren weiblichen Körpers. Gleich in den ersten Zeilen der Trilogie wird in den Worten des Königs deutlich, dass Mütterlichkeit auf perverse Weise als zerstörerisch empfunden und mit Krieg und Blutvergießen gleichgesetzt wird: *„No more the thirsty entrance of this soil / Shall daub her lips with her own children's blood"*(1HIV, 1.1.5-6), (2HIV, 1.2.11-12). Es geht hier nicht um eine einfache Vermeidung des Weiblichen, sondern es muss unterworfen und unterdrückt werden, so wie die Belagerung einer Stadt, die als Vergewaltigung einer Jungfrau imaginiert wird (HV, 3.3.7-35).

In der umfassendsten psychoanalytischen Studie der Beziehung von Hal und Falstaff argumentiert Valerie TRAUB, Falstaffs Körper und die damit verbundene somatische Bildhaftigkeit mache ihn zum unterbewussten präödipalen Mütterlichen, gegen das Hal sich absetzten muss, um zum „Mann" zu werden. Demnach würde Falstaff für Hal nicht ein alternatives Vater-Bild darstellen, sondern eine projizierte Phantasie von einer prä-ödipalen Mutterfigur, deren Zurückweisung die Basis für seine maskuline Subjektivität ist, die ja gerade in den Historien über die Dominierung der Frauen konstruiert wird.

> Hal's rejection of Falsatff serves simultaneously to temporarily assuage anxieties, first, about male homoeroticism and, second, about a heterosexuality based on the equation of woman and maternity.[142]

In seiner doppelten Signifikanz als homoerotisches oder weibliches Objekt der Begierde stellt Falstaff eine ernste Bedrohung für Hal's erwachsene Heterosexualität dar, die er durch dessen Verstoßung auslöschen will.

Nur Blutvergießen in martialisch-männlicher Schlacht kann Hal von dieser Beschmutzung durch das Mütterliche und das Homoerotische säubern, denn der Weg zu einer rein männlichen Identität führt in dieser Welt des Krieges natürlich über das Schlachtfeld, wie nach einer zweiten Geburt, gesäubert von allen kindlichen Sünden will Hal aus der Schlacht zurückkehren, um endlich seines Vaters Sohn sein zu können: *„When I will wear a garment all of blood, / And stain my favours in a bloody mask, / Which, wash'd away, shall scoure my shame with / It"*

---

[142] Traub, S. 465.

(1 HIV, III.2.135-37). Nachdem Hal sich in einer düsteren, grotesken Geburtsphantasie von der erdrückenden „Mutter" befreit hat („*by breaking through the foul and ugly mists / Of vapours that seem to strangle him*", 1HIV, 1.2.195-96), wird das minderwertige Mütterliche durch Prinzessin Katharine ersetzt, denn ihr jungfräulicher Körper stellt keine Bedrohung für Hal's heterosexuelle Männlichkeit dar. Als die Verkörperung einer idealisierten männlichen Vorstellung von Weiblichkeit wird sie ganz ähnlich beschrieben wie Miranda in *The Tempest*, nämlich als „fair" (HV, 5.2.104), „*fair flower-de-luce*" (HV, 5.2.210-11), „*angel*" (HV, 5.2.110): „*Katherine is positioned, in the space of one hundred lines, as far as possible from the ‚grotesque' maternal body*"[143].

Die Ersetzung von Falstaffs groteskem mütterlichen Körpers durch den idealisierten jungfräulichen Katharines ist jedoch eine instabile und problematische Lösung, denn, wie auch Prospero an seiner eigenen Tochter erkennen muss, trägt jede Frau in sich die doppelte Bedrohung durch die mütterliche Allmacht und „monströse" weibliche Sexualität.

Auch wenn am Ende mit Falstaffs Verstoßung das „Weibliche" aus der Welt des neuen Königs ausradiert und entmachtet wurde: Die männliche Angstphantasie von defekter „Männlichkeit" und ihrer grotesken Verbindung mit dem „Weiblichen" als Bedrohung der patriarchalischen Ordnung existiert weiter – in der Hypersignifikanz der monströsen Körper von Richard, Caliban und Falstaff, der sich abermals in eine Parallelwelt geflüchtet hat und uns in *The Merry Wives of Windsor* wiederbegegnet:

> The desire to bypass the maternal, then, seems to be a doomed project; if anything, these texts demonstrate the inevitable return of the repressed – oftentimes with a vengeance.[144]

---

[143] Traub, S. 469.
[144] Ebd., S. 470.

Schlussbetrachtung

Madam, I have a touch of your condition (RIII, IV.4.158)

Disability kann, wie die Schicksale von Richard III., Caliban und Falstaff zeigen, niemals gleichzeitig eine vollwertige Mitgliedschaft in der männerdominierten Welt bedeuten, denn ein „Monster" kann kein „Mann" sein. Obwohl keiner von ihnen durch seine *disabilities* tatsächlich ernsthaft körperlich eingeschränkt ist und sie alle, auch Caliban, über eine bemerkenswerte Intelligenz verfügen, ist ihnen der Zugang zur Sphäre der männlichen Gesellschaft versperrt.

Unter den frühneuzeitlichen Vorstellungen vom männlichen als dem perfekten menschlichen Körper steht das „Monster" auf der selben Stufe wie die Frau, denn beide besitzen eine deformierte, minderwertige Version des männlichen Idealkörpers, *„unfinished"* und *„scarce half made up"*, wie Richard es selbst ausdrückt. Alle drei Charaktere sind „monströs", weil sie sich in einem Zustand zwischen fertig und unfertig und damit zwischen männlich und weiblich befinden, ein Bereich zwischen den beiden grundlegenden Polen der menschlichen Selbstdefinition, der nicht geduldet werden kann, daher muss die Gesellschaft ihre „Monster" ausstoßen oder vernichten.

Das gesellschaftlich Inakzeptable, Beängstigende an diesen „monströsen" Männern ist nicht allein ihre Assoziation mit dem weiblichen „Anderen", sondern dass sie darüber sogar noch hinausgehen, dass sie die mit aller Macht aufrecht zu erhaltenden Grenzen zwischen männlich und weiblich zu durchbrechen scheinen. Was Jonathan Goldberg über Falstaffs Körper sagt, gilt ebenso für Richard und Caliban: Der „monströse" männliche Körper ist *„simultaneously male, female, and hermaphroditic, gross, engrossing and engrossed, desired, desiring and disgusting."*[145]

Die Körper der männlichen „Monster" ist eine Projektionsfläche für die Ängste des Patriarchats vor der zerstörerischen weiblichen Sexualität und Mütterlichkeit, die sie in mehrfacher Form verkörpern.

Die zentrale Rolle in der somatischen Signifikanz des männlichen Monsters spielt dabei die Macht der Mutter: Sie sind allesamt Produkte vom „monstrous births", also die Folgen der perversen Sexualität ihrer Mütter, zu denen sie kein oder ein gestörtes Verhältnis besitzen. Gleichzeitig weisen ihre durch ihren pathologischen

---

[145] Jonathan Goldberg, *Sodometries. Renaissance Texts, Modern Sexualities*. Stamford (Canada), 1992, S. 173.

Zustand ohnehin als „unmännliche" gekennzeichneten Körper unheimliche Ähnlichkeiten mit dem grotesken mütterlichen Leib auf. Durch bestimmte Attribute, Aussagen oder Situationen werden alle drei als „Schwangere" charakterisiert: Richard durch seinen Buckel, Caliban in der grotesken „Geburtsszene" mit Trinculo und Stephano und vor allem Falstaff durch seinen angeschwollenen Bauch. Ihre Körper sind gleichsam „bedeutungsschwanger".

Sie selbst besitzen zwar eine Sexualität, die zwar meist uneindeutig, aber an sich nicht dezidiert monströs ist, weil sie dem natürlichen Wunsch nach Vermehrung entspricht. Sie haben jedoch keinen Zugang zu einer heteronormativen Sexualität, daher müssen sie diese entweder erzwingen, wie Richard und Caliban, oder sich ihr ganz entziehen, wie Falstaff, der zugleich eine homoerotische und eine asexuelle, kindliche Seite zu haben scheint und dessen heterosexuelle Kontakte sich auf Maulheldentum und komödiantische Episoden beschränken.

Die Problematik des außergewöhnlichen männlichen Körpers besteht also nicht in einer über den Körper nach Außen transportierten innerlichen „Deformiertheit", sondern in der direkten Verbindung von imperfektem Körper und imperfekter Männlichkeit. Der Besitzer des „monströsen" Körpers kämpft im Patriarchat einen Kampf um Status und Anerkennung, den er aufgrund seiner offensichtlichen „Impotenz" nicht gewinnen kann, ohne zu kriminellen, unmoralischen Mitteln zu greifen.

Shakespeares männliche „Monster" können keine Könige, Liebhaber, Ehemänner und Väter sein, doch sie alle sind Söhne, Söhne der Frauen, die aus der Welt der Historien und der Romanzen verbannt wurden, weil ihre Sexualität und die geheimnisvolle Macht, die ihre Körper ihnen verleihen, eine Gefahr für die von Männern konstruierte und dominierte Gesellschaft darzustellen scheinen. Der Prozess des Ausschlusses der Frauen aus historischen und politischen Vorgängen ist jedoch niemals vollendet, alles Verdrängte kehrt bei Shakespeare stets in neuer Form zurück: als Traum, als Wahnvorstellung, als Geist – und als *monstrous birth*, als deformierte Produkte des gefürchteten und verbannten weiblichen Körpers.

In einer Zeit in der die traditionellen Ideologien, religiösen Vorstellungen, und sozialen Konstruktionen sich dramatisch zu verändern beginnen, in der althergebrachte *Gender*-Rollen und sexuelle Tabus ihre Grenzen zu durchbrechen drohen, sind die außergewöhnlichen Körper von Richard III., Caliban und Falstaff einerseits drohende Vorzeichen für gesellschaftliches Chaos, andererseits Hoffnungsschimmer für die Möglichkeit einer neuen autonomen Individualität, die eine Brücke über die wachsende Kluft zwischen der überholten patriarchalischen Weltordnung und den neuen Entfaltungsmöglichkeiten der modernen Gesellschaft darstellen könnte – dies gilt für Shakespeares Zeit ebenso wir für unsere.

Bibliographie

Quellen

Sämtliche Zitate aus Shakespeares Dramen entstammen:

Richard Proudfoot, Ann Thompson und David Scott Kastan (Hrsg.), The Arden Shakespeare: Complete Works. (Revised and Reprinted Edition), London, 2007.

Sekundärliteratur

ADELMANN, Janet: Suffocating Mothers. Fantasies of maternal origin in Shakespeare's plays, Hamlet to The Tempest. New York, 1992.

AUDEN, W.H., "The Pince's Dog", in: G.K. Hunter (Hrsg.), Shakespeare: Henry IV Parts I and II. London, 1970, S.187-211.

BACON, Francis, Essays, Civil and Moral. Vol. III, Part 1. The Harvard Classics, hrsg. von Charles W. Eliot. New York, 1909–14; online unter www.bartleby.com/3/1/ [12.03.2008].

BAMBER, Linda, Comic Women, Tragic Men. A Study of Gender and Genre in Shakespeare. Stanford, 1982.

BARKER, Francis and Peter Hulme, "'Nymphs and reapers heavily vanish': The Discursive Contexts of The Tempest", in John Drakakis (Hrsg.), Alternative Shakespeares, London, 1985, S. 191-205.

BERRY, Philippa, Of Chastity and Power. Elizabethan Literature and the Unmarried Queen. London/ New York 1989.

BREITENBERG, Mark, Anxious Masculinity in Early Modern England. Cambridge 1996.

BURNETT, Mark Thornton, Constructing "monsters" in Shakespearean drama and early modern culture. Basingstoke 2002.

BUTLER, Judith, Bodies that Matter: On the Discursive Limits of "Sex". New York, 1993.

CARRIGAN, Tim, R.W. Connell & John Lee, „Ansätze zu einer neuen Soziologie der Männlichkeit", in: BauSteineMänner (Hrsg.), Kritische Männerforschung, Neue Ansätze in der Geschlechtertheorie. Berlin, S.38-76.

COHEN, Derek. "The Culture of Slavery: Caliban and Ariel", Dalhousie Review 76.2 (1996): S. 153-175.

DREHER, Diane Elizabeth, Domination and Defiance: Fathers and Daughters. Lexington (Kentucky), 1986.

EVERETT, Barbara, The Fatness of Falstaff: Shakespeare and Character, in: Proceedings of the British Academy 76 (1990), S.109-28.

FEHER, Michael, Ramona Nadaff & Nadia Tazi (Hrsg.), Fragments for a History of the Human Body. 3 Bde, New York, 1989.

FIEDLER, Leslie A., The Stranger in Shakespeare. London, 1973.

FINDLAY, Heather, "Renaissance Pederasty and Pedagogy: The 'Case' of Shakespeare's Falstaff", in: Yale Journal of Criticism 3 (1989), S.229-38.

FISHER, Will, "The Renaissance Beard: Masculinity in Modern England", in: Renaissance Quarterly 54 (2001), S. 155-187.

GAINES, Barry. "What Did Caliban Look Like?", in: Shakespeare Yearbook 1 (1990), S. 50-58.

GARLAND THOMSON, Rosemarie (Hrsg.), "Introduction: From Wonder to Error – A genealogy ofFreak Discourse in Modernity", in: Dies. (Hrsg.), Freakery: Cultural Spectacles of the Extraordinary Body. New York, 1996.

GILMAN, Sander L., Fat Boys. A Slim Book. Lincoln (Nebraska), 2004.

GOLDBERG, Jonathan, Sodometries. Renaissance Texts, Modern Sexualities. Stanford (Canada), 1992, S.173.

GRADY, Hugh, "Falstaff: Subjectivity between the Carnival and the Aesthetic", in. The Modern Language Review 96, Nr. 3 (Juli, 2001), S. 609-623.

GROEBER, Valentin, „Körper auf dem Markt. Söldner, Organhandel und die Geschichte der Körpergeschichte", in: Mittelweg 36. Zeitschrift des Hamburger Instituts für Sozialforschung, (Dezember 2005), S. 69-84.

HANKINS, John E., "Caliban the Bestial Man", in: PMLA 62, Nr. 3 (1947), S. 793-801.

KAHN, Coppélia, Man's Estate. Masculine Identity in Shakespeare. Berkeley/Los Angeles, 1981.

KERMODE, Frank (Hrsg.), William Shakespeare: The Tempest. (New Arden Edition). London, 1954.

KLEE, Ernst, . Behindert. Über die Enteignung von Körper und Bewusstsein. Frankfurt a. M. 1980, online eingestellt unter:

http://bidok.uibk.ac.at/library/klee-behindert.html?hls=Klee#id2701497 [14.12.2007].

LAMB, Michael E., u.a., "The Father-Daughter Relationship", in: Claire B. Kopp und Martha Kirkpatrick (Hrsg.), Becoming Female. New York 1979, S.80-106.

LAQUEUR, Thomas, Auf den Leib geschrieben. Die Inszenierung der Geschlechter von der Antike bis Freud. Übers. v. H. Jochen Bußmann, Frankfurt/New York, 1990

LARA, Irene, "Beyond Caliban's Curses: The Decolonial Feminist Literacy of Sycorax", in: Journal of International Women's Studies 9, (November 2007), S.80-98, online eingestellt unter: www.bridgew.edu/SoAS/jiws/Nov07/Caliban.pdf [20.01.2008].

LORENZ, Maren, Leibhaftige Vergangenheit. Eine Einführung in die Körpergeschichte. Tübingen, 2000.

MASON VAUGHAN, Virginia, "'Something Rich and Strange': Caliban's Theatrical Metamorphoses", Shakespeare Quarterly 36, Nr. 4 (1985), S. 390-405.

MEUSER, Michael, Geschlecht und Männlichkeit, Soziologische Theorie und kulturelle Deutungsmuster. Opladen, 1998.

MITCHELL, David T. and Sharon L. Snyder (eds), The Body and Physical Difference: Discourses of Disability. Michigan, 1997.

MOULTON, Ian Frederick: "A Monster Great Deformed": The Unruly Masculinity of Richard III", in: Shakespeare Quarterly 47 (3), 1996.

PARE, Ambroise, Des monstres et prodiges. (Paris, 1573), Engl. Übers.: On Monsters and Marvels. Translation, Introduction and Notes by J. R. Pallister. Chicago, 1982

PLASSE, Marie A., Corporeality and the Opening of Richard III. In: Willson, Robert F. Junior, Entering the Maze: Shakespeare's Art of beginning. New York, 1995.

RHODES, Neill; Elizabethan Qrotesque. London, 1980.

ROPER, Lyndal, Oedipus and the Devil. Witchcraft, sexuality and religion in early modern Europe. London/New York, 1994.

SAINT-HILAIRE, Isidore Geoffroy, Histoire générale et particuliére des anomalies de l'organisation chez l'homme et les animaux ou Traité de tératologie. Paris/Brüssel, 1832-37.

SARASIN, Philipp, Reizbare Maschinen. Eine Geschichte des Körpers 1765 1914. Frankfurt/M. 2001.

SEMONIN, Paul, "Monsters in the Marketplace: The Exhibition of Human Oddities in Early Modern England", in: Rosemarie Garland Thomson (Hrsg.), Freakery: Cultural Spectacles of the Extraordinary Body. New York, 1996, S.69-83.

SCHOENFELDT, Mark, Bodies and Selves in Early Modern England. Physiology and Inwardness in Spenser, Shakespeare, Herbert, and Milton. Cambridge 1999.

SCHÖNWIESE, Volker, „Perspektiven der Disability Studies", Behinderte in Familie und Gesellschaft 5 (2005), S. 16-21.

SHEPARD, Alexandra, Meanings of manhood in early modern England. Oxford, 2003.

SMITH, Bruce R., Shakespeare and Masculinity. Oxford, 2000.

SPIVACK, Bernhard, "Falstaff and the Psychomachia", in: Shakespeare Quarterly 8 (1957), S.449-459.

STEWART, Douglas J., "Falstaff the Centaur", in: Shakespeare Quarterly 28 (1977), S. 5-21.

THOMAS, Keith, Man and the Natural World. London, 1983.

TRAUB, Valerie, "Prince Hal's Falstaff: Positioning Psychoanalysis and the Female Reproductive Body", Shakespeare Quarterly 40.4 (1989), S.456-474.

VADDE, Aarthi, "On the Absent Presence of Mothers in The Tempest", online verfügbar unter The Association of Young Journalists and Writers (AYJW), http://ayjw.org/articles.php?id=605901 [20.01.2007].

VAUGHAN, Alden T. und Virginia Mason Vaughan, Shakespeare's Caliban: A Cultural History. Cambridge, 1991.

WALTER, Tilmann, Unkeuschheit und Werk der Liebe. Berlin, 1998.

WISCHERMANN, Clemens, „Geschichte des Körpers oder Körper mit Geschichte?", in: Clemens Wischermann. & Stefan Haas (Hrsg.), Körper mit Geschichte. Münster/Konstanz, 2000, S.7-31.

WOMERSLEY, David, "Why Is Falstaff Fat?", Review of English Studies 47 (1996), S. 1-22.

Internet-Quellen (in der Reihenfolge ihrer Erwähnung im Text)

http://www.disability-studies-deutschland.de/dsd.php [18.12.2007]

http://www.openlibrary.org/details/collectionofseve00lillrich [12.12.2007]: Elektronische Edition von Joseph Lilly's A collection of seventy-nine blackletter ballads and broadsides. (London, 1867)

http://www.richardiii.net/begin.htm [17.12.2007]: Online-Auftritt der Richard III.- Society

http://www.sciencenews.org/sn_arc99/5_15_99/bob2.htm [13.01.2007]: Zum Fish-Odour-Syndrome

The Construction of Feminity and Masculinity in Shakespeare's *Macbeth*

Vinzent Fröhlich, 2007

Foreword

The title of this paper is "The Construction of Femininity and Masculinity in Shakespeare's *Macbeth*". As this title suggests, I will analyze how Shakespeare construed female and male identity in *Macbeth*. As in many Shakespearean dramas, the play starts with the destruction of order leading to a crisis and ending in the restoration of order at the end of the play (Gelfert 32). The political order, which is destroyed in the play is King Duncan's order, where a unique set of masculine and feminine values is cherished. Macbeth murders King Duncan in order to usurp his throne. Macbeth's reign turns Duncan's order into chaos and moral order cannot return to Scotland until the tyrant ruler Macbeth is defeated by troops who fight for the restoration of Duncan's order, through the coronation of his son Malcolm. This essay will question the roles Shakespeare gives female and male characters in the destruction and restoration of this order. However, I will also raise questions such as:

- Which historical concepts does the author use to construe his male and female characters?
- Does he construe "typical" roles of men and women?
- Moreover, what happens when gender boundaries are crossed, if men develop feminine traits and women male?

With special regard to the marriage of Macbeth and Lady Macbeth, I will analyze the interaction between the genders. In the course of my analysis, I will use the term "gender", originating from Anglo-American feminist discourse, meaning "the social, cultural, and psychological meaning imposed upon biological sexual identity" (Showalter 1-2).

Interpreting femininity and masculinity as "gender" constructions allows a more thorough analysis of the various processes involved in the "making" of men and women. Whilst the term "sex" suggests that children naturally acquire the appropriate masculine or feminine behavioural norms of their society, the term "gender" can also indicate that some people feel discrepancies between their "anatomical sex and experiential sense of gender and sexuality" (Showalter 2). After a short historical introduction about the origins of the play, I will analyze the masculine world of chivalry that the play takes place in. Understanding the world of chivalry, its values and codes is required as most of the male characters are construed as chivalrous knights serving in the corps of King Duncan.

The Sources of the Play

Although the sole authority for the text of this play is the first edition published in the 1623 volume of Shakespeare's *Comedies, Histories, and Tragedies*, the play was most likely first performed at the *Globe* Theatre in 1606 to compliment and entertain King James I and his visitor, the King of Denmark (Brown 9). The script of *Macbeth*, Shakespeare's only play set in Scotland, includes many stage directions such as directions for sound and lighting. This could perhaps indicate that the text of the play had been used as a prompt text before it was printed and included in the collection (Brown 10).

James was a fan of Raphael Holinshed's *Chronicles of England, Scotland, and Ireland* (1587) (Brown 13). Perhaps for this reason, Shakespeare also wanted to write a dark and gripping play for James I.

The *Chronicles* were condensed, shaped, and augmented specifically to create an exciting, entertaining and gripping plot. Shakespeare's *Macbeth* is a play that deals with regicide and the horrible consequences that regicide has on both the murderer and the country. Although it is the "shortest and bloodiest" Shakespearean drama, it has been immensely successful and has attracted huge audiences from all over the world since its time (Phillips / Douthat 2). Shakespeare wrote this play to compliment the "self-proclaimed anti-militarist" King James I (Wells 117).

James I was a "genuine peacemaker" whose dearest ambition was for a united Europe (Wells 133). Still James was not ignorant to the fact that any military aristocracy needed control (Ibid.). At the beginning of his reign, James I was very popular as his policy of promoting "piety, peace and learning" gave hope after the final years of Elizabeth's reign, which was marked by "the inbred factionalism of the court and the aggressively militant nationalism fostered by the war party" (Ibid.). According to James I a "wise ruler" should strive for peace and "justice tempered by mercy" (as he emphasizes in *Basilicon Doron*) (Wells 134). However, how exactly did Shakespeare alter his original sources? According to Mabillard, Shakespeare's alterations of his sources served three purposes: "the dramatic purpose of creating a more exciting story than is found in the sources; the thematic purpose of creating a more complex characterization of Macbeth; and the political purpose of catering to the beliefs of the reigning monarch, King James I" (Mabillard 1).

In order to create a "direct" plot Shakespeare reduced Duncan's wars to only one and also ignored Macbeth's "ten years of prudent rule" and gave Macduff "less prominence until after the slaughter" of his family (Brown 13). He concentrated on the topic of regicide and its consequences (Ibid.).

Furthermore, he "carefully modified" the characters and ignored Macbeth's "harsh temperament before aiming at the crown" in the *Chronicles* (Ibid).

In the Chronicles "the naming of Malcolm as Duncan's heir was a just ground for Macbeth's hostility"; Shakespeare also dropped this and presented King Duncan as a most saintly King (Ibid.). Shakespeare also changed the nature of the crime "from open political assassination carried out with the support of Banquo and others" to "murder in Macbeth's own castle", which Macbeth carries out with his wife (Ibid).

Shakespeare's own inventions were "Macbeth's 'horrible imaginings' in his very first scene after hearing the witches' prophecies, his helplessness immediately following the crime, the long talk with the murderers of Banquo, the appearances of Banquo's ghost, the subsequent scenes between Macbeth and his wife, Lady Macbeth's sleepwalking and her reported suicide" (Brown 14). Shakespeare accepts the political background and adds a supernatural one (Brown 15). Shakespeare knew that King James I believed in witchcraft. He reshaped Holinshed's "nymphs" who were "unequivocally female" and "attractive" and turned them into androgynous forces of evil (Rackin 132). To conclude, Shakespeare "contrived from the *Chronicles* a historical, political, spiritual, sexual and mental tragedy (Brown 15).

Its topic is the "sacrilegious nature of regicide" and its fatal consequences, a topic Shakespeare chose to compliment King James I (Wells 136).

Masculinity in Shakespeare's *Macbeth*

Shakespeare lived in a time that had seen chivalry in decline (Wells 12). During the Renaissance in England chivalry was an "antiquated system" bearing little resemblance to contemporary social and military reality (Wells 13). Although horsed knights with helmets, swords, lances and breastplates had already been replaced with troops of soldiers with guns and pistols, the image of the chivalrous knight was by far not out of society's mind and contemporary fashion (Smith 44). It was immensely popular among noblemen and gentlemen in Renaissance England to have their portraits painted in the style of chivalry (Ibid.). This may be the reason why Shakespeare decided to place another tragedy in "a ceremonial feudal world", in which the chivalrous knight epitomizes the ideal of manliness (Smith 45).

Macbeth is not the first Shakespearean play set in the world of chivalry. However, why did Shakespeare create another play, in which the chivalrous knight is the masculine ideal? Firstly, Shakespeare was fascinated by the world of chivalry and in favour of the humanist ideas of chivalry (Meron 5). Secondly, staging a play in a historical setting gave Shakespeare "a greater literary freedom" to express critical ideas (Ibid).

In *Macbeth*, masculinity equals chivalry. An ideal knight showed more than "loyalty" to those he served. He also showed "solidarity" to his kinsmen and "orthodoxy" in the conduct of his duties (Long 54).

In the following section, I will explain the values of chivalry more thoroughly and how they were translated into customs of warfare.

The Values of Chivalry

In the Middle Ages, chivalry was an "ideal" of masculinity rather than an institution (Schofield 3). Chivalric values became the new ideal of masculinity in medieval England (Wells 11). The chivalric premise and rites were based on "justice, loyalty, courage, honour and mercy" (Meron 5). Of all theses principles, honour was considered the most important one. The honour code is the most enduring legacies of chivalry and bound knights to act honourably in civil society and warfare (Wells 11). Justice, loyalty, courage, honour and mercy shaped the customs of warfare and in the Middle Ages and the Renaissance and influence today's laws and practices of warfare (Meron 3-4). These chivalric virtues were translated into a behavioural code which was to be applied both in civil society and on the battlefield by "knights, nobility and the entire warring class" (Meron 5).

Any chivalrous knight had to swear "to renounce the pursuit of material gain, to do nobly for the mere love of nobleness, to be generous of his goods, to be courteous to the vanquished, to redress wrongs, to draw his sword in no quarrel but a just one, to keep his word, to respect oaths, and above all, to protect the helpless and to serve women" (Schofish 5). Chivalry was a normative ideal, which applied to knights and nobles regardless of nationality, but did not protect commoners, peasants and non-Christians (Meron 6). Some of the rules of chivalry were manifested by royal ordinances, for example Henry V's ordinances of 1419, which explicitly made illegal "assault, robbery, and capture" of people belonging to the Church as well as the rape of women (Meron 5).

Chivalrous knights had the "duty to grand quarter on the battlefield in exchange for ransom, treat prisoners humanely and protect women, children and other non-combatants" (Ibid.). Warring men had to conform to chivalric rules. The international order of chivalry established courts to re-enforce the principles of chivalry and any warrior could report breaches on these rules committed by enemies (Meron 6).

The Duties of Chivalrous Knights

In the world of chivalry "physical courage and military prowess" were considered the "guarantors of justice and honour" (Wells 11). As was mentioned, the most important duty for any chivalrous knight was to conduct humanitarian and responsible behaviour in both peace and war in order to seek honour and to avoid shame (Meron 108). He had to "defend the faith against unbelievers, defend the temporal lord and protect the weak, women, widows and orphans. Furthermore, he was compelled to pursue robbers and malefactors, uphold justice and train to acquire the virtues necessary to perform these duties: "wisdom, charity, loyalty and courage" (Meron 108). "Pride, false-swearing, idleness, lechery and treason" were to be avoided (Meron 109). On the battlefield chivalrous knights had to accept and apply certain standards. Both belligerents were (ideally) granted an equal position in their battlefield at an arranged time and place (Meron 109). Proving loyalty meant "fidelity to one's lord and the Church" as well as to the order of chivalry and its customs (Ibid).

The notion of justice did not allow knights to fight in unjust war as only the participation in just war was supposed to gain fame (Meron 112). Just war was considered as a means to right wrongs (Ibid.).

Civilized manners in warfare included the duty to respect the bodies of the dead and to grant them an honourable burial and to search for the missing (Meron 115). As the duties of chivalrous knights were plenty, several lists were written down during the Middle Ages to remind the knights of their duties and to give them advice in crucial situations. One of these lists is contained in the book *Chivalry* by the French historian Léon Gautier:

- Thou shalt believe all the Church teaches, and shall observe all its directions.
- Thou shalt defend the Church.
- Thou shalt respect all the weak, and shalt constitute thyself the defender of them.
- Thou shalt love the country in which thou wast born.
- Thou shalt not recoil before thine enemy.
- Thou shalt make war against the infidel without cessation, and without mercy.
- Thou shalt never lie, and shall remain faithful to thy pledged word.
- Thou shalt be generous, give largess to everyone.

- Thou shalt be everywhere and always the companion of the right and the good against injustice and evil. (http://en.wikipedia.org/wiki/Chivalry)

Chivalric codes set high standards and expectations. A chivalrous knight had to be as noble-minded as a priest and as strong and courageous as a hero. Before describing the depiction of Macbeth, Banquo, Macduff, and Malcolm as chivalrous knights, I will concentrate on King Duncan's "natural order" as the destruction of his life and thus reign is the starting point of the tragedy.

King Duncan's "Natural Order"

King Duncan is a benevolent King who represents a "moral and political order rooted in a natural order established by God" (Blits 1). God was supposed to see everything and know everyone's secrets and secret thoughts, to protect the innocent and punish the guilty (Ibid). Duncan's personality combines both male and female traits.

The audience sees his male traits through his appreciation of valour in warfare. He compliments and honours to the bleeding Sergeant who fought to free his son from his capture:

> So well thy words become thee, as thy wounds:
> They smack of honour both. (1.2.44-5)

On the other hand, his female traits are revealed through his desire of peace and harmony. He speaks in metaphors of nurturing, hope and fecundity, for instance, when he praises Banquo's bravery in the fight against Norway with the words:

> [...] Noble Banquo,
> That hast no less deserv'd, nor must be known
> No less to have done so, let me infold thee,
> And hold thee to my heart. (1.4.29-32)

Duncan symbolizes "legitimate authority, gentle fathering, maternal nurturing, social accord and childlike trust" (Stockholder 100). He is fond of his servants and delights in their company. His love for his knights extends onto families and can almost be seen as "motherly" at the banquet, where he greats Lady Macbeth warmly as "fair and noble hostess" (1.6.23) and says:

> Give me your hand;
> Conduct me to mine host: we love him highly,
> And shall continue our graces towards him.
> By your leave, hostess. (1.6.28-31)

Never knowing that Lady Macbeth had previously conjured up murderous spirits so she could kill him, he seems to delight in her company. Although he has been deceived before, he loves and trust his knights.

Referring to the treacherous Thane of Cawdor, Duncan even comments on his inability to judge people correctly:

> There's no art
> To find the mind's construction in the face:
> He was a gentleman on whom I built
> An absolute trust. (1.4.11-13)

However, at no point in the play does Duncan try to find a way to check the loyalty of his knights. His "naive faith in the appearance of loyalty in his followers" is a "mistaken faith", which will make Duncan transfer both Cawdor's title and his "absolute" trust to Macbeth (Hays 103-4). He is "simply fooled by false appearance" (Jorgensen, *Sensational Art* 46).

In Rogers's interpretation, Duncan represents "the successful amalgamation of the masculine and feminine gender principles" (Rogers 4). Rogers believes that it is Duncan's feminine qualities which eventually kill him. She argues that the society described in *Macbeth* is a strictly patriarchal one in which "male supremacy is being protected by brute force" (Ibid.). She claims that in order to survive in this world, characters have to rid themselves off "any connection to the feminine sphere" as exemplified by Macduff who was not "of a woman born" (Rogers 3). Although I agree with Rogers that King Duncan possesses both masculine and feminine qualities and that the world of *Macbeth* is a strictly patriarchal one, I would not say that it is Duncan's feminine values which eventually kill him. King Duncan is a benevolent King who naturally favours peace and harmony over war and terror. But was it really Duncan's feminine values that made him too blind to see any evil in his county and among his servants?

The fact that it is Macduff who can put an end to Macbeth's tyranny because he was not of "of woman born" (4.1.80) is crucial. However, Macduff did not intentionally cut this "connection to the feminine sphere". It is not true that Macduff negates his own feminine qualities. In the course of the play, he will reveal innate feminine qualities. In my opinion, it is not exclusively King Duncan's feminine qualities that will cost his life, but a tendency to be too uncritical towards his servant's true ambitions combined with a too close relationship to them. Duncan does not develop an "appropriate" distance to his knights. By treating his servants like his sons, he might increase some knight's readiness to defend Scotland, but it, on the other hand, increases certain unrealistic hopes and expectations among others, especially Macbeth. Although he returns as the "hero" of the battle against Macdonwald, Duncan's son Malcolm, successor to the throne, is crowned the new King of Scotland. The fact that Malcolm lacks maturity and so far has not proved any male qualities increases Macbeth's envy towards the legitimate heir of the crown.

I think that Shakespeare deliberately portrays Duncan as a naïve and trusting character as a strong contrast to the tyrannical ruler Macbeth, "idealizing Duncan and demonizing Macbeth" (Hays 104). Thus, King Duncan is the embodiment of both a beloved King and father figure as well the embodiment of innocence and victimhood. His female qualities are undeniable. His caring female qualities perhaps raise the question to the audience of whether he has a spouse, and if so, where she is. Again it is Macduff who informs the audience about her life and death:

> ... the Queen ...
> Oft'ner upon her knees than on her feet,
> Died every day she liv'd. (4.3.109-111)

The audience gets the impression that she must have been a pious wife who was deeply religious. Maybe Duncan possesses some of her gentle qualities. Duncan's loyal subjects regard their king's body to be "The Lord's anointed Temple" (2.3.67) and that any attack upon him would be a sacrilege. Murdering him means "striking at the elements of life itself: it means murdering sleep, "Chief nourisher at life's feast" (2.2.38)" (Long 49). The death of this gentle and ideal king means the loss of "natural order" based on "love, trust, hospitality, gentleness, procreation and the divine" (Blits 51).

Macbeth's Development from Scotland's Saviour to Scotland's Criminal King and Bloody Tyrant

In this play about the "loss and recovery of right rule", Macbeth is the main protagonist, who at the beginning is described as Scotland's saviour (Hays 100). However, at no point in the play Macbeth is depicted as a true chivalrous knight. He may be "a knight of surpassing prowess in battle", but his conduct is "less than chivalrous" and "his character [is] less than morally or religiously correct" (Hays 107). Being a warrior in the fight against Norway, he literally slays his enemies without remorse. In Act I, Scene II a wounded Sergeant reports King Duncan how Macbeth defended Scotland and won the fight against the Norwegian rebel Macdonwald. The description of this deed reveals that Macbeth delights in executing his enemies:

> For brave Macbeth (well he deserves that name),
> Disdaining Fortune, with his brandish'd steel,
> Which smok'd with bloody execution,
> Like Valour's minion, carv'd out his passage,
> Till he fac'd the slave;
> Which ne'er shook hands, nor bade farewell to him,
> Till he unseam'd him from the nave to th'chops,
> And fix'd his head upon our battlements. (1.2.16-23)

This scene describes Macbeth as a cruel and remorseless warrior whose fighting strategy reminds one of the way professional butchers produce "cutlets or pieces of meat" (Foakes 149). Indeed, Macbeth kills Macdonwald with unnecessary brutality, "he unseam'd him from nave to th'chops" (1.2.22-3), meaning that Macbeth cuts open the entire torso of his enemy and thus presents himself as an enormously brutal warrior without scruples. His ferocity is "unrestrained by the customs and methods of chivalric combat" (Hays 107). In his confrontation with the rebel Macdonwald, he "omits the courtesies of chivalric combat between knights"; he "ne'er shook hands, nor bade farewell to him" (1.2.21), suggesting "both murder and mutilation" rather than depicting Macbeth as an honourable chivalrous knight (Hays 108). From the beginning, Macbeth proves military ability but also moral ambiguity (Ibid.). However, his brutality as a warrior is translated as bravery by his kinsmen and rewarded by the Scottish King who makes him Thane of Cawdor as was predicted by the witches (in Act one, scene three).

The mere fact that Macbeth rises in the Scottish society because of his omnipresent reputation as a brave soldier, indicates that this society is marked by warship and that masculinity is measured by the number of enemies a man is able to kill. Showing unrestrained brutality on the battlefield, or creating "strange images of death" (1.3.97), as Ross puts it, is rewarded rather than criticized by Macbeth's kinsmen. Thus Ross' reference to Macbeth as "Bellona's bridegroom" (1.2.55), the newly wedded husband to the Roman goddess of war, is a compliment, not a criticism (Foakes 149).

King Duncan acknowledges Macbeth's valour and gives him the title of Thane of Cawdor almost immediately after the witches' prophecy that he will be "Thane of Cawdor ... and King hereafter" (1.3.49-50).

Ironically, Macbeth's predecessor was executed for treason as he had helped the military forces of Norway during the battle. Now dark thoughts of regicide haunt Macbeth. He assumes that this crime is the prerequisite for becoming King of Scotland himself, the mere thought of this deed gives him a "horrid image" (1.3.135), which makes him feel uncomfortable and leads him to the conclusion:

> If Chance will have me King, why, Chance may crown me,
> Without my stir. (1.3.142-4)

Still this idea will not leave Macbeth alone. Macbeth is confused about his inner drive to murder Duncan and does not entirely understand this impulse (Foakes 151). Being "the product of a culture of violence" he has proved his outstanding bravery in the fight against Norway, but killing Duncan is something different (Foakes 149). It is treason to kill one's kinsman and a guest. Killing Duncan means crossing a line he has never crossed before. Now Macbeth is suffering from his idea to kill Duncan in order to gain the crown himself. Macbeth's mental turmoil at the thought of killing King Duncan and his subsequent conclusion to become the new King of Scotland by "chance" and "without his stir" indicate that it takes Lady Macbeth's initiation to persuade him to commit regicide.

I will explain how Lady Macbeth influences her husband to commit regicide in the section "Macbeth and Lady Macbeth: Marital Fulfillment in Regicide". After Macbeth's coronation he "alternates between a "manly readiness" (2.3.133) to rid himself of all those who stand in his way and a condition in which a "torture of the mind" (3.2.21) unmans him" (Foakes 152).

Despite being the new King of Scotland, Macbeth is unable to enjoy his newly achieved status. Instead, he develops a paranoia-like psychological condition, which makes him suspicious towards his kinsmen (Ibid.). He fears that he has revealed his guilt to the entire court and therefore feels the urge to kill more and more of his kinsmen.

He has his agents kill Banquo as his sons were prophesied to become the future Kings of Scotland. Lady Macduff and her children are also slaughtered. In order to protect his positions as King, Macbeth is forced to fight the English troops who come to break his tyranny (Foakes 153). Returning to battlefield against the English forces gives him new energy. Before this last battle, he had lost his ability to feel emotion. He is neither able to feels sympathy for his wife who committed suicide nor for his victims. But the prospect of fighting against the English invading troops, who are lead by Duncan's son Malcolm, gives him new strength to protect not only his power but also his honour and dignity. He obviously delights in renewing the cycle of violence for he fights strongly against his enemies although his life has become "a walking shadow" (5.5.24). During this last battle "a heroic conception of manliness centered on courage... becomes valued again" (Foakes 154). Ironically, young Siward is praised for dying "like a man" in confronting Macbeth (Foakes 153). Macbeth's self-conception as a man is deeply rooted in his ability to fight against his enemies, a quality which marks masculinity in a war-ridden society.

I would like to conclude that masculine violence is an underlying theme in the tragedy *Macbeth*. Violence epitomizes the concept of masculinity in Macbeth's world. It is socially accepted within the realm of warfare. Violence is expected to be shown by men, especially to defend their King and family. Macbeth became a "war hero" for showing "loyalty, valour and service kinship" to Duncan (Foakes 155).

Indeed, he proved to be a strong and successful warrior whose brutality was part of his glory. He was feared by his enemies and admired by his kinsmen. He delighted in killing his enemies and showed no remorse or sympathy for his victims. In the beginning of the play, his remorselessness was limited to warfare. However, in his quest for power, his remorselessness was numbed. Although he was longing for the crown, he was actually not able to be a real King. Macbeth was an able soldier in the Scottish troops whose valour made him legendary among his kinsmen, but he proved unable to keep his manly composure and sanity. Displaying violence once gave Macbeth strength and established his glory among his kinsmen as long as he fought to protect his county. It is upon his reflection of the bloody murder of Duncan that he began to lose his sanity. This regicide killed "the root of this own life as isolation and the loss of his mental health [was] the price he [had] to pay for it" (Eagleton 7). Madness weakened his mind and turned him into a person people both fear and pity. The murder of the King was triggered by his own ambition and re-enforced by the confusing prophecy of the three witches as well as by his wife's deadly ambition. Macbeth ended as a "shrinking, superstitious, bragging, hysterical wrench at Dunsinane who [could not] look his enemies in the face" (Dusinberre 285).

I think there is another contributing factor as Macbeth's violence increases so drastically in the course of the play, and that is that of his sterility.

Sterility as the Underlying Reason for Macbeth's Violence

In his dissertation about the relationships between parents and children in various Shakespearean dramas, Götz Ahrendt describes Macbeth as a "hero" whose kingdom becomes worthless as he is a "childless father" (250).

Ahrendt claims that Macbeth gradually comes to the realization that his achievements are worthless unless he has sons to inherit his kingdom (Ibid.). Macbeth considers his crown as a reward for his endevours, but his achievements are pointless unless he has a son to inherit his throne (250). To his mind, having no children is a shame, because a kingdom is worthless without potential heirs. In his soliloquy in Act three, Scene one, he expresses his bitterness about his childlessness:

> Upon my head they plac'd a fruitless crown,
> And put a barren sceptre in my gripe,
> Thence to be wrench'd with an unlineal hand,
> No son of mine succeeding. If't be so,
> For Banquo's issue have I fil'd my mind;
> For them the gracious Duncan have I murther'd;
> Put rancours in the vessel of my peace,
> Only for them; and mine eternal jewel
> Given to the common Enemy of man,
> To make them kings, the seed of Banquo kings!
> Rather than so, come, fate, into the list,
> And champion me to th' utterance! (3.1.60-71)

It is indeed ironic that Macbeth expresses despair about not fathering a son as this has not been changed by any events during the play. He is desperate because Banquo's sons will inherit a crown he had to fight and murder for. Instead of expressing remorse for murdering Duncan, he feels sorry for himself.

He first blames the three witches for placing "a fruitless crown" upon his head, then the devil ("the common Enemy of man") and finally "Faith" itself, which he decides to challenge (Ahrendt 250). In challenging "Fate", it is clear that he will continue to murder to hold on to his power. His determination seems rather shortsighted as although he might succeed in killing Banquo's children, he still would not have sons of his own to pass the crown on to.

Macbeth is blinded by his desire for power that he is not able to reach this conclusion. His ambition is now to fight against the fulfillment of the prophecy the witches gave to Banquo that his sons will be kings.

Macbeth cannot be happy with a crown which he cannot pass on to his own "issue". In the eyes of the contemporary society, a family is not complete without children as they nurture the hope for the continuation of the prosperity and success of a family (Ahrendt 251). Realizing that his kingdom is worthless without having his own heir to the crown, Macbeth begins to envy and detest all of his kinsmen who are fathers, no matter if their children may be a threat to his crown or not (Ahrendt 251). This obsession seems irrational since he knows that only Banquo's sons were foretold to become kings and that no man born under natural circumstances can threaten his royal power. Still his final question to the witches at their second meeting deals with Banquo and his sons (Ibid.):

> ... Yet my heart
> Throbs to know one thing: tell me (if your art
> Can tell so much), shall Banquo's issue ever
> Reign in this kingdom? (4.1.100-3),

he insists to get a response to his question:

> I will be satisfied: deny me this,
> And an eternal curse fall on you! Let me know. (4.1.104-5)

The "show of eight Kings" from Banquo's lineage and the bloodstained ghost of Banquo laughing at him gives him the "horrible" awareness that his crown is in fact worthless (Ibid.):

> Horrible sight! - Now, I see, 'tis true;
> For the blood-bolter'd Banquo smiles upon me,
> And points at them for his. (4.1.122-4)

After this meeting with the witches and the apparitions, Macbeth is ready to challenge his fate. After being warned of Macduff, Macbeth hires murderers to kill Macduff's family. I think this is an irrational decision for he knows that it is Banquo's sons who are a threat to his crown (Ahrendt 251). Macbeth's fight against potential enemies contributes inevitably to his downfall and will not turn him into a father, only into a tyrant people fear. Macbeth becomes more and more isolated. Alone and dejected in the castle of Dunsinane, Macbeth reflects on his misery, which, to his mind, is due to a lack of "honour, love [and] obedience" (5.3.25) of his kinsmen and due to the fact that he has no next of kin (Ahrendt 252). In his soliloquy:

> I have live'd long enough: my way of life
> Is fall'n into the sear, the yellow leaf;
> And that which should accompany old age,
> As honour, love, obedience, troops of friends,
> I must not look to have; but in their stead,
> Curses, not loud, but deep, mouth-honour, breath,
> Which the poor heart would fain deny, and dare not. (5.3.22-7)

Macbeth realizes that his life will soon be over. Although he is depressed, he is not suicidal. Even after he realizes that a troop of enemies is approaching his castle in the form of a leafy forest, he is not willing to surrender. Instead he renews the circle of violence he started and runs amok fighting his enemies as he did when he was a brave soldier under King Duncan's rule. Macbeth has become a tyrant whose ambition and need for power has driven him to murder. Even after it is clear to him that his reign has become void of meaning, he still defends it with his life. This last fight gives him the chance to do what he is good at, namely killing, and thereby regain some of his dignity.

Macbeth's sterility is a leitmotif in the play symbolizing Macbeth's sterility of morals (Ahrendt 254). In his selfish ambition to kill Banquo and Fleance, Macbeth appeals to the fatherly and protective instincts of his hired killers, telling them it is Banquo that is responsible for their poverty and thus the poverty of their children. Macbeth relies on their roles as fathers to provoke them into a readiness to kill Banquo and his son Fleance (Ahrendt 252):

> ... Are you so gospell'd,
> To pray for this good man, and for his issue,
> Whose heavy hand hath bow'd you to the grave,
> And beggar'd yours for ever? (3.1.87-9)

Despite their fraternity, Macbeth does not seem to accept the murderers as men and gets angry when one of them claims "We are men, my Liege." (3.1.90). Macbeth responds that they are "men" as far as the "catalogue" goes, as any breed of dog (3.1.91-6). This would suggest that Macbeth's concept of manliness is not solely based on fraternity. Instead Macbeth favours a definition of masculinity based on noble qualities, such as valour, "love, honour [and obedience]" (5.3.25) and does so until his death. Although he himself lacks these very virtues that he values, he still defines himself as a man who is entitled to the respect of his kinsmen. Macbeth's deep envy towards fathers haunts him until his bitter end. He proved to be especially envious towards Banquo whose concepts of manliness is very different from his own. At the first glance, Banquo seems to perfectly match the standards of chivalry.

In the following section, I will explain why I regard Banquo's concept of masculinity to be dubious.

Banquo: Perfect Knight or Villain ?

At the beginning of the play, Banquo seems to be Macbeth's closest confidant and "the only figure Macbeth identifies with" (Stockholder 102). Banquo is depicted as an ambitious knight who, as the bloody Sergeant reports, "was as involved as Macbeth in the bloodshed and slaughter of the battle against the forces led by Macdonwald" (Hays 109). Macbeth and Banquo are delineated as an indistinguishable pair; both are ambitious "captains" (1.2.33) who, in order to fight the Norwegian troops (Kahn 175):

> Doubly redoubled strokes upon the foe:
> [...] they meant to bathe in reeking wounds,
> Or memorize another Golgotha. (1.2.39-41)

Banquo is described as a warrior who just like Macbeth is able to "kill large numbers of soldiers" (Hays 108). Although Banquo's fighting methods are also less than chivalric, his allegiance to King Duncan is stronger than Macbeth's. Banquo honestly declares his love for Duncan. In response to Duncan's praises:

> [...] Noble Banquo,
> That hast no less deserv'd, nor must be known
> No less to have done so, let me infold thee,
> And hold thee to my heart. (1.4.29-32),

Banquo warmly replies:

> There if I grow,
> The harvest is your own. (1.4.33-4)

The witches' prophecy to Banquo that he will "get kings, though ... be none" (1.3.67) initially does not affect Banquo's loyalty to Duncan.

Shakespeare delineates Banquo as an honourable knight who succeeds in "succumbing to the instruments of darkness, the witches" (Jorgensen, *The Tragedies* 86). The witches' prophecies that Macbeth shall be "Thane of Cawdor" and "be King hereafter" (1.3.49-50) and that Banquo shall "get kings, though ... be none" (1.3.67) turn both Macbeth and Banquo into "noble men ... who are told ... of great futures [and who know that] some tainted action seems necessary in each case" (Ibid.). The prophecy haunts Banquo. Having "dreamt ... of the three Weird Sisters" (2.1.20), Banquo cannot, or rather would not, sleep; he tells his son Fleance:

> A heavy summons lies like lead upon me,
> And yet I would not sleep: merciful Powers!
> Restrain in me the cursed thoughts that nature
> Gives way to in response! (2.1.6-9)

The "merciful Powers" (2.1.7) Banquo prays to are probably the "order of angels appointed by God to guard against and restrain demons" (Curry 81). However, Banquo is able to overcome these "cursed thoughts", which strengthens his solidarity to King Duncan. When Macbeth asks him for his support, which would "make honour" (2.1.26) for him, his proud reply is:

> So I lose none
> In seeking to augment it, but still keep
> My bosom franchis'd, and allegiance clear,
> I shall be counsell'd. (2.1.26-9)

Unlike Macbeth, Banquo is not dissatisfied with the witches' prophecy to him. He seems "content merely with the prospect of transmitting a royal inheritance" (Kahn 182). In the course of the play, Banquo will become Macbeth's rival because Banquo "will get kings" and fraternity is "the ultimate manly satisfaction in this play, which [Macbeth] never achieves" (Ibid.).

According to the witches' prophecies, it is not Banquo, but rather his sons who may be a threat to Macbeth's crown. Banquo and his sons are more than a threat to Macbeth's crown. Banquo is "Macbeth's ideal image", a "man of conscience as well as courage" (Kahn 182-3). Macbeth envies Banquo's fraternity and manly composure and therefore Macbeth considers Banquo to be his greatest enemy. In his soliloquy, Macbeth outlines why he now considers Banquo as his enemy:

> Our fears in Banquo
> Stick deep, and in his royalty of nature
> Reigns that which would be fear'd: 'tis much he dares;
> And, to that dauntless temper of his mind,
> He hath a wisdom that doth guide his valour
> To act in safety. There is none but he
> Whose being I do fear: and under him
> My Genius is rebuk'd. (3.1.47-55)

Macbeth is not only envious towards Banquo because he is a father to sons prophesied to become kings, but also for his chivalric qualities such as courage, fairness, wisdom, and valour. Banquo's noble masculine qualities make "Macbeth shrink pitifully" (Long 87). Interestingly, he is especially envious of Banquo's soundness and "temper" of mind which contrasts to the tortured and distressed mind of Macbeth.

Banquo seemingly epitomizes a brave warrior, a chivalrous knight with loyalty and strength of character. However, Banquo does not protest after Duncan's murder although he knows that it was Macbeth, not Donalbain and not Malcolm, who committed this crime.

It is Macduff, not Banquo, who shows the expected reaction of a true and loyal chivalric knight on hearing the news of Duncan's murder. Macduff is outraged:

> O horror! horror! horror!
> Tongue nor heart cannot conceive, nor name thee!
> [...]
> Confusion now hath made his masterpiece!
> Most sacrilegious Murther hath broke ope
> The Lord's anointed Temple, and stole thence
> The life o'th'building! (2.3.62-3, 65-8)

Banquo's silence after the murder is inexplicable (Hays 110). Bradley speculates that Banquo hopes to "profit ... by acquiescing in Macbeth's accession to the throne", which would jeopardize his political idealism (306-7). Alfar argues to the same point: "Banquo is willing to wink at regicide when his heirs' acquisition of the throne is in view." (134). In addition, Jorgensen agrees that "morally Banquo becomes a passive sharer of the evil fortunes of Macbeth, which are linked by the witches with his own" (136). However, Banquo's silence after the regicide is not absolute. Banquo speaks about his suspicion to Macbeth and thereby expresses his hope for the fulfillment of the prophecy the witches gave to him:

> Thou hast it now, King, Cawdor, Glamis, all,
> As the Weird Women promis'd; and, I fear,
> Thou play' dst most foully for' t; yet it was said,
> It should not stand in thy posterity;
> But that myself should be the root and father
> Of many kings. If there come truth from them
> [...]
> Why, by the verities on thee made good,
> May they not be my oracles as well,
> And set me up in hope? [...]. (3.1.1-10)

Banquo is thus depicted as a chivalric knight who stresses his loyalty and valour to King Duncan, but his true ambition is to become the "root and father of many kings" (3.1.5-6).

His political idealism as well as his morality make him strong enough to challenge his dark thoughts. He refuses to use violence against King Duncan in order to hasten the witches' prophecy. This enables him to keep his "bosom franchis'd, and allegiance clear" (2.1.28). Unlike Macduff, Banquo's loyalty to his King ends with Duncan's death. He then proves to be an opportunist who seeks to profit from Macbeth's crime. The fact that Macbeth and Banquo were once comrades, influences the way Macbeth plots to kill Banquo and Fleance. Instead of killing Banquo and Fleance himself, he decides to keep their blood "safely remote" by hiring murderers to perform this deed (Jorgensen, *The Tragedies* 88). Banquo's murder is quick and Shakespeare does not give him a "great death speech" (Long 90). Banquo's dying words emphasize his fraternal pride and his wish for his "issue" to survive and possibly revenge his father:

> O, treachery! Fly, good Fleance, fly, fly, fly!
> Thou may'st revenge – O slave! (3.3.16-7)

It is impossible for Macbeth to keep Banquo's blood remote from him and his conscience as the hired murderers bring it to the banquet and turn the occasion into a bloody affair. The news that Banquo is dead, but Fleance survived makes Macbeth ill; he exclaims:

> [...] I had else been perfect;
> Whole as the marble, founded as the rock,
> As broad and general as the casing air:
> But now, I am cabin'd, cribb'd, confin'd, bound in
> To saucy doubts and fears. [...]. (3.4.20-4)

Banquets traditionally symbolize political and social order (Long 90). Therefore, Banquo's unexpected appearance as a ghost at the banquet makes him the moral winner of Macbeth's lethal intrigue as his ghost is able to make Macbeth look "quite unmann'd in folly" (3.4.73). His appearance makes him look like a crazed boy among men. Without words Banquo's ghost is able to demonstrate his "invulnerability to death" (Long 86). Banquo is immortal to Macbeth as he is able to haunt his mind and Banquo's "issue" also eluded the hired murderers (Long 87). It is therefore ironic that Macbeth cannot maintain his composure when he is confronted with Banquo's ghost.

This confrontation is more shocking to Macbeth than facing "the rugged Russian bear, / The armed rhinoceros, or th' Hyrcan tiger" (3.4.99-100). Banquo's ghost makes it impossible for Macbeth to be a good host. He is unable "to grace [his guests] with [his] royal company" (3.4.43) and thus fails to establish any royal order. On the contrary, Banquo's ghost takes "Macbeth's royal seat of honour and ... is, as Macbeth says, crowned with "twenty mortal murders" (3.4.82)" (Calderwood 126). Thus Banquo shortly becomes "King of Scotland" and creates a prophetic image that forecasts the reign of his son (Ibid.). Feeling "unmanned" by the frightening sight of Banquo's ghost, which cannot be seen by his guests, Macbeth seems to regret his murder and expresses his readiness to "return life to the Ghost" to regain his own manliness and fight a duel with the living Banquo (Calderwood 127):

> [...] be alive again,
> And dare me to the desert with thy sword;
> If trembling I inhibit then, protest me
> The baby of a girl [...]. (3.4.102-5)

Banquo's ghost increases Macbeth's longing for a clear and manly order of the world. Macbeth would rather die in a duel against his enemy than face a ghost.

Macbeth's "manliness" does not return until Banquo's ghost disappears (Calderwood 127):

> Why, so; - being gone,
> I am a man again. (3.4.107-8)

But Macbeth will not regain his "manliness" because Banquo's ghost "never fully makes an exit from his mind" (Calderwood 130). Banquo's ghost is able to threaten Macbeth's manliness. As Banquo's ghost keeps haunting Macbeth, he returns to the witches "to find certitude" (Long 93). Macbeth is longing to know if "... Banquo's issue [shall] ever reign in this kingdom" (4.1.102-3). The witches' "show of eight Kings" (4.1.111) of Banquo's lineage scares Macbeth. However, he does not consider this vision as a "punishment for his sins, but rather a partial horror of future doom" (Jorgensen, *Sensational Art* 180). The "show of kings" puts an end to Macbeth's ambition in the form of own children (Ibid.).

To conclude, Banquo may not be a perfect chivalrous knight as he does not expose Macbeth as Duncan's murder. But his guilt is a minor one compared to Macbeth's. Although he also entertained dark thoughts, he musters not to give into them. He does not consider regicide, but he is willing to tolerate Macbeth's crime and hence profit from it. His loyalty to King Duncan ended with Duncan's death, which makes him less chivalrous than Macduff. Still he is virtuous enough not to ally with the witches. His relative independence from the witches spares him their punishment: barrenness (Jorgensen, *Sensational Art* 154). In *The Discoverie of Witchcraft*, Reginald Scot explains that witches can

> produce barrennesse in man, woman, and beast. These can throwe children into water, as they walke with their mothers, and not be seene [...]. These can take awaie mans courage, and the power of generation (6).

Banquo's relative innocence spares him the loss of his potency. He is fruitful in that he can proudly point at a line of eight kings descending from him, while Macbeth is punished with sterility.

Macduff: The Epitome of Chivalry?

Macduff's concept of masculinity opposes Macbeth's as it is not (directly) linked to violence. Fairness and freedom from tyranny for his country are important values to Macduff. He is the embodiment of true chivalric manliness and during the course of the play he takes on a unique form of manliness which goes beyond the ideals of chivalrous masculinity. He is represented as an honourable knight whose valour and service to King Duncan does not end after his violent murder. He judges Macbeth's ambitions justly and acquires the courage to develop female qualities such as sensitivity, sympathy and empathy without losing the courage of a chivalrous knight fighting heroically against the tyrannical ruler Macbeth in just war. He identifies Macbeth as what he really is: "an untitled tyrant bloody-scepter'd" (4.3.104) (Jorgensen, *Sensational Art* 91). From the beginning of the play, he symbolizes fairness and a cry for humane circumstances in a morally corrupted Scotland.

He is the one who cries out the moral horror of King Duncan's murder. His cry for humane values and fairness is repeatedly associated with the trumpet. Both Macbeth and Macduff share the quality of fighting recklessly in war. Macbeth fights an unjust war in his pursuit and defense of his illegitimate crown. However, Macduff risks his life fighting for humanity and out of love and loyalty to King Duncan in just war.

Macbeth fights in order to conceal his crimes and uphold his illegitimate kingdom, Macduff, on the other hand, does not fight for egoistic purposes. Instead, he fights for his country and the noble values King Duncan represents. Ironically, he wants to protect Lady Macbeth from hearing about the bloody crime against King Duncan. He gently warns her:

> O gentle lady,
> 'Tis not for you to hear what I can speak:
> The repetition, in a woman's ear,
> Would murther as it fell. (2.3.81-4)

This proves that he shows gentlemanly behaviour to women even in times of severe distress. He later fights for the interests of the legitimate heir of the crown, Duncan's elder son Malcolm. In order to restore natural principles, he organizes the revolt against the tyranny of Macbeth whose reign he refuses to accept. After Banquo is murdered, Macduff becomes Macbeth's antagonist and biggest enemy. Throughout the entire play, Macduff proves to be a chivalrous knight whose devotion to King Duncan does not stop after his death "as he aligns himself with

Duncan and Malcolm, and alienates himself from Macbeth" (Hays 110). Fighting for fairness and humane values as formerly represented by King Duncan is his goal in life and he sees it as his duty to end Macbeth's reign of terror.

Macduff travels to Malcolm to organize a revolt against Macbeth. Despite Lady Macduff's supposition that he abandoned his family, Macduff did not intentionally leave his family to be slaughtered. On the news that the tyrant ruler Macbeth had killed his entire family, Macduff initially does not strive for revenge, as one would expect.

Instead, he seems rather weak and mournful. He is stunned and cannot believe that he has lost his entire family. He asks Ross, the messenger of this tragic news:

> My children too? (4.3.211),
>
> My wife killed too? (4.3.213),
>
> All my pretty ones?
> Did you say all? - O Hell-kite! - All?
> What all my chickens, and their dam,
> At one fell swoop? (4.3.216-8)

It is Malcolm who urges him to "Dispute it like a man" (4.3.219), to which Macduff replies: "I shall do so; / But I must also feel it like a man" (4.3.220-1) (Eagleton 100). Whilst violence and a longing for revenge would be the more natural manly response to this atrocity, Macduff refuses to confirm automatically to the stereotype (Ibid.). His first impulse is to mourn the loss of his family and not to take revenge on his family's murderer. Malcolm does not seem to understand Macduff's sadness. To him, Macduff is acting weakly, as Malcolm's concept of manliness is based on the assumption that men should always be in control of their feelings and act bravely. Malcolm is the embodiment of a "patriarchal stereotype of courage and emotional control", whereas Macduff goes "beyond this ideology of gender" by showing his depressed feelings and demanding the right to mourn the loss of his beloved ones (Ibid.).

Macduff's rapid decision to fight back (4.3.230-4) comes as a surprise echoing his own surprised response to Malcolm on hearing that Malcolm follows fair ambitions. Having won the final battle against Macbeth, Macduff represents his manly pride by sticking the defeated tyrant's head on a pole and celebrating his success. Still he does not claim the throne for himself as Macbeth did.

Instead, he "hails" the new King of Scotland (Malcolm) with warm words:

> Hail, King! for so thou art. Behold, where stands
> Th'usurper's cursed head: the time is free.
> I see thee compass'd with thy kingdom's pearl,
> That speak my salutation in their minds;
> Whose voices I desire aloud with mine,
> Hail, King of Scotland! (5.9.20-5)

Through the character of Macduff, Shakespeare creates the embodiment of a chivalrous knight. Still Macduff is more than a stereotype. He inherits feminine values he is not inhibited to express. He thus alters the picture of a chivalrous knight and makes it more natural. Macduff goes beyond traditional chivalric values as "courage, valour and manliness", in his concept of masculinity "manly valour must be tempered by the more civilized virtues of feeling and compassion" (Wells 117). Macduff is depicted as the personification of chivalric valour, he is "honourably by his profession of allegiance to [King Duncan] adhering to the line of succession, and placing the county's interests ahead of his own" (Hays 110). He is a knight "servable to his king, loyal to the throne, and devoted to his county – all points shown throughout the play and stressed in the Court Scene" (Hays 111). Only at one point in the play does Macduff seems morally shallow. This is when Malcolm tests Macduff's political idealism and Macduff signals that he will support Malcolm's legitimate claim to the throne regardless of his selfproclaimed lasciviousness and tyrannical tendencies (Alfar 132). Malcolm claims

> In my voluptuousness: your wives, your daughters,
> Your matrons, and your maids, could not fill up
> The cisterns of my lust; and my desire ... (4.3.61-3),

to which Macduff responds to in a misogynist way:

> We have willing dames enough; there cannot be
> That vulture in you, to devour so many
> As will to greatness dedicate themselves,
> Finding it so inclin'd. (4.3.73-6)

However, Macduff is the one "chivalric champion" in this play who eventually will "seek and confront Macbeth, defeat him offstage, and re-appear with his head on the sword", just to be "the first to hail Malcolm as king" (Hays 111). In Hays assertion, it is due to Macduff's political idealism that Scotland's right rule can be restored (98).

Malcolm: Hope for a Restored "Natural Order"?

Malcolm is the legitimate heir of the benevolent King Duncan whose reign promised a "natural order" of humanity. It is with Malcolm's coronation that the play ends. However, does Malcolm really have the format to become a humane king? How does he define masculinity? Eagleton argues that Malcolm's understanding of the term "man" equals the "patriarchal stereotype of courage and emotional control" and is therefore referring to Malcolm's response to Macduff's very emotional reaction on the news that his entire family was killed by Macbeth's hired killers (Eagleton 100). In Act four, Scene three Macduff seems temporarily "unmanned" by his sorrow and cannot stop whining and mourning his loss. Malcolm feels uncomfortable about Macduff's emotional reaction, which to him seems unnatural and effeminate. So he taunts Macduff to "Dispute it like a man" (4.3.219). This advice echoes the chivalric notion of masculine courage and readiness to fight against tyranny in fair warfare.

Ironically, Malcolm's expressed "need to combat treason with manly readiness" reminds the audience of Macbeth as the brave warrior he was at the beginning of the play and who remorselessly slew Macdonwald (Wells 120). At this point, Malcolm reveals to the audience that he does not have the "feminine" qualities which his father possessed, otherwise he would certainly have expressed his sympathy and consoled his friend. However, Malcolm's apparent lack of feminine qualities does not, on the other hand, disqualify him as a fair King of Scotland who will eventually restore his father's "natural order".

In his very critical characterization of Malcolm, Stanley Booth clearly states that Malcolm is unable to nurture any hope for that. Booth's argument is that in order to represent hope for a restored "natural order" in Scotland, Malcolm would have to win the audience's attention and affection and accordingly become a real antagonist to Macbeth (Booth 105-7). But "for the play's length" the audience practically sees the action "through Macbeth's eyes" (Booth 106). Booth states that being "audience to *Macbeth* is virtually to *be* Macbeth" (106). He also claims that due to Malcolm's scarcity of appearances on stage as well as the quality of his speeches Malcolm cannot be considered a strong and manly character (107). Indeed, Malcolm has little chance to win the heart of the audience. He first appears in Act one, Scene two to greet the bleeding Sergeant who informs King Duncan of Macbeth's heroism in the fight against Macdonwald:

> This is the Sergeant;
> Who, like a good and hardy soldier, fought '

> Gainst my captivity. - Hail, brave friend!
> Say to the King the knowledge of the broil,
> As thou didst leave it. (1.2.3-7)

His praises for the bleeding Captain, who has saved him on the battlefield, show Malcolm's appreciation of chivalric values such as courage, honour and relentlessness in fair warfare. In the same scene, he greets another Scottish nobleman (Rosse):

> The worthy Thane of Rosse. (1.2.47),

and in Act one, Scene four, he informs his father of the execution of the treacherous Thane of Cawdor. Again his speech expresses his chivalric definition of masculinity, which praises courage in fair warfare and despises treason:

> ... I have spoke
> With one that saw him die: who did report,
> That very frankly he confess'd his treasons,
> Implor'd your Highness' pardon, and set forth
> A deep repentance. Nothing in his life
> Became him like the leaving it: he died
> As one that had been studied in his death,
> To throw away the dearest thing he ow'd,
> As 'twere a careless trifle. (1.4.3-11)

Booth argues that in these scenes "Malcolm shows signs of just the sort of spiritual energy he would need if he were to separate the audience's soul from Macbeth" and perhaps be seen as an able knight and worthy successor to his father's throne (Booth 107). Malcolm next appears on stage after his father's murder, a scene in which, according to Booth, this "potential hero [is rendered] theatrically impotent", especially because of his detached response on hearing the news that his father has been killed (Ibid.):

> Macduff: Your royal father's murther'd.
> Malcolm: O! by whom? (2.3.97-8)

Booth claims Shakespeare follows a specific strategy to "undo" Malcolm completely as a "potential hero" and to make his "presence painful to his moral allies, the audience" (107). He argues that, for example, Malcolm's long and strenuous testing of Macduff's idealism in the England scene (Act four, Scene three) reflects this strategy (Booth 106).

Although Booth's assumption that Malcolm is not a real antagonist to Macbeth - at least not until he aligns himself with Macduff - is true, on the other hand, Booth's insistence on Malcolm's "theatrical impotence" seems too harsh.

Malcolm's escape to England after his father's murder is understandable, as "[...] there is no mercy left" (2.4.144) in Scotland. This may be a decision, which does not epitomize him as a hero who will fight to save his country and be as great a king as his father was. It takes Macduff's initiative to make Malcolm take a stand against Macbeth's tyranny. In addition, Malcolm is not a charismatic man.

However, in the course of the play Malcolm develops a set of values, which differs from his father's and perhaps makes him the symbol of a restored "natural order" in Scotland. Knowing that his father's unlimited trust was part of the reason why he was killed, Malcolm develops a watchfulness, which makes him test Macduff's ambitions before he aligns himself with him. However, Malcolm's long testing of Macduff's integrity (in Act four, Scene three) may be tedious to the audience as this scene fails to keep up with the velocity of the previous scenes. Nevertheless, I disagree with Booth who interprets that "Malcolm's behaviour in [this scene] is the most perverse element in a perverse scene [in which he vilifies] himself to test Macduff's political idealism" (Booth 107). Watchfulness and suspicion have become Malcolm's prevalent traits.

In this scene, Malcolm denies that he possesses any king-becoming graces such

> As Justice, Verity, Temp'rance, Stableness,
> Bounty, Perseverance, Mercy, Lowliness,
> Devotion, Patience, Courage, Fortitude. (4.3.92-4),

He emphasizes that he would be a tyrannical king, just like Macbeth:

> ...were I King,
> I should cut off the nobles for their lands;
> Desire his jewels, and this other's house:
> And my more-having would be as a sauce
> To make me hunger more; that I should forge
> Quarrels unjust against the good and loyal,
> Destroying them for wealth. (4.3.78-84),

and exemplifies his (pretended) "lust" and "desire" in a misogynist way:

> In my voluptuousness: your wives, your daughters,
> Your matrons , and your maids, could not fill up
> The cistern of my lust; and my desire [...]. (4.3.61-3)

He also reiterates that he is "bloody, luxurious, avaricious, false, deceitful, sudden, malicious" and lecherous (4.3.58-9). In actuality, Malcolm does not present his own sinful attributes. He rather depicts the tyranny of Macbeth's realm. Malcolm's testing of Macduff's "idealism" is indeed very intense. At first Malcolm pretends to be fond of Macbeth's tyranny. Malcolm calls Macbeth "an angry god" (4.3.17) and recommends Macduff

> To offer up a weak, poor, innocent lamb,
> T'appease [him]. (4.3.16-7)

Macduff's assertion "I am not treacherous." (4.3.18) does not convince Malcolm of Macduff's noble causes. Part of his suspicions arises from the fact that Macduff left his wife and children "unprotected". Therefore, Malcolm asks Macduff:

> Why in that rawness left you wife and child
> (Those precious motives, those strong knots of love),
> Without leave-taking? (4.3.26-8)

Malcolm continues to test Macduff's morality. However, it becomes obvious that in his definition of manliness a man should never leave his family unprotected. Malcolm's tedious self-accusation does not stop until Macduff brings up the topic of Malcolm's "royal father" and pious mother (4.3.108-111) and desperately declares that Scotland's "hope ends here!" (4.3.113). All of a sudden, Malcolm takes back his self-accusation as his "first false speaking" (4.3.130) and reveals his "true" identity. To Macduff's great surprise, Malcolm declares:

> Macduff, this noble passion,
> Child of integrity, hath from my soul
> Wip'd the black scruples, reconcil'd my thoughts
> To thy good truth and honour. [...]
> I put myself to thy direction, and
> Unspeak mine own detraction; here adjure
> The taints and blames I laid upon myself,
> For stranger to my nature. (4.3.114-25)

He stresses his innocence by claiming to be

> ... yet
> Unknown to woman; never was forsworn;
> [...]
> At no time broke my faith. (4.3.125-8)

He then begins to take control of his country and orders English troops to challenge Macbeth.

Malcolm's "false speaking" is highly ambiguous. Alfar states that the audience never really learns about Malcolm's own integrity. She suggests that it is hard to tell how much truth lies in Malcolm's lengthy self-accusations (131-2). In Alfar's view, Malcolm needs Macduff to support his "claim to power militarily, despite his rights to it as a heir", so he needs to "reverse his claim to depravity [when] Macduff renounces his support" (Alfar 131). Furthermore, she claims that "it is only when Macduff rejects Malcolm ... that Malcolm repudiates that evil in himself, crediting the goodness he sees in Macduff ... and claiming a sinless life heretofore" (Alfar 132). Indeed, Malcolm never outlines his definition of what a gentle and noble king is. The audience can only speculate if Malcolm really has "tyrannical tendencies" (Alfar 131) or if he is a chivalric man, just like Macduff.

However, Hays draws a completely different picture of this scene. He states that in this scene Malcolm establishes "his qualifications for rule by successfully testing Macduff and converting his grief [over the loss of his family] into anger so that Macduff's vengeance may serve political purposes as well as give personal satisfaction" (Hays 112). Unfortunately, Hays does not explain which "qualification" Malcolm establishes exactly. Does he establish the "king-becoming graces" (4.3.91-4) he previously denied possessing?

Despite the ambiguity of this scene and although Malcolm may not develop into a real antagonist to Macbeth, it seems that he follows noble political ambitions. He wants to free Scotland from tyranny.

It is hard to say if Malcolm is free from any "tyrannical tendencies" himself and if he really aspires to develop "king-becoming graces", which would make him the symbol of hope for a restored Scotland based on "natural order". Malcolm's idea of masculinity is based on chivalric values. Especially before his coronation, he emphasizes chivalric values of manliness, such as a masculine readiness to revenge. Confronted with Macduff's sorrow, he advices him to

> Be comforted:
> Let's make us med'cines of our great revenge,
> To cure this deadly grief. (4.3.213-5),

as well as to

> Dispute it like a man. (4.3.219)

Having convinced Macduff to revenge his slain family, Malcolm acknowledges his restored masculinity:

> This tune goes manly.
> Come, go we to the King: our power is ready;
> Our lack is nothing but our leave. Macbeth
> Is ripe for shaking. (4.3.235)

However, after his lengthy testing of Macduff's true ambitions it is hard to make out if these chivalric values do really represent Malcolm's genuine definition of manliness. Malcolm's changing concept of manliness in this act is remarkable. Malcolm's transformation from a lecherous villain to a true chivalric man might seem surprising, if not contrived. However, his strong appeal to masculine values based on chivalry does not translate in a corresponding participation in actual warfare.

Although Scottish nobleman Mentieth (in 5.2) exclaims that

> The English power is near, led on by Malcolm, His uncle Siward, and the good Macduff. (5.2.1-2),

Malcolm stays on the periphery of the battlefield.

To conclude, Malcolm does not seem to develop a unique set of values epitomizing him to be the symbol of hope for a restored "natural order" in Scotland. However, he manages to team up with noble Macduff and Siward and thus organizes the revolt against Macbeth. By the end of the play, Malcolm is able to express his sympathy to Siward who lost his son in the final battle against Macbeth:

> Siward.   Why then, God's soldier be he!
> Had I as many sons as I have hairs,
> I would not wish them to a fairer death:
> And so, his knell is knoll'd.
> Malcolm.   He's worth more sorrow,
> And that I'll spend for him. (5.9.13-8)

This could perhaps indicate that Malcolm's definition of masculinity is just developing. Knowing that he will need help to develop the "king-becoming graces" required to restore his father's "natural order", he seems to bind himself closer to his "thanes" and "kinsmen" by declaring them

> Earls; the first that ever Scotland
> In such an honour nam'd. (5.9.29-30)

Malcolm's first political gesture is a gesture of gratitude, which alienates him from Macbeth's political style. Malcolm represents himself as a king who is willing to share political responsibility and possessions.

Femininity in Shakespeare's *Macbeth*

Although the title of this essay is *The Construction of Femininity and Masculinity in Shakespeare's Macbeth* I chose to start my analysis with the male characters in this play as the world of Macbeth is a men's world. There are only three "natural women" in the play, Lady Macduff, Lady Macbeth and her assistant. Although Shakespeare's *Macbeth* is placed in the world of chivalry, the women are construed like Elizabethan housewives. In the following section, I will explain this concept of femininity.

The Elizabethan Housewife

During the 16th century the concept of family shifted from the "Open Lineage Family" to the "Restricted Patriarchal Nuclear Family" (Stone 652). The "Open Lineage Family" had welcomed "aid and direction from the kin and the community", but lacked "domestic privacy", close relations between the spouses as well as between parents and children" (Ibid.). The "Restricted Patriarchal Nuclear Family" substituted "loyalties to lineage, kin, patrons and local community" by "more universalistic loyalties" to state and Church (Stone 7).

The "Restricted Patriarchal Nuclear Family" consisted of husband and wife and the children, which strengthened men's patriarchal power over the family to an extent that made him a "legalized petty tyrant within the home" (Stone 7). The wife and the children had no autonomy in this family structure whatsoever. By marriage, the husband and the wife became one person in law: the person of the husband (Stone 195).

The wife was her husband's inferior, so she was expected to be submissive to her husband at all times. An ideal woman had a "servile nature" and was "weak, submissive, charitable, virtuous and modest" (Stone 198). Her function was "housekeeping and the breeding and rearing of children" (Ibid.). She was to show chastity, modesty, altruism and obedience to her husband (Märtin 9).

Furthermore, she was expected to be silent in Church and at home and at all times obedient to her husband (Stone 200). The ideal Renaissance woman proved to have values such as obedience, silence, sexual chastity, piety, humility, constancy, and patience to her husband. Her husband was entitled to apply "moderate correction" in case she failed to show these qualities (Ibid.). A woman's place was either in her husband's or her father's house (Stone 198). Whilst women occupied the domain of "private, domestic affairs" as wives and mothers, husbands occupied "the male domain of public, economic and political action (Rackin 131). Men were soldiers, politicians, or leaders; they lived duty-bound lives. Moreover, they were supposed to be well-educated, show cultural grace, be gentlemen, understand arts and science and to prove refinement and courage.

Whilst men took over active roles in society, women were expected to fulfill a passive role. They were considered as the "weaker vessels", which means weaker than men both physically, emotionally, intellectually and morally (Klein 240). Furthermore, they were believed "to be prone to fears and subject to the vagaries of their imagination" (Ibid.). Women's inferior role in the family was justified with reference to the "second account of the creation in Genesis", where it says that "the perfect woman" was created later than the perfect man, shaped from his rib in order to forestall his loneliness and to be a "help meet for him" (Chapter II, verse 20) (Klein 240).

Because of "the curse of the Fall", women "were bound by nature and law to obey their husbands as well as their God" (Ibid.). Women could disobey their husbands only when husbands acted "in opposition to divine law" (Ibid.). In the 16th century, a man, his wife, and their children became the most "basic foundation of society", and it was the proper and moral ordering of this unit that would bring perfection and order to the Church and state in a time of immense transition and overlapping sensibilities (Rogers 2).

Humble Lady Macduff

In *Macbeth* Lady Macduff is portrayed as the most natural and humble woman although her appearance on stage is very short and tragic. The audience sees her on stage in one scene only, the scene in which she and her children are killed by Macbeth's brutal agents. She is the only female character in the play who has a living child and who despite her very short appearance on stage epitomizes "natural" femininity, which is very distinct and different from the witches and Lady Macbeth (Rackin 134). She is both a wife and a mother and thus represents life and hope for the survival of the next generation. On the other hand, she embodies victimhood in a society dominated by warfare and brutal males. She personifies "feminine helplessness" as her husband left her and her children "unprotected in a dangerous situation" (Ibid.). Lady Macduff misinterprets this fact when she jumps to the bitter conclusion:

> ... He loves us not:
> He wants the natural touch; for the poor wren,
> The most diminutive of birds, will fight,
> Her young ones in her nest, against the owl:
> All is the fear, and nothing is the love. (4.2.8-12)

Lady Macduff does not teach her son to honour his father. Instead, she stresses the "obligations he has to his family" and the fact that he fails to fulfill them (Bamber 93). The thought that her husband might have left the family to flee from his enemies adds to her anxiety. Shakespeare presents Lady Macduff as a "domesticated modern wife" who is incapable of defending her family from attacking forces, not as "a medieval noblewoman" who typically had the ability to "lead the defense of the castle in her husband's absence" (Rackin 135). As Rackin points out, the Macduff's household resembles a modern house "rather than a feudal stronghold" (135). Lady Macduff's crucial situation does not remain unnoticed by men who might have given her protection instead of her husband. But instead of protecting Lady Macduff, Ross tells her:

> You must have patience, Madam. (4.2.2)

Ross' advice to Lady Macduff does not help her. The messenger's warning to Lady Macduff seems more useful; he warns her of the approaching attackers and tells her to flee:

> I doubt, some danger does approach you nearly:
> If you will take a homely man's advice,
> Be not found here; hence, with your little ones. (4.2.66-8)

In her self-justification she explains why she does not take the messenger's advice to flee from her house:

> Whither should I fly?
> I have done no harm. But I remember now
> I am in this earthly world, where, to do harm
> Is often laudable; to do good, sometime
> Accounted dangerous folly: why then, alas!
> Do I put up that womanly defence,
> To say, I have done no harm? (4.2.72-8)

She is not naïve to the fact that the world she lives in follows the principle of "fair is foul, and foul is fair" (Dusinberre 282). Before she is murdered, she expresses that she worries about her husband and hopes that he does not have to face murderers like she has to:

> First murderer: Where is your husband?
>
> Lady Macduff: I hope, in no place so unsanctified,
> Where such as thou may'st find him. (4.2.79-81)

Macduff is horrified when he hears that his entire family was killed (Bamber 94). By contrast, Macbeth's reaction on hearing that his wife committed suicide is not emotional at all; he casually says:

> She should have died hereafter. (5.5.17)

Macduff's intense mourning proves that he really loved his wife although she was very critical towards his endavours. In my characterization of King Duncan, I mentioned that Duncan symbolizes victimhood. Lady Macduff shares this feature with him. Indeed, they both become victims to the tyrant Macbeth. Still Lady Macduff becomes King Duncan's antithesis in two respects. Lady Macduff does not share King Duncan's political shortsightedness. She is absolutely aware of the cruel political reality she has to face. And whilst King Duncan trusts too much, Lady Macduff trusts too little. She dies thinking that her husband deceived her and her children. It is however interesting that Shakespeare gave Lady Macduff, a seemingly common housewife, more awareness of the social and political dangers in Scotland than he gave to King Duncan, whose absolute trust and optimism eventually kill him.

Lady Macduff's personality is Shakespeare's original invention as Holinshed's *Chronicles* do not characterize her at all, but only explain that she, her children and her attendants were brutally killed by Macbeth's agents (Rackin 134). Sir William Davenant (1606-1668), the English poet and dramatist who "rewrote" and "updated" Shakespeare's *Macbeth* for Restoration audiences, gave Lady Macduff much more prominence by adding "three new scenes", in which Lady Macduff was given the role of "her husband's confidant, advisor, and inspiration", a strategy he chose to ensure that "the good people would have a good, modern marriage" (Rackin 136).

Whilst Davenant's adaption of the play, the prevalent stage version "from the 1660s to 1774", gave Lady Macduff more prominence, Lady Macduff is a "minor character" in Shakespeare's *Macbeth* and symbolizes a cry for civility (Rackin 136). Her character reminds the audience of Macduff's noble ambitions and his protests against the murderous tyranny arising from Macbeth's bloody rule (Ibid). She is construed as a woman "restricted to the private, domestic sphere" whose "natural vocation" is to be a wife and mother (Rackin 134). Thus Shakespeare shaped her to match the contemporary image of "women's nature", which was just beginning to establish in his time (Rackin 135).

Witches as a Social and Political Problem in Shakespeare's England

Witches were a severe social and political problem in Shakespeare's England. They were not considered as fictitious characters who were able to "hex", which means that they could cast spells on other people. People of this time were generally very suspersticious. They believed that witches could fly, make people ill, conjure visions, make themselves invisible, conjure storms and cause shipwrecks.

Mostly old women, ill and poor women were accused of being witches, especially if they were "unfortunate enough to be crone-like, snaggle-toothed, sunken-cheeked and having a hairy lip" (Ibid.). Also melancholy was frequently interpreted as a symptom of "susceptibility to the temptations of the devil" during the Renaissance and Reformation (Neely 14). These women were said to have the "evil eye". Cats were seen as their most likely "familiars", so that having cats was taken as proof that they were indeed witches (Ibid.). Bodily marks such as "warts, moles, or even a flea-bite" were seen as marking features and were interpreted as "devil marks" proving women's connection to the devil (Ibid). Legend had it that in order to become a witch a woman had to sell her soul to the devil. A witch was usually matched with a familiar in the form of a small animal without a tail. Reginald Scot depicted witches as "leane and deformed, shewing melancholie in their faces, to the horror of all that see them" (Jorgensen, *Sensational Art* 118). Women who failed to have a lovely face were easily identified as witches by their fellow people. In order to match the Elizabethan ideal of femininity, a woman had to have "ivory skin, rosy cheeks, a round face, rounder hips and yielding flesh" (Papp / Kirkland 75).

Between the Genders: The Witches in *Macbeth*

Defining the witches' (gender) identity and tracing their influence on the main-protagonist's actions is a task generations of literary critics have struggled with. It is an extremely difficult task as the witches raise more questions than they give answers. In the following, I will comment on different approaches to the witches in order to find answers to the following questions:

- Who or what are the witches?
- Which role do they play in the drama *Macbeth*?
- How do they influence Macbeth's decisions?
- Are they guilty for the crimes committed by Macbeth?

Some critics, Blanche Coles for example, interpret the witches as part of Macbeth's imagination or rather subconscious. Coles considers that the witches are "symbolic representations of the thoughts and desires which have slumbered in Macbeth's breast and now rise into consciousness and confront him" (55). This interpretation would imply that the witches are non-real creatures, which cannot be experienced by any other person than Macbeth as they are "embodiments of Macbeth's own evil" (Jorgensen, *Sensational Art* 234).

Furthermore, the question of guilt could not be answered sufficiently as, in this approach, the witches are seen as part of Macbeth's own personality. Bradley refutes this approach; he argues that Macbeth could not have possibly dreamt about such detailed prophecies as "[...] / The power of man, for none of woman born / Shall harm Macbeth" (4.1.80-1) (Bradley 303). Another aspect refuting Coles' approach is that the most important and thorough description of the witches comes from Banquo, not from Macbeth (1.3.39-47). Thus the witches cannot be considered as mere "embodiments of Macbeth's own evil" or part of Macbeth's own personality.

Other approaches tend to see the witches as victims who, due to their androgynous appeal, became societal outcasts. Some of these approaches tend to downplay the witches' evil impact on Macbeth. Terry Eagleton, for example, states that the three witches are the true "heroines" of the play although the play itself and literary critics hardly ever recognize this fact (Eagleton 2).

The weird sisters constitute their own "sisterly community", which is an exile from official society; the witches are therefore indifferent to the policy of the Scottish court (Eagleton 4). Accordingly, the weird sisters are societal outcasts because they fail to be "natural women" living in a home, the traditional place of Renaissance women (Rackin 131).

In fact, Shakespeare does not even construe them as women. In contrast to the "three women in strange and wild apparel, resembling creatures of elder world" in Holinshed's *Chronicles*, Shakespeare does not construe "his" witches as unequivocally female creatures, but rather as creatures whose appearance makes it hard to identify them as either women or men (Rackin 131-2). When Banquo and Macbeth first meet the weird sisters, Banquo is confused as he is unable to categorize them. He says:

> ... What are these,
> So wither'd and so wild in their attire,
> That look not like th'inhabitants o'th'earth,
> And yet are on't? ...
> ... You seem to understand me,
> By each at once her choppy finger laying
> Upon her skinny lips: you should be women,
> And yet your beards forbid me to interpret
> That you are so. (1.3.39-47)

Banquo's description of the witches is the most detailed physical description of any characters in the play the audience gets. It identities the witches as both "unwomanly and unnatural" (Rackin 131). The witches' outward appearance confuses Banquo. In this speech, Banquo emphasizes their gender ambiguity due to the witches' "beards" (1.3.46), but also their unattractive physique: they have "choppy fingers" (1.3.44) and "skinny lips" (1.3.45). Thus Banquo's description of the witches does not only raise questions about the witches' gender identity, but also disqualifies them from contemporary society's notion of what a woman is.

Their "beards" are "visible physical marks" establishing the witches' defectiveness as women (Rackin 131-2). Their "gender ambiguity" is entirely Shakespeare's invention (Rackin 132). In Holinshed's *Chronicles* they were unequivocally female and, as an illustration in the 1577 edition shows, portrayed as "attractive and elaborately gowned women" (Ibid.). Their gender ambiguity alienates the witches from the natural female characters, especially Lady Macduff. Thus Shakespeare's weird sisters are not expected to display the prototypical female "qualities of gentleness and pity", which were assumed to be naturally grounded in women's bodies (Rackin 132).

On the other hand, the witches are also disconnected from the masculine gender role, which is to be a hero on the battlefield. Eagleton assumes that their androgyny makes the witches societal outcasts who inhabit their own world, which intersects with Macbeth's (Eagleton 3). Another question Banquo's description of the witches raises is whether they are "inhabitants of the earth" or not (1.3.41). Despite their independence from official society, the witches have remarkable intuitive perception of the world. They see it as what it really is: "a pious self-deception of a society based on routine oppression and incessant warfare" (Eagleton 2). They also outline the reality of the world of *Macbeth*: "Fair is foul, and foul is fine" (1.1.11) proving a fundamental political awareness King Duncan fails to develop. Their speeches are full of riddles, contradictions and double-meanings and develop an immense power over Macbeth's mind. Eagleton rightly claims that "the witches strike at the stable social, sexual and linguistic forms" society needs to survive, as they are "androgynous, multiple ("threein-one") and imperfect speakers" (2). He further argues that official society fears the witches as they are embodiment of what is evil and that society cannot deal with the "amount of creativity" the witches unfold (4-6).

In *Macbeth* official society values "meek women, military carnage and aristocratic titles" (Eagleton 4). Emphasizing the witches' creativity, Eagleton seems to acquit the witches of any participation in the murder of King Duncan and of any evil in the world of Macbeth (4). In this respect, Terry Eagleton's characterization of the witches is too positive. Indeed, the witches are highly creative as their riddling and ambiguous wordplays suggest, but they are not entirely innocent. They may not have the ability to kill humans, but they are able to harm society. In Act three, Scene one, one of the witches replies to the question:

> 1. Witch.   Where hast thou been, Sister?
> 2. Witch.   Killing swine. (1.3.1-2)

The witches have the ability to do evil and also delight in punishing people as the report of the first witch (in the same scene) suggests:

> 1. Witch.   A sailor's wife had chestnuts in her lap,
> And mounch'd, and mounch'd, and mounch'd:
> 'Give me', quoth I: -
> 'Aroynt thee, witch!' the rump-fed ronyon cries.
> Her husband's to Aleppo gone, master o'th'Tiger:
> But in a sieve I'll thither sail,
> And like a rat without a tail;

> 2. Witch. I'll do, I'll do, and I'll do.
> 2. Witch. I'll give thee a wind.
> 1. Witch. Th'art kind.
> 3. Witch. And I another.
> 1. Witch. I myself have all the other;
> And the very ports they blow,
> All the quarters that they know
> I'th'shipman's card.
> I'll drain him dry as hay:
> Sleep shall neither night nor day
> Hang upon his penthouse lid; He shall live a man
> forbid. (1.3.3-26)

This episode shows that the witches delight in revenge. Instead of forgiving the woman for not sharing her nuts, which may perhaps be expected from a gentle, noble and natural woman, the witch rather punishes her by punishing her husband.

The words "I'll drain him dry as hay" (1.3.18) indicate that the witch is trying to trouble the sailor's potency or at least his self-confidence as he will discover his own incompetence as a sailor. The stingy woman's punishment will thus be a husband who lost his manly pride or fertility. In this respect, Shakespeare construes "his" witches conventionally as witches were typically associated with incidents such as "interference with livestock, weather and male sexuality" (Neely 58). Eagleton's approach is partly true. The witches do "inhabit their own world" apart from official society (Eagleton 3). Official society fails to appreciate the high "amount of creativity" of the witches. But the witches are not innocent of the violence that unfolds in the play.

Many literary critics, such as Neely, describe the witches more aptly. They neither depict the witches as victims of their own gender ambiguity doomed to be societal outcasts, nor do they underestimate the malicious nature of the witches. Neely defines the witches as "sources of malevolence" who, just like Lady Macbeth, are "catalysts to Macbeth's actions" and thus help unfold "the unnaturalness, disorder, and violence" in the play (57). She emphasizes that the witches are more than "social misfits" as they are able to do "preternatural travels" and are provided with the usual "accouterments" of witches: they have "familiars", apply "spells, potions, fortune-telling, and successful conjuring" and show "submission to Hecate" (58).

However, the witches do not intend to support Macbeth; the witches clearly "wish Macbeth to fail" (Neely 58). In Kahn's consideration, the witches are "sources of [Macbeth's] sexual confusion ... who direct their mischief toward him" (173).

Kahn sees the witches as primarily female creatures who, just like Lady Macbeth, "ally themselves with destruction, not creation" (Ibid.).

Alfar emphasizes that the "witches' gender instability, supernatural powers and malevolence towards men embody typical early modern anxieties about female agency", yet she makes concessions to the fact that it is unclear whether the witches are really "human, female, or male" (117). However, it is clear that they "hold power over mortal men" (Ibid.).

According to Proser, the witches are "unnatural creatures with an anarchic power" who embody "the power of evil" in this play and whose aim it is to possess "Macbeth's soul" (52-4). The witches' anarchic power makes them "appeal to desire alone; and for those ... who submit themselves to their power, desire alone becomes a standard of action" rendering values such as "justice and humanity" irrelevant (Proser 54). Jorgensen considers the witches as "imperfect women", "embodiments of evil" who have a part in Macbeth's fall" (*Sensational Art* 116-7). They "cast their stench of evil over much of the play" (Jorgensen, *Sensational Art* 120).

What these different approaches share is that they do not portray the witches as natural women sentenced to lifelong banishment for their gender instability by an intolerant society, which misunderstands their creativity. Furthermore, they do not refute that the witches are (at least indirectly) responsible for the violence which unfolds in the course of the drama.

The play starts with the witches intending to meet Macbeth, which, according to Proser, proves the witches' interest in "Macbeth's soul" (52-4):

    1. Witch.   When shall we meet again [...]
                   Where is the place?
    2. Witch.   Upon the heath
    3. Witch.   There too meet with Macbeth (1.1.1.-7)

Whilst this passage proves the witches' interest in Macbeth's soul, it also proves their indifference towards Banquo's as he is not mentioned. And from the beginning, the witches seem to succeed in gaining power over Macbeth's subconscious as Macbeth's very first sentence in the play (spoken to Banquo, right before their first encounter with the witches) proves; he says:

> So foul and fair a day I have not seen. (1.3.38),

echoing the witches' motto "Fair is foul, and foul is fair" (1.1.11). At the beginning, Macbeth is fascinated by the witches. Unlike Banquo, Macbeth is not repelled by the witches' gender ambiguity and apparent ugliness, which in turn suggests that there is something dark within Macbeth's soul. He feels drawn into their net of supernatural powers, which he refers to as "strange intelligence" (1.3.76). After their magical disappearance, Macbeth says "Would they had stay'd!" (1.3.82). This passage also shows the witches' independence from mortal men as they refuse to listen to Macbeth's command "Speak, I charge you." (1.3.78) and vanish instead. The witches' prophecy leaves the recipient uncertain of its exact meaning and never outlines how to react in the face of it. Their first prophecy to Macbeth and Banquo initially seems a very fair one. Macbeth is prophesied to become "... Thane of Cawdor ... and shalt be King hereafter" (1.3.49-50). Banquo's prophecy seems far less prosperous:

> 3. Witch. Hail!
> 1. Witch. Lesser than Macbeth, and greater.
> 2. Witch. Not so happy, yet much happier.
> 3. Witch. Thou shalt get kings, though be none. (1.3.64-7)

It is also a prophecy which does not affect Banquo's future, but his sons'. It calls neither for any direct action nor any action at all. However, the witches' prophecy makes Banquo suffer mental pain he prays to overcome:

> A heavy summons lies like lead upon me,
> And yet I would not sleep: merciful Powers!
> Restrain in me the cursed thoughts that nature
> Gives way to in response! (2.1.6-9)

Banquo suffers from insomnia and "cursed thoughts" although his prophecy gives no direct indications as to how strong the witches' supernatural powers are. They have the ability to cause mental suffering. The witches prophecies haunt both Macbeth and Banquo. Yet only Banquo is able to let his morals overcome his desire for a prosperous destiny. Although Macbeth seems more susceptible to the witches' prophecies, Macbeth initially seems strong enough to overcome his dark thoughts, too. He comes to the peaceful conclusion:

> If Chance will have me King, why,
> Chance may crown me Without my stir. (1.3.143-4)

It will take Lady Macbeth's initiation to makes Macbeth put his dark thoughts into practice. However, the witches' prophecies will be the "point of departure for both the inner and outer action [as they] will set in motion ... hopes and desires ... fears and doubts of Macbeth" (Clemen 77). I will later discuss Lady Macbeth's influence on her husband and their relationship more thoroughly in the section "Macbeth and Lady Macbeth: Marital Fulfillment in Regicide".

The price Macbeth has to pay for his alliance with the witches is the deterioration of his peace of mind and his sanity. The witches cast a spell on Macbeth. His actions, as a result of their prophecies, have strained his nervous system with symptoms of "excruciating agitation, shaking, and "starting" of the body" (Jorgensen, Sensational Art 158-9). Faced with Banquo's ghost, Macbeth displays these symptoms in the banquet scene. Macbeth cannot hide his severe mental turmoil from his guests.

Still he tries to excuse it as "a strange infirmity, which is nothing / To those that know me" (3.4.84-5) (Jorgensen 159). At this point, the witches' strategy of ruining Macbeth by "sending" him fits is recognizable. Macbeth's fits, which Lady Macbeth clumsily tries to justify:

> ... My Lord is often thus,
> And hath been from his youth: ...
> The fit is momentary; ...
> He will again be well. If you much note him,
> You shall offend him, and extend his passion (3.4.52-6),

His fits reveal that Macbeth has become a severely mentally ill person whose condition makes him unpredictable (Ibid.). Thus instead of establishing a new royal order, he is doomed to reveal his total incompetence as a king to the entire Court. Jorgensen defines Macbeth's "fit" as "an emotional condition" associated with shaking", which is not caused by "epilepsy, or even a fever", but rather by "guilt" and "fear" (*Sensational Art* 159). On the news that Fleance "has escaped" Macbeth exclaims (Ibid.):

> Then comes my fit again: I had else been perfect;
> Whole as the marble, founded as the rock, [...]
> But now, I am cabin'd, cribb'd, confin'd, bound in
> To saucy doubts and fears. (3.4.20-4)

Macbeth shows these symptoms even earlier in the play. In his soliloquy, Macbeth reflects upon his dark desire to kill King Duncan (Jorgensen, *Sensational Art* 159): My thought, whose murther yet is fantastical,

> Shakes so my single state of man. (1.3.139-40)

After the regicide and while he is plotting the murders of Banquo and Fleance, Macbeth mentions his "terrible dreams, / That shake us nightly" (3.2.18-9) (Ibid.). As I already mentioned, Macbeth's "shaking" is accompanied with his "starting", which is probably a short, quick movement caused by intense anxiety. Macbeth "starts", for instance, at the sight of Banquo's ghost "in the banquet scene and later again "in painful realization at the sight of the Apparitions (4.1.116)" (Jorgensen, *Sensational Art* 159). However, Macbeth does not seem to sense that the witches actually "wish [him] to fail" (Neely 58). On the contrary, Macbeth's alliance with the witches gains special importance after the regicide. After this crime, Macbeth decides to spare his wife the knowledge of his future atrocities. He probably wants her to be natural again so that she can bear sons to follow him on the thrown. Macbeth wants her to be "innocent of the knowledge" (3.2.45) that he is plotting to kill Banquo and Fleance in order to prevent Banquo from "getting kings" as was predicted by the witches (1.3.64-9).

For their second meeting with Macbeth, the witches prepare a brew including such gruesome ingredients as the "Finger of birth-strangled babe" (4.1.30) and "sows blood, that hath eaten / Her nine farrow" (4.1.64-5). This reflects the unnaturalness of the witches and reminds the audience of Lady Macbeth's readiness to "dash" her suckling babies' "brain out" (1.7.56-8). Jorgensen brilliantly comments on the magic charm the witches prepare for Macbeth:

> The Witches, too, sacrifice a babe for their brew, and this particular brew differs from Lady Macbeth's sacrifice only in being deliberately prepared for Macbeth's ruin. It will be, like the naked feelings Lady Macbeth sacrifices in the imagined form of a baby, an agent of retribution. (*Sensational Art* 105)

Jorgensen's assertion that the witches sacrifice a (living) baby may be a bit farfetched; in fact the brew includes "the finger of a birth-strangled baby", not the corpse of a baby they reportedly killed themselves. However, the ingredients of the witches' brew align the witches with "destruction" and alienate them from "creation" (Kahn 173).

In Renaissance England "infanticide was not treated as homicide" and was rather "dealt with in the secular courts" as a "lesser crime" (Stone 474). However, in the eyes of a contemporary audience, the witches would have seemed suspicious of infanticide. In order to find certitude and maybe to stabilize his nerves, which are severely stressed, Macbeth conjures the witches to foretell him his fate. However, Hecate, the goddess of witchcraft and "contriver of all harms" (3.5.7) prepared "deceitful oracles", which will give Macbeth a false sense of security and thus "lead him to his self-destruction" (Blits 126-7). In Act three, Scene five, Hecate chides the three witches for having dealt with Macbeth without her permission:

> How did you dare
> To trade and traffic with Macbeth,
> In riddles, and affairs of death;
> And I, the mistress of your charms,
> And the close contriver of all harms,
> Was never call'd to bear my part,
> Or show the glory of our art? (3.5.2-9)

The witches "worship and fear" Hecate, who, in contrast to the other witches, does not "speak in grim and bloody images" (Blits 124). Shakespeare does not construe Hecate as a witch who is especially repulsive. "Despite her connection to evil ... there is nothing terrifying or ugly about Hecate in this scene (Ibid.)." Although she is angry with the witches for "having violated the power order of things by overstepping the appropriate bounds of their art" (Blits 125), she is more troubled by Macbeth's evil and rebukes the witches for having "traded" with

> ... a wayward son
> Spiteful, and wrathful; who, as others do,
> Loves for his own ends, not for you. (3.5.11-3)

Hecate thinks that Macbeth is a selfish, thankless and "wrongheaded" fool and that the witches behaved towards him as a "thoroughly indulgent mother" and they will "receive nothing in return for their actions" (Blits 126). Hecate senses that Macbeth is "acting as though he has nothing to fear ... from [the witches]" as he believes in "the sufficiency of his virtues" (Blits 126). In Hecate's eyes, Macbeth's behaviour disdains "her divine power" (Ibid.). Therefore, Hecate feels urged to punish him. Hecate knows that Macbeth will come "to the pit of Acheron in the morning to learn "his destiny" (3.5.17) (Ibid.). So she orders the witches to "prepare their cauldrons with the spells [and] charms ..., while Hecate herself will take to the air and catch a falling drop of moon-vapor" (Blits 126), which distilled by her magic arts

> Shall raise such artificial sprites,
> As, by the strength of their illusion,
> Shall draw him on his confusion. (3.5.27-9)

Hecate's plan is to give Macbeth a false sense of security (Blits 127). She wants him to feel invincible. She says

> He shall spurn fate, scorn death, and bear
> His hopes 'bove wisdom, grace, and fear;
> And you all know, security
> Is mortals' chiefest enemy. (3.5.30-3)

Instead of giving Macbeth certitude, the prophecies given by "artificial spirits" (3.5.27) the witches conjured, will contribute to Macbeth's mental torment. Hecate plays a minor role in the Cauldron scene. The witches' brew will produce the "artificial spirits" without Hecate's "falling drop of moon-vapor". In this scene she is rather a "bystander" (Blits 134). Although Macbeth desperately wants the witches to foretell his fate, he addresses them in a rather hostile way, as "secret, black, and midnight hags" (4.1.48).

He demands to hear the witches' prophecy even if it brought "utter chaos and ruin upon the earth" (Blits 135-6). In this scene the witches pretend to be servile, if not selfsacrificing. They pretend to be eager to listen to Macbeth's commands:

> 1. Witch. Speak.
> 2. Witch. Demand.
> 3. Witch. We'll answer. (4.1.61)

It seems that the witches' readiness to obey Macbeth's commands is part of their malicious "glee" (Jorgensen, Sensational Art 179). Macbeth demands to hear the prophecy from the witches' (masculine) masters, which reflects Macbeth's royal pride (Blits 137). The witches have to "strengthen their cauldron with the blood of a sow that has eaten her young [and] add to the flame congealed sweat taken from a murderer's gallows (4.1.64-7), ingredients that ... remind us of Lady Macbeth and Macbeth" (Ibid.). The witches' brew produced three apparitions, which are "foul in form, but fair in promise" (Jorgensen, Sensational Art 179).

The first apparition is an armed head. It is the only adult among the three apparitions and symbolizes "manly virtue itself", or rather "the warrior's kind of manhood" (Blits 137). It warns Macbeth

> Macbeth! Macbeth! Macbeth! beware Macduff;
> Beware the Thane of Fife. (4.1.71-2)

This apparition is a reflection of Macbeth's inner turmoil. It symbolizes that Macbeth found the new localization of his fear in Macduff. Macbeth seems to delight in this prophecy and thanks the first apparition with the words "Whate' er thou art, for thy good caution, thanks: / Thou hast harp'd my fear aright" (4.1.72-3). Although the next apparition is a babe figure, one of the witches declares that this one is "More potent than the first" (4.1.76).

Voicing what could be considered "the manly ethic's motto" (Blits 138) it recommends Macbeth to

> Be bloody, bold, and resolute: laugh to scorn
> The power of man, for none of woman born
> Shall harm Macbeth. (4.1.79-81)

Jorgensen claims that the "bloody child" most likely represents Macduff who was "untimely ripped from his mother's womb" (*Sensational Art* 106). Blits sees another possible reading as to this apparition; he claims that it might as well represent "the nursing son Lady Macbeth would have killed rather than to forswear her resolve" (138). He argues that it is "unclear whether the blood on the child is that of birth or death" (Ibid.). However, this apparition may be the most influential one as it "helps to lead Macbeth, through willful blindness, to destruction" (Jorgensen, *Sensational Art* 106).

Macbeth interprets this prophecy as a "universal assurance" of his invincibility (Blits 138). Temporarily, this prophecy gives him a sense of security, which makes him lose his fear of Macduff:

> Then live, Macduff: what need I fear of thee? (4.1.82)

But then again he feels tempted to

> ...make assurance double sure,
> and take a bond of Fate. (4.1.83-4),

meaning that he desperately tries to "bind Fate to its promise" (Blits 139). The third apparition is another babe figure: "a child crowned with a tree in his hand", which later becomes clear that this is Malcolm (Jorgensen, *Sensational Art* 106). The prophecy of the third apparition resembles the second prophecy. It is designed to give Macbeth a universal sense of security tempting him to feel unassailable. The apparition says:

> Be lion-mettled, proud, and take no care
> Who chafes, who frets, or where conspirers are:
> Macbeth shall never vanquish'd be, until
> Great Birnam wood to Dunsinane hill
> Shall come against him. (4.1.90-4)

At this point, Macbeth cannot guess that this prophecy "foreshadows Malcolm's camouflaging of his troops with branches of Birnam wood in their hands" (Blits 139). Macbeth is convinced that these are impossible conditions and thus feels delighted by these "Sweet bodements" (4.1.95). After this show of "artificial sprites" Hecate's goal should be fulfilled; Macbeth should now "spurn fate, scorn death and bear his hopes 'bove wisdom, grace and fear" and have a (false) sense of "security, moral's chiefest enemy" (3.5.27-33). But Macbeth's anxiety is stronger than Hecate expected. After these fair promises, Macbeth needs to know if Banquo's sons will become kings in Scotland (4.1.100-3). At first, the witches refuse to answer this question. They give him the advice "Seek to know no more." (4.1.104). However, the witches can hardly hide their malicious "glee" as they present "A show of eight Kings" (4.1.111) descending from Banquo (Jorgensen, Sensational Art 179):

> 1. Witch. Show!
> 2. Witch. Show!
> 3. Witch. Show!
> All. Show his eyes, and grieve his heart;
> Come like shadows, so depart. (4.1.107-11)

The Show of Kings tortures Macbeth's eyes. He desperately exclaims:

> ... filthy hags!
> Why do you show me this? ... Start, eyes!
> ... I will see no more
> What! Will the line stretch out to th'crack of doom? (4.1.115-7)

The witches pretend to be astonished by Macbeth's intense reaction and offer to cheer him up (4.1.125-32) with a "grotesque dance" (Blits 143). Macbeth's meeting with the witches and the news that Macduff fled to England leads Macbeth to his fatal resolution:

> From this moment,
> The very firstlings of my heart shall be
> The firstlings of my hand. (4.1.146-8),

meaning that from now on "he will act without a moment's thought or hesitation" (Blits 144). This decision leads Macbeth to murder Macduff's entire family. The fact that after his meeting with the witches, Macbeth makes "war on children or ... on generation itself" leads me to the question if the witches are to blame for Macbeth's crimes. At the first glance, it seems that the witches tempt Macbeth into killing whoever stands in his way. Reportedly, the witches delight in "Killing swine." (1.3.2), but they do not kill human beings. They may be supernatural powers of evil, but it definitely takes human agency to commit homicide. Besides, it is not impossible to resist the witches' temptations as Banquo proved. Therefore, I agree with Lucy's assumption:

The Weird Sisters, the Evil Passions, may lay snares, deceive, tempt have no authority with fatalistic power to do violence to the human will; they are the embodiments of the inward temptation, and can never be man's fate until he delivers himself into their keeping" (16).

Macbeth and Lady Macbeth: Marital Fulfillment in Regicide

In this part of my essay, I would like to analyze the marriage of Macbeth and Lady Macbeth with a focus on the regicide they commit. We have seen that initially Macbeth tried to overcome his mortal desire to kill King Duncan after the witches prophesied that Macbeth will be king. At first, he came to the peaceful conclusion:

> If Chance will have me King, why, Chance
> may crown me,
> Without my stir. (1.3.142-4)

It is due to the interaction between the spouses that Macbeth changes his mind. As the title of this section suggests, the deed Macbeth and his wife commit is influenced by "an aura of sexualized violence" that entwines the couple (Stockholder 107). This title is inspired by Stockholder's statement that "rather than being the source of procreation and love, Macbeth's relation to his wife is fulfilled in the murder of Duncan" (100). He states that the fact that Duncan represents "legitimate authority" and "gentle fathering" makes the crime look like a patricide (Stockholder 101).

Additionally, Märtin suggests that the regicide symbolizes the sexual fulfillment of the spouses, which is based on their love and intimacy (155). She claims that most literary critics consider the relationship of Macbeth and his wife as a very close, stable and intimate one, some of them even suggest that the spouses have a symbiotic relationship (Märtin 155-6). One of them is A.C. Bradley. He believes that the spouses are entwined by the guilt they share as "they have the makings of one murderer between them" (Bradley 377). However, even before their crime they seem to be a unique couple by contemporary standards. The couple lives in "a medieval feudal household" (Märtin 157). This is a household which hardly allows for privacy and individuality as it is "constantly spied upon and interrupted by their domestic servants" (Stone 6). Contemporary relations between husband and wife were therefore often "fairly remote" and based on socio-political obligations (Stone 6). Husband and wife were rather "members of a functioning social universe" than lovers and were "rarely in private together" (Ibid.).

Despite these obstacles, Macbeth and Lady Macbeth share a very close and intimate relationship, which even isolates them from the rest of the world (Märtin 150). Their deep love and affection must have seemed odd to a contemporary audience (Märtin 162). The way they talk to each other shows that they really love each other and know each other very well. Berry states that Macbeth and his wife "have no difficulty in comprehending the obliquities and nuances of their communication" (92). In his letter, Macbeth uses tender words and calls her "my dearest partner of greatness" (1.5.11). It is important for Macbeth to inform his wife about what the witches prophesied him and to make her "rejoice" at the brilliant future perspective he was foretold: "This I have thought good to deliver thee (my dearest partner in greatness) that thou might'st not lose the dues of rejoicing" (1.5.9-12). This letter might indicate how much Macbeth loves and trusts his wife. Although Lady Macbeth does not have a living child, she fulfills her role to be a loving wife and perfect hostess (Märtin 157).

But why do Macbeth and his wife become a pair of accomplices in regicide? And how is their sexuality connected to this deed? Märtin argues that Shakespeare deliberately combines the couple's drive for royal power with the notion of sexual desire and fear of failing (166). She refers to scenes in the play that suggest that for both spouses the deed is connected to sexuality (Märtin 165-6), for example, in his letter to his wife, Macbeth describes his feelings at his first meeting with the witches:

> ... I burned in desire to question them further. (1.5.3-4)

In his soliloquy in Act one, Scene seven, Macbeth reflects on his desire to murder King Duncan in images, which perhaps may be seen as phallic images (Märtin 166). Macbeth says:

> I have no spur
> To pick the sides of my intend, but only
> Vaulting ambition, which overleaps itself
> And falls on th'other. (1.7.25-8)

This speech is very significant as it underlines that killing King Duncan is tempting to Macbeth. In his view, this deed may be the proof for his outstanding bravery and manliness. Biggins states: "The slaying of Duncan is, indeed, to be the proof of Macbeth's manliness in this particular double sense, of sexual potency and courage (264). Lady Macbeth similarly uses sexual images to provoke her husband into regicide (Märtin 166). She aks him:

> What cannot you and I perform upon
> Th'unguarded Duncan? What not put upon
> His spongy officers, who shall bear the guilt
> Of our great quell? (1.7.70-3)

A quell is usually something that is put to an end through violence. Used as a verb it is often used in militarily contexts, for instance, you can quell a revolt. But in this speech it seems that Lady Macbeth uses this term metaphorically, suggesting a sexual act in the vicinity of a corpse. Part of the reasons why this couple turns into a murderous one lies in Lady Macbeth's concept of manliness. At the beginning of the play, Lady Macbeth is "more committed [than her husband] to a code of manliness that emphasizes power, honour, war and revenge" (Bamber 91). She prefers a "bloody sort of honour over traditional feminine values in general and womanly love in particular" and pretends to be tougher than her husband (Ibid.). In her value system transgression is the most important quality of manly behaviour (Eagleton 4).

Dusinberre argues that Lady Macbeth's concept of masculinity is "devastatingly conventional" as in Lady Macbeth's perception, "a man is one who acts", which is illustrated in Act one, Scene seven, when she tries to provoke her husband into regicide and therefore asks him (Dusinberre 284):

> Art thou afeard
> To be the same in thine own act and valour
> As thou art in desire? (1.7.39-41)

Lady Macbeth's question is meant to provoke her husband into committing regicide by questioning his virility, a strategy Lady Macbeth continues to follow until the actual regicide in Act two, Scene two.

Bamber analyzed the marriage of Macbeth and Lady Macbeth. In her approach, she differentiates a "masculine Self" from a "feminine Other" (2-6). The masculine Self denotes the tragic hero's world, his beliefs, ambitions, drives and emotions. The "feminine Other" stands for the females equivalents offering an alternative order. Bamber discovered that in *Macbeth* it is the tragic hero who has the "privilege" of being "concerned with himself" and to develop an "extra Self" to comment on his beliefs, ambitions, drives and emotions (Bamber 6). Thus it is Macbeth who reveals an "inner life" with "thoughts and feelings" that he expresses in soliloquies (Bamber 7). Bamber argues that Lady Macbeth does not represent a "feminine Other" as an alternative order to her husband's reality. In Bamber's interpretation, Lady Macbeth does not have an independent "self-interest" and solely serves as her husband's "collaborator" (Bamber 92). This assumption is partly true. In my opinion, it is wrong to believe that Lady Macbeth does not have any "self-interest" and only exists in order to back her husband's interests.

Lady Macbeth's interest is to become the Queen of Scotland and thus share incredible wealth and power with her husband. But this "self-interest" happens to be linked with her husband's position in the court of Scotland.

Therefore, she strives for her husband's power. Lady Macbeth's aim may be to share power with her husband and perhaps be her husband's political adviser. Macbeth's desire for power may be strong, but Lady Macbeth's desire for power is even stronger. Having received her husband's letter and knowing of Macbeth's chance to be King of Scotland, she cannot understand why her husband hesitates to kill Duncan in order to "steal" his crown. She knows that her husband, despite his attested valour in warfare, is too gentle to commit regicide. In her soliloquy in Act one, Scene five, she expresses her deep distrust about her husband's "manly" nature:

> ... Yet do I fear thy
> nature: It is too full o'th'milk of human
> kindness, To catch the nearest way. (1.5.16-8)

Denying to have any moral revulsion towards regicide herself, she questions her husband's manly readiness to pick "the nearest way", meaning to murder King Duncan. Fearing that her husband may be too "full of the milk of human kindness", Lady Macbeth considers that Macbeth is "as innocent as a new-born baby" and thus "lacks the manly qualities required to use violence for his own good" (Eagleton 4). She dislikes her husband's "weak, milky-natured aspect, which she associates with the benign and foolishly trusting Duncan" (Stockholder 105). This bond of maternal images and brutal images in Lady Macbeth's speech will repeat only a few lines later, when she herself crosses a line by praying to be "unsexed" (Eagleton 4). Her unrestrained ambition is for royal power.

Therefore, she prays to be "unsexed" by the "murth'ring ministers" to be able to inspire her husband to overcome his moral revulsion toward killing Duncan or even kill Duncan herself:

> ... Come, you Spirits
> That tend on mortal thoughts, unsex me here,
> And fill me, from the crown to the toe, top-full
> Of direst cruelty! Make thick my blood,
> Stop up th'access and passage of remorse;
> That no compunctious visitings of Nature
> Shake my fell purpose ...

> ... Come to my woman's breasts,
> And take my milk for gall, you murth'ring ministers. (1.5.40-8)

In this scene, Lady Macbeth "renounces womanly love for the spirit of murder (Bamber 91). Her plea to be "unsexed" reflects her desire to rid herself of the typical female attributes, such as gentleness and pity (Rackin 132). Instead of cherishing feminine values, she prays for manly attributes such as "power, honour, war, and revenge" and eventually murder (Bamber 91). She feels trapped by her own gender role, which makes her mind soft and weak. Therefore, she sacrifices her maternal qualities and trades them for an evil masculine nature enabling her to kill or rather inspire her husband to commit regicide for the sake of power and wealth. Her appeal to the murdering ministers both estranges her from womanhood and Christianity (Asp 59). From this moment on, "no nourishment will flow from her breasts, in wanting freedom from any "compunctious visitings of Nature", she relates herself to ... barren infertility" (Stockholder 105). Although Lady Macbeth knows of her husband's invocation to the weird sisters, she never tells him about her own invocation to the "murth'ring ministers" (Märtin 150). Interestingly, Lady Macbeth casts herself into a sexually dominant role when she wants to "pour my spirits in thine ear, / And chastise with the valour of her tongue / All that impedes thee from the golden round" (I.v.26-8) (Stockholder 107).

She is highly manipulative and virtually brainwashes Macbeth when she tries to persuade him to murder Duncan, she claim to him:

> ... I have given suck, and know
> How tender 'tis to love the babe that milks me:
> I would, while it was smiling in my face,
> Have pluck'd my nipple from his boneless gums,
> And dash'd the brains out, had I so sworn As
> you have done t this. (1.7.54-9)

Indeed, Macbeth has never sworn that we would kill Duncan, at least not on stage. She repeatedly challenges him by questioning his manliness. To her mind, masculinity is bound to be violence. Rackin states that "Lady Macbeth connects manliness and murder" (Rackin 136). She is similar to the weird sisters as she is able to manipulate Macbeth's decision (Ibid.). Her bloodthirsty ambition for the crown seems unnatural in the realm of the contemporary society.

After the deed, in which she returns the bloody daggers and smears the sleeping grooms' faces in order to makes them suspicious of this treason, Lady Macbeth collapses; she cries

Help me hence, ho! (2.3.117),

which visually dramatizes her weakness and her unsuccessful attempt to "unsex" herself (Eagleton 4). Eventually, she cannot be manly and is after all "no more than a woman in a man's world" (Foakes 155). She cannot rid herself of her female qualities and conscience and becomes a somnambulist reliving her mental horrors at night. Her somnambulism is a reflexion of her "mental alienation" culminating in her suicide, which does not raise questions by society (Neely 56). Her suicide is "feminized and guilt-ridden" (Ibid.). One might say that the regicide committed by Macbeth and Lady Macbeth was supposed to intensify their love (Märtin 150).

However, it fails to do so. The deed does not prove Macbeth's manliness and potency, but it marks the beginning of his downfall. Lady Macbeth can not "repudiate her womanhood to make Macbeth a man; seeking to be more than a woman she becomes less than one [and thus becomes] as unsexed as the witches themselves" (Dusinberre 284).

Conclusion

In the course of this essay, I argued that the world of *Macbeth* is a world of chivalry, which prefers a specific concept of manliness, which is the concept of the chivalrous knight. This concept is linked with an honour code and a code of conduct in warfare. Valour and prowess in just warfare in the defense of Scotland are the most important values under King Duncan's rule. Although King Duncan is a benevolent king whose combination of masculine and feminine qualities promises a fair society, he has to witness the decay of morals due to treacherous knights in his country which is marked by blood and brutality. Indeed, the first human words in the play are "What bloody man is that?". The answer describes Macbeth (French 242). In the course of the play, the main-protagonist will change his manly identity. He wants to be more than a chivalrous knight. In his pursuit of power, he will divide the manly characters into those he fears and thus kills and those whose valour and noble qualities enable them to challenge Macbeth's tyranny. Remarkably few of the chivalrous men do really act in a chivalrous way. For some of the male characters in the play treason seems tempting. As I mentioned, Macbeth's Scotland experiences a time of incessant warfare. The world of men is thus occupied with battles. But which roles do the female characters play in this society? We have seen that "natural" women in Macbeth are "domesticated housewives" (Rackin 134-6).

It is noteworthy that Shakespeare used a rather new concept of femininity, which was just beginning to develop in Elizabethan England and links it with an ancient concept of masculinity (Ibid.). The role of the wife was reduced to the domestic space. Women were supposed to be natural and caring mothers as well as loving wives. Despite the patriarchal structure of contemporary families, Shakespeare did not construe women who need their husband's permission to express themselves (in this play). They know what they want although they may be unaware of the consequences of their actions. We have seen that the world of Macbeth follows the motto "Fair is foul, and foul is fair" (1.1.11). This seems to apply to all characters. Shakespeare does not really construe "perfect" characters although some literary critics describe Macduff as the epitome of chivalry, ignoring his (few) moral failures. The world of Macbeth is a manly world, in which women do not have many options. They can either be housewives and mothers (Lady Macbeth) or develop fantasies of power they might use for their own purposes (Lady Macbeth).

The witches play a central role in the drama. They provoke mortals with their ambiguous prophecy and witchcraft and shock people with their filthiness and gender ambiguity. They confuse mortals with their strange appearance and bring them misery unless they are morally sound.

Works Cited

Primary Source

Shakespeare, William. Macbeth. [English / German edition; translated and edited by Barbara Rojahn-Deyk]. Stuttgart: Reclam, 2005.

Secondary Sources

Ahrendt, Götz. For our fathers's sake, and mother's care: Zur Eltern-Kind-Beziehung in den Dramen Shakespeares unter Berücksichtigung zeitgenössischer

Traktatliteratur und Porträts. Frankfurt am Main.: Peter Lang, 2003.

Asp, Carolyn. 'Be bloody, bold and resolute': The Tragic Action and Sexual Stereotyping in Macbeth. Studies in Philology. 88:2 (1981 Spring, 153-169).

Bradley, A.C. Shakespearean Tragedy. Cleveland: World Publishing Co., 1964.

Bamber, Linda. Comic Women, Tragic Men: A Study of Gender and Genre in Shakespeare. Stanford, California: Stanford University Press, 1982.

Barker, Doborah E., and Ivo Kamps, eds. Shakespeare and Gender: A History. London and New York: Verso, 1995.

Berry, Ralph. Shakespearean Structures. London: Macmillan, 1981.

Blits, Jan H. The Insufficiency of Virtue: Macbeth and the Natural Order. Lanham, USA and London: Rowan & Littlefield, 1996.

Biggins, Dennis. "Sexuality, Witchcraft and Violence in Macbeth." Shakespeare Studies 8 (1975): 255-77.

Booth, Steven. King Lear, Macbeth, Indefinition, and Tragedy. New Haven and London: Yale University Press, 1993.

Bradley, Andrew Cecil. Shakespearean Tragedy: Lectures on Hamlet, Othello, King Lear, and Macbeth. Harmondsworth, Middlesex: Penguin Books, 1991.

Brown, John Russell. Shakespeare's Dramatic Style. London: Heinemann, 1972.

Calderwood, James L. If It Were Done: Macbeth and Tragic Action. Amherst: The University of Massachusetts Press, 1986.

Castiglione, Baldassare. The Book of the Courtier. Translated by Sir Thomas Hoby. London: Dent, 1928.

Clemen, Wolfgang. Shakespeare's Dramatic Art: Collected Essays. London and New York: Methuen, 1980.

Coles, Blanche. Shakespeare Studies: Macbeth. New York: Smith, 1938.

Curry, Walter Clyde. Shakespeare's Philosophical Patterns. Baton Rouge: Louisiana State University Press, 1937.

Dusinberre, Juliet. Shakespeare and the Nature of Women. London: Macmillan, 1975.

Eagleton, Terry. Rereading Literature: William Shakespeare. Oxford, UK and Cambridge, USA: Blackwell, 1997.

Foakes, R.A. Shakespeare and Violence. Cambridge, UK: Cambridge University Press, 2003.

French, Marilyn. Shakespeare's Division of Experience. New York: Ballantine Books, 1981.

Hays, Michael L. Shakespearean Tragedy as Chivalric Romance: Rethinking Macbeth, Hamlet, Othello, and King Lear. Cambridge: Brewer, 2003.

Jorgensen, Paul A. William Shakespeare: The Tragedies. Boston: Twayne Publishers, 1985.

- - - . Our Naked Frailties : Sensational Art and Meaning in Macbeth. Berkley, Los Angeles, London: University of California Press, 1971.

Kahn, Coppélia. Man's Estate: Masculine Identity in Shakespeare. Berkley, Los Angeles, London: University of California Press, 1981.

Klein, Joan Larsen. "Lady Macbeth: Infirm of purpose". In: C.R.S. Lenz, G. Greene and C.T. Neely (ed.). *The Woman's Part. Feminist Criticism of Shakespeare*. Urbana, Chicago, London: University of Illinois Press, 1980, pp.240-55.

Long, Michael. Harvester New Critical Introductions to Shakespeare: Macbeth. New York, London, Toronto, Sydney, Tokyo: Havester Wheatsheaf, 1989.

Lucy, Margaret. Shakespeare and the Supernatural. Liverpool: Shakespeare Press, 1906.

Mabillard, Amanda. An Analysis of Shakespeare's Sources for Macbeth. Shakespeare. Online 2000. (20/1/2007) <http://www.shakespeareonline.com/playanalysis/macbethsources.html>

Märtin, Doris. Shakespeares 'Fiend-like Queens'. Heidelberg: Carl Winter, 1992.

McCoy, Richard. The Rites of Knighthood: The Literature of Elizabethan Chivalry. Berkley: University of California Press, 1989.

Meron, Theodor. Bloody Constraints: War and Chivalry in Shakespeare. New York, Oxford: Oxford University Press, 1998.

Neely, Carol Thomas. Distracted Subjects: Madness and Gender in Shakespeare and Early Modern Culture. Ithaca and London: Cornell University Press, 2004.

Papp, Joseph, and Elizabeth Kirkland. Shakespeare Alive!. New York: Banton Books, 2001.

Phillips, Brian, and Ross Southat. William Shakespeare: Macbeth. New York: SparkNotes LLC, 2002.

Proser, Matthew N. The Heroic Image in Five Shakespearean Tragedies. Princeton, New Jersey: Princeton University Press, 1965.

Rackin, Phyllis. Shakespeare and Women. New York: Oxford University Press, 2005.

Rogers, Nicole. Mutuality and Patriarchy in the Renaissance Family and Shakespeare's *Macbeth*. Victoria: University of Victoria, 1996. 18 January 2007 <http://www.engl.uvic.ca/Faculty/MBHomePage/ISShakespeare/Resources/Women/m>.

Schabert, Ina, ed. Shakespeare-Handbuch. 2nd edition. Stuttgart: Kröner, 1978.

Scot, Reginald. The Discoverie of Witchcraft. (1584). Reprint, Carbondale: Southern Illinois University Press, 1964.

Schofield, William Henry. Chivalry in English Literature: Chaucer, Malory, Spenser and Shakespeare. Cambridge: Harvard University, 1912.

Showalter, Elaine. Speaking of Gender. New York, London: Routledge, 1989.

Smith, Bruce R. Shakespeare and Masculinity. New York: Oxford University Press, 2000.

Stockholder, Kay. Dream Works: Lovers and Families in Shakespeare's Plays. Toronto, Buffalo, London: University of Toronto Press, 1987.

Stone, Lawrence. The Family, Sex and Marriage in England 1500-1800. London:

Weidenfeld and Nicolson, 1979.

Wells, Robin Headlam. Shakespeare on Masculinity. Cambridge: Cambridge University Press, 2000.

Online Sources

http://en.wikipedia.org/wiki/Chivalry (28/11/06).

http://www.etymonline.com/index.php?search=chivalry&searchmode=none (28/11/06).

http://www.etymonline.com/index.php?search=knight&searchmode=none (28/11/06).

www.historic-uk.com/CultureUK/witches.htm (28/12/2006).

Gender Politics in *Macbeth*

Katharina Herrmann, 2008

Introduction

Renaissance tragedy does to a large extent deal with common political, religious and social questions of the time. In most cases, authors use tragedy as the place to question and even criticize those issues, and thus use it as a political space. In Jacobean England, society was profoundly hierarchical with the king on top of the state, and the father or husband as head of the family. "[W]omen were clearly socially subordinate, and the preponderance of discourse on the gender hierarchy was misogynistic"[146]. *Macbeth* is one of Shakespeare's late tragedies, written in 1606, and presented at the Globe Theatre later that year. In Shakespeare's plays sex and gender are crucial for defining human identity and political power.

In the course of this essay, I will first take a closer look at gender ideology in the English Renaissance and in Renaissance tragedy and see how society justified the social subordination of women, and what kind of behaviour was considered appropriate for women. As *Macbeth* is a play that hugely builds on gender stereotyping, I will afterwards work out the play's definition of masculinity and femininity in the medieval social context the tragedy is set in, and subsequently analyse the characters of the three witches and king Duncan regarding their hermaphroditism and androgynity, and see whether the blurring of fixed gender roles might be interpreted as an indication that gender politics in *Macbeth* are unusual for the medieval Scottish context. The main part of this essay will be dedicated to the Macbeths, two strongly individualized characters. I will examine the characters of Lady Macbeth and Macbeth first, take a look at how their ambition leads to their downfall and afterwards discuss whether it is possible to talk about an inversion of the traditional gender roles since especially Lady Macbeth oversteps the boundaries of appropriate female behaviour and is, at least in the beginning, the more powerful character of the two spouses.

---

[146] Dympna Callaghan. *Woman and Gender in Renaissance Tragedy: A Study of King Lear, Othello, The Duchess of Malfi and The White Devil.* (London: Harvester Wheatsheaf, 1989) 12.

Gender ideology

Gender ideology in the English Renaissance

In Renaissance society, women did not exist as individuals, but as part of their fathers' or husbands' possessions. Marriage in those days was a mere transfer of power from one male to another. Besides, it was seen as the foundation of the family and, at the same time, the basis of the whole state.[147] The social subordination of women has its roots in the Creation story of the Bible, which serves as proof of women's innate inferiority. As the "broken rib of mankind"[148] a woman is "a purely derivative creation, she is less than man, merely a portion of his anatomy, and yet at once more than man since she is an overspill of Adam, created from a bone which was in excess of his needs"[149]. In general, the Church attached great importance to the patriarchal hierarchy since this form of society was already described in the Decalogue and other biblical texts, which proclaim the father, who is given his authority by God himself, as the head of the family.[150] A good wife or daughter had to be submissive and obedient, she had to do what the head of the family demanded without ever complaining. Rebellion of any kind was regarded as treason and especially rebellion over the issue of marriage constituted a serious threat to the order of the state. In Jacobean England, society was profoundly hierarchical. The family was seen as a domestic microcosm reflecting the order of the society or the macrocosm. Rebellion or disorder within the family was seen as treason since it might have had repercussions on society as a whole. In *The Trew Law of Free Monarchies* published in 1598, King James I uses the analogy of the king as father and argues that the former considers his subjects his children: "... a naturall Father to all his Lieges ... And as the Father by his fatherly duty is bound to care for the nourishing, education, and vertuous government of his children; even so is the king bound to care for all his subjects"[151].

Almost one hundred years earlier Christine de Pizan, a 15th century writer, counsels women to live in complete submission:

---

[147] Cf. Callaghan, *Woman and Gender in Renaissance Tragedy*, 14.

[148] Middleton, Thomas, William Rowley, *The Changeling*. (London: Nick Hern Books, 2000) 99.

[149] Callaghan, *Woman and Gender in Renaissance Tragedy*, 102.

[150] Cf. ibid. 17.

[151] Ibid. 18.

> she will humble herself toward him, in deed and word and by curtseying; she will obey without complaint; and she will hold her peace [...] suppose he is unloving towards his wife or strays into a love affair [...] she must put up with all this and dissimulate wisely, pretending that she does not notice it and that she truly does not know anything about it.[152]

While Pizan's statement from *The Treasure of the City of Ladies* (1405) stresses the importance of female submission, obedience and discretion, Baldassare Castiglione, in *The Book of the Courtier* (1528), remarks about male and female conduct:

> We ourselves have set a rule that a dissolute life in us is not a vice, or fault, or disgrace, while in women it means such utter opprobrium and shame that any woman of whom ill is once spoken is disgraced forever, whether what is said be calumny or not.[153]

The attitudes towards women and appropriate female behaviour described above are also mirrored in 15th and 16th century tragedy.

Gender ideology in Renaissance tragedy

In Shakespeare's plays sex and gender are crucial determinants of human identity and political power. The hierarchical nature of the Early modern household and women's natural inferiority are reflected differently in the plays: *The Taming of the Shrew*, for example, is an extreme example of the acceptance of the codes of female behaviour as mentioned above.

After his marriage to Katherine Petruccio calls her "my goods, my chattels. She is my house, / My household-stuff, my field, my barn, / My horse, my ox, my ass, my anything" (III.ii.229231)[154]. At the end of the play Katherine seems to have

---

[152] Bear, R. S. "Pamphilia to Amphilanthus". *Renascence Editions: An Online Repository of Works Printed in English Between the Years 1477 and 1799*. Homepage: http://darkwing.uoregon.edu/~rbear/mary.html. Called up on 24 February 2008.

[153] Bear, R. S. "Pamphilia to Amphilanthus". *Renascence Editions: An Online Repository of Works Printed in English Between the Years 1477 and 1799*. Homepage: http://darkwing.uoregon.edu/~rbear/mary.html. Called up on 24 February 2008.

[154] Shakespeare, William. *The Taming of the Shrew*. In: Richard Proudfoot, Ann Thompson and David Scott Kastan. *The Arden Shakespeare: Complete Works* (London: Thomson Learning, 2001), 1058.

lost her initial rebelliousness and complies with the norms society imposes on women. She tells other women:

> Thy husband is thy lord, thy life, thy keeper,
> Thy head, thy sovereign; one that cares for thee,
> And for thy maintenance; commits his body
> To painful labour both by sea and land,
> To watch the night in storms, the day in cold,
> Whilst thou liest warm at home, secure and safe;
> And craves no other tribute at thy hands But
> love, fair looks, and true obedience;
> Too little payment for so great a debt. (V.ii.147-155)[155]

The subordination of women to the prescriptive power of patriarchal doctrine required them to strive for four virtues, for obedience, chastity, silence and piety. Especially chastity was very important for the social status. This is reflected in *Hamlet*, in Laertes's warning to his sister Ophelia about Hamlet's amorous intentions:

> Then weigh what loss your honour may sustain
> If with too credent ear you list his songs Or
> lose your heart, or your chaste treasure open
> To his unmastered importunity.
> Fear it, Ophelia, fear it, my dear sister,
> And keep you in the rear of your affection
> Out of the shot and danger of desire. (I.iii.28-34)[156]

As dramatic action depends on conflicts, Shakespeare's plays show disruptions of the social order, of the household or the state as a whole. "Dramatic conflict is located within familial, social, and political transitions, particularly in moments of marriage, death and genealogical succession."[157] Such a conflict becomes obvious in *Macbeth*, where Lady Macbeth is responsible for the male hero's downfall. "The masculinity of Shakespeare's tragic heroes is paradoxically vulnerable,

---

[155] Ibid., 1069.

[156] Shakespeare, William. *Hamlet*. (ed. Ann Thompson and Neil Taylor). London: Thomson, 2006. All references in brackets refer to this edition.

[157] Traub, Valerie. "Gender and sexuality in Shakespeare". Eds. Margareta de Grazia and Stanley Wells. *The Cambridge Companion to Shakespeare*. (Cambridge: CUP, 2001) 132.

dependent on women's confirmation and approval. If their masculine self-image is challenged, male characters descend into rage, tyranny, even madness."[158]

In the following, I am going to take a closer look at the way *Macbeth* challenges the typical conceptions of femininity and masculinity.

---

[158] Ibid., 134, f.

Gender stereotyping in *Macbeth*

Masculinity

As *Macbeth* is a play that hugely builds on gender stereotypes, I would first of all like to take a closer look at how the play and the characters themselves define the norms and conducts of appropriate male and female conduct. Afterwards, I will go over to an examination of the Weird Sisters and King Duncan as those characters, from the very beginning of the play, hint at a blurring of the traditional categories of male and female.

The heroic world of *Macbeth* is established in the opening scenes describing the Scottish victory in the battle against the Norwegian army. They are crucial for the play's definition of manhood in terms of valour, prowess in battle and violence. The first impression of Macbeth is based on the Captain's report of Macdonald's murder:

> [...] but all's too weak,
> for brave Macbeth – well he deserves that name –
> Disdaining Fortune, with his brandished steel
> Which smoked with bloody execution,
> Like Valour's minion carved out his passage
> Till he faced the slave –
> Which ne'er shook hands nor bade farewell to him,
> Till he unseamed him from the nave to th' chops,
> And fixed his head upon our battlements. (I.ii.15-23) [159]

The very anonymity of the Captain, who relates Macbeth's deed to the king makes the latter's glorification in "Homeric terms"[160] as an eagle, a lion, "Valour's minion" and even Bellona, the Roman goddess of war's bridegroom, seem objective. In the heroic world of medieval Scotland, violence is fully accepted and Macdonald's severed head is a symbol thereof. On hearing of the murder of the treacherous nobleman King Duncan praises Macbeth as "valiant cousin, worthy gentleman" (I.ii.24) since the execution of the Thane of Cawdor is fully legitimate and necessary to secure Duncan's throne. Loyalty to king and country, courage in war and the readiness to sacrifice one's life for a noble cause are the virtues a man's

---

[159] Shakespeare, William. *Macbeth*. (Ed. Nicholas Brooke) Oxford: OUP, 1990. All references in brackets refer to this edition.

[160] Sadowski, Piotr. *Dynamism of Character in Shakespeare's Mature Tragedies*. (London: Associated University Presses, 2003) 274.

valour is judged by. To die a hero's death is confirmation of manhood. This becomes especially clear towards the end of the play when young Siward, the Earl of Northumberland's son, is killed in combat. Rosse consoles Old Siward with the thought that his son died a hero's death:

> Your son, my lord, has paid a soldier's debt;
> He only lived but till he was a man,
> The which no sooner had his prowess confirmed
> In the unshrinking station where he fought,
> But like a man he died. (V.vii. 69-73)

The touchstones by which manhood is defined are not solely violence, prowess in battle and loyalty to the king; manhood is comprised of more. This view is taken by the Scottish nobles, whose definition of manhood is not as narrow as that of Macbeth and his wife. For the nobles power cannot be regarded as immune from cruelty and crime, and especially after Macbeth's regicide they have to use violence in order to re-establish order in Scotland but they build on

> [t]he king-becoming graces,
> As justice, verity, temp'rance, stableness,
> Bounty, perseverance, mercy, lowliness,
> Devotion, patience, courage, fortitude[.] (IV.iii. 91-94)

Allowing oneself to be sensitive and to feel grief is, according to Malcolm and Macduff, also an essential part of manhood. The total absence of feelings as in Macbeth's definition of manliness is the prerequisite for failure since power in the hands of a man who does not show human feelings inevitably leads to a character's downfall and to political chaos in the kingdom. Although Macduff abandons his family in order to go to England and convince

Malcolm to return to Scotland as their legitimate king, he is Shakespeare's exemplar of heroic manhood. "Dramatically and psychologically, he takes on full masculine power only as he loses his family and becomes energized by the loss, converting his grief into the more 'manly' tune of vengeance [...]; the loss of his family here enables his accession to full masculine action even while his response to that loss insists on a more humane definition of manhood."[161] Bearing the loss of his wife and children means allowing for feelings. Macduff's grief clearly is

---

[161] Adelman, Janet. "'Born of Woman': Fantasies of Maternal Power in *Macbeth*". Eds. Nelson Garner, Shirley and Sprengnether, Madelon. *Shakespearean Tragedy and Gender*. (Bloomington and Indianapolis: Indiana University Press, 1996) 120.

the turning point to full humanity. Only by feeling it as a man is Macduff able to come to terms with the horrible murder of his family and can start to "[d]ispute it like a man" (IV.iii. 219) by seeking vengeance. Thus, taking revenge for injustice is fully compatible with the nobles' code of manliness. "The manly stereotype in this play exceeds the limits of soldierly valor and embraces the extreme of retaliatory violence. This attitude permeates society from noble to bondsman."[162] On the one hand, Macduff's cry "He has no children!" voices his frustration at not being able to take complete revenge and wipe out the murderer's family. Macbeth, on the other hand, makes a clear distinction between the catalogue of men and the "valued file" (III.i.95) and demands constant proving of one's manhood by manly deeds.

As mentioned above, Macbeth's understanding of manhood is different. In the beginning of the play, it is basically the same as the Scottish nobles' definition of manliness but due to his own ambition and his wife's influence, it evolves as the play progresses. I will come back to the character of Macbeth and its dynamism later.

Femininity

The stereotypical role of women in the play defines them as passive, weak, dependent, and incapable of dealing with violence, except to become its victims. In the whole play, natural femininity is only represented by Lady Macduff although her role in the tragedy is only minor. Even though Macduff and his wife seem to be the "normative couple"[163], they never appear on stage together and there is no communication between the two of them, at least not in the sense in which the Macbeths talk to and understand each other. As a medieval noblewoman, Lady Macduff "would have been expected to lead the defence of the castle in her husband's absence, but this lady is represented as a domesticated modern "wife", helpless without her husband's protection, easy prey to the assassins who violate her domestic space"[164]. Although confined to passivity, Lady Macduff publicly expresses her feelings after having been told about her husband's departure for

---

[162] Asp, Carolyn. "'Be bloody, bold and resolute': Tragic Action and Sexual Stereotyping in *Macbeth*". Ed. Schoenbaum, Samuel. *Macbeth: Critical Essays*. (London and New York: Garland Publishing, Inc., 1991) 379.

[163] Ibid., 382.

[164] Rackin, Phyllis. *Shakespeare and Women*. (Oxford and New York: OUP, 2005) 135.

England and thus leaving her and the children unprotected. She expresses her total helplessness by lamenting

> He loves us not,
> [...] For the poor wren,
> The most diminuitive of birds, will fight,
> Her young ones in her nest, against the owl.
> All is the fear and nothing is the love;
> As little is the wisdom, where the flight
> So runs against all reason. (IV.ii.8-14)

Irene G. Dash argues that, by including Lady Macduff and contrasting her to Lady Macbeth, the play examines the sources for a woman's moral decisions. Lady Macbeth fully supports her husband in seizing the Scottish throne although he has no title to it; Lady Macduff, however, condemns her husband for fleeing to England and leaving his family in mortal danger.[165]

Not only is the characterization of women in terms of conventional prejudices and stereotypes supported by the portrayal of Lady Macduff, but also by male attitudes towards women, which are now and then uttered in the course of the play. In I.vi. Duncan addresses Lady Macbeth as "[f]air and noble hostess" (I.vi.25), thus indirectly telling her what he considers to be her role and what he expects from her, i.e. to be looked after well. Later, after the murder of Duncan is detected and Lady Macbeth wants to know what had happened before, Macduff warns her by describing the typical feminine reaction to such dreadful news:

> O gentle lady,
> 'Tis not for you to hear what I can speak:
> The repetition in a woman's ear
> Would murder as it fell. (II.iii.85-88)

Lady Macbeth acts accordingly, she reacts exactly the way she is expected to. On hearing Macbeth's moving description of his discovery of the dead king she almost faints and needs help to leave the room.

However, appearances are deceptive since Lady Macbeth is not the dutiful submissive woman she pretends to be in public. In a world in which femininity is reduced to passivity and weakness, obedience and the embodiment of humane

---

[165] Cf. Dash, Irene G. *Women's Worlds in Shakespeare's Plays*. (London: Associated University Presses, 1997) 161, f.

virtues, a strong woman like Lady Macbeth who would like to assert herself in a world dominated by men and who would like to see herself as her husband's equal has to leave the domain she is traditionally confined to and overstep the mark to manly behaviour.

Blurring of categories

The view that *Macbeth* is a play structured by antitheses and clear-cut black and white structures, representing good and evil or male and female respectively, is deconstructed in post-modern criticism. Taking a closer look at the figures of the Weird Sisters and King Duncan, this approach is justified since Shakespeare does identify them as female and male in the dramatis personae but, nevertheless, there are direct and indirect hints in the play which make the clear cut boundaries of at least the witches' biological sex disappear.

Apart from the fact that they are servants of Hecate, the witches' true identity is left unclear throughout the play. As they are frequently referred to as "sisters" and "witches" they seem to be female. Banquo is the only one to question their biological sex when saying "You should be women. / And yet your beards forbid me to interpret / That you are so" (I.iii.45-47). It is not at all clear whether the witches are female or male; the only thing that can be said with certainty about them is that they hold power over mortal men and that their "gender instability, uncanny powers, and malevolence towards men embody typical early modern anxieties about female agency"[166]. Their language of contradiction mirrored by "[f]air is foul, and foul is fair" (I.i.11) may also be taken as a hint at the mingling of categories, moral standards and at the fact that nothing is quite what it seems.

Although King Duncan's biological sex remains undisputed, he nevertheless combines in himself the attributes of both father and mother. Duncan is the "androgynous parent"[167] who, on the one hand is the centre of authority as he confers titles to the nobles and is the source of honour and lineage. On the other hand, he is the source of nurturance who plants his children on the throne and makes them grow. King Duncan is the source of all good and he is opposed to the witches' poisonous cauldron and Lady Macbeth's gall-filled breasts. Duncan makes the existence of a mother unnecessary and in the end he is killed for his typically female softness, his naïve trust and his inability to read peoples' minds in their faces. After the

---

[166] León Alfar, Christina. *Fantasies of Female Evil: The Dynamics of Gender an Power in Shakespearean Tragedy.* (London: Associated University Presses, 2003) 117.

[167] Adelman, "'Born of Woman' Fantasies of Maternal Power in Macbeth", 108.

regicide, male and female become realms apart: the female characters are either merely helpless as in the case of Lady Macduff or merely poisonous as Lady Macbeth; the males become cruel and bloodthirsty. So, the harmonious relationship between the genders as combined in the king fails.[168]

As demonstrated above, *Macbeth* is a play based on gender roles, and their blurring or even inversion. Stereotypes generally intensify opinions, roles and appropriate patterns of behaviour but they simultaneously narrow the free development of characters or personalities by insisting on conventionalised roles men and women have to play in social interaction. In the following, I am going to demonstrate how Macbeth and his wife overstep the boundaries of suitable behaviour which their society imposes on them.

---

[168] Cf. ibid., 108, f.

Gender conflict in *Macbeth*

Lady Macbeth, the "fiendlike queen"

Macbeth is unusual among Shakespeare's great tragedies since a woman is one of the leading characters. The play explores the relationship between gender and power, portraying male characters as strong-willed and courageous, but at the same time giving a female character, Lady Macbeth, a ruthless and over-ambitious personality which is typically more associated with masculinity. But it is exactly the relationship between gender and power which is the key to reading Lady Macbeth's character.

The exploration of gender roles starts in Act I. Scenes v-vii are dominated by Lady Macbeth, whose soliloquies give an insight into her determination and strength of will, which completely top that of her husband. From the moment Lady Macbeth receives her husband's letter telling her about the witches' prophecy and his "promotion" to the Thane of Cawdor it becomes clear that the Macbeths are an unusual couple for their time. Calling her his "dearest partner of greatness" clearly hints at the fact that Macbeth does not regard his wife as his inferior but rather as his equal. Macbeth is promised greatness in form of the Scottish kingship but, as becomes clear from his statements, he apparently intends to share it with his wife, to establish a kind of joint-rule. Yet, immediately after reading the message, Lady Macbeth critically remarks:

> Glamis thou art, and Cawdor, and shalt be
> What thou art promised; yet do I fear thy nature,
> It is too full o'th' milk of human kindness
> To catch the nearest way. Thou wouldst be great,
> Art not without ambition, but without
> The illness should attend it. What thou wouldst highly,
> That wouldst thou holily; wouldst not play false,
> And yet wouldst wrongly win. (I.v.15-21)

It is obvious that Lady Macbeth feels attracted by the prospect of coming to and exercising power but she feels that that she must convince her husband to take the steps necessary for seizing the crown. Diagnosing her husband's nature as "too full o'th' milk of human kindness" Lady Macbeth indicates that "on the dynamic scale her husband's character is less mature than hers, so that [… in the following] Lady Macbeth deliberately exaggerates her husband's weakness to steal his heart to action"[169]. Throughout the play, her power remains merely rhetorical, and she is aware thereof since she remarks:

> That I may pour my spirits in thine ear,
> And chastise with the valour of my tongue
> All that impedes thee from the golden round[.] (I.v.24-26)

In her probably most famous soliloquy in which she calls on spirits to "unsex" her, she resolves to put her natural femininity aside in order to be able to take the measures necessary to seize the crown:

> Come, you spirits,
> That tend on mortal thoughts, unsex me here,
> And fill me from the crown to the toe, top-full
> Of direst cruelty. Make thick my blood,
> Stop up th' access and passage to remorse,
> That no compunctious visitings of nature
> Shake my fell purpose, not keep peace between
> Th' effect and it. Come to my woman's breasts
> And take my milk for gall, you murd'ring ministers,
> Wherever, in your sightless substances,
> You wait on nature's mischief. Come, thick night,
> And pall thee in the dunnest smoke of Hell,
> That my keen knife see not the wound it makes,
> Nor Heaven peep through the blanket of the dark
> To cry, 'Hold, hold'. (I.v.39-53)

Lady Macbeth seems to have internalized the male values of her society and these remarks are a manifestation of her belief that manhood is defined by violence and murder. "Because her function is predicated on renunciation of her own desire, Lady Macbeth *unquestioningly* seeks to confirm Macbeth's ambition, notwithstanding her inability ever to do so. With the promises of the weird sisters [...] and the knowledge of her husband's "burnt...desire" [...] for the power promised him, Lady Macbeth recognizes the requirements of her role."[170]

As Macbeth is reluctant to consent to the regicide immediately after his return, Lady Macbeth takes on Machiavellian traits, instructs her husband to "look like th' innocent flower, / But be the serpent under't" (I.v.64-65) and to leave all the

---

[169] Sadowski, *Dynamism of Character in Shakespeare's Mature Tragedies*, 285.

[170] León Alfar, *Fantasies of Female Evil*, 125.

rest to her. Being torn between the desire for power on the one hand and moral reservations on the other, Macbeth has to be forced into murdering the king and Lady Macbeth achieves her aim by first calling him a coward and subsequently questioning his masculinity. Hers are the most striking statements of the society's cult of manliness and accepted by all the major characters:

> Wouldst thou have that
> Which thou esteem'st the ornament of life,
> And live a coward in thine own esteem,
> Letting 'I dare not' wait upon 'I would',
> Like the poor cat i'th' adage? (I.vii.41-45)

She goes on:

> When thou durst do it, then you were a man;
> And to be more than what you were, you would
> Be so much more the man. (I.vii.49-51)

Lady Macbeth's whole argument to murder is built on sexual taunting. She describes Macbeth as a husband and, above all, a lover who looks so "green" and "pale" (I.vii.37) and who will thus never be able to snatch the glory he is offered. "[S]he challenges an essential element of his self-image, that of potent male, which is the foundation of all his other roles. To be the heroic warrior, to be king, he must first act the man with her. When this role is threatened by her scorn, when the symbol of his whole enterprise is found to be flaccid or unacceptable [...], the collapse of what might be called the male ego is imminent."[171] Her question "Art thou afeard / To be the same in thine own act and valour / As thou art in desire?" (I.vii.39-41) expresses that she will despise him if he is not man enough to commit the murder. She says that the hopes she has placed in him were too great and that he will probably never live up to her expectations.

Immediately after facing Macbeth with his effeminacy, she uses the most violent picture of the whole play to embarrass his manhood by presenting herself more manly than he is:

> I have given suck, and know
> How tender 'tis to love the babe that milks me;
> I would, while it was smiling in my face,

---

[171] Asp, "'Be Bloody, bold and resolute': Tragic Action and Sexual Stereotyping in Macbeth", 384.

> Have plucked my nipple from his boneless gums
> And dashed the brains out, had I so sworn
> As you have done to this. (I.vii.54.59)

Claiming this she "'unsexes' herself psychologically"[172] by conjuring up an image of a mother killing her own child. In a drastic way she makes clear to Macbeth that she would ignore all her womanly traits like tenderness and weakness to kill her baby, and that he should be man enough to use violence to achieve his aims, and thus act like a real man. For Lady Macbeth the murder of the king becomes a proof of her husband's masculinity. Her vows mark her as the more ruthless character of the two, and inevitably the audience's sympathy moves towards Macbeth. Macbeth's resistance to his wife's manipulations is not strong enough; she clearly is in control of the situation and Macbeth becomes the executor of her plan.

Shortly before Macbeth commits the regicide, Lady Macbeth appears to be vulnerable for the first time in the play. She confesses that she had to give herself Dutch courage but in the decisive moment could not stab the king since he resembled her father while he was asleep. After the murder, however, Lady Macbeth regains her manliness for, by disposing of the murder weapon, she is doing what has to be done. Exhorting Macbeth "A little water clears us of this deed. / How easy is it then!" (II.ii.66-67), she appears as the voice of calculating reason. Her pragmatism facing the just committed murder portrays her as a brutal and cold-blooded criminal. Duncan's murder may be regarded as a turning point in the play since afterwards Lady Macbeth recedes from centre stage and Macbeth takes her place. The banqueting scene, the hour of triumph for the Macbeths, is the last scene in which Lady Macbeth actively intervenes in the happenings on stage. Macbeth, who is appalled at the sight of Banquo's ghost, feels that he is now doomed, and in his horror unconsciously gives away the murders he has committed and commissioned. Lady Macbeth tries to bring him back to his senses by questioning his manhood and asking if he was "quite unmanned in folly" (III.iv.74). She tries to gloss over the situation by claiming that fits like the ones the whole court are witnessing are just "a thing of custom" (III.iv.98), nothing to be worried about. But after the crimes were irrevocably revealed, all she can do is bid the nobles to leave.

As Macbeth has now taken over not only Lady Macbeth's role but also adopted her ruthlessness, she loses her importance and all that is left for her is the descent

---

[172] Sadowski, *Dynamism of Character in Shakespeare's Mature Tragedies*, 287.

into madness and the disintegration of her personality. All of a sudden her dramatic role as the driver of the action is eliminated and she is confined to helpless passivity. In the sleepwalking scene, her "somnambulism offers a version of complete alienation from life and human relations to which her complicity in Macbeth's crimes has led her"[173]. The doctor describes her state as a "slumbery agitation" (V.i.11) "[a] great perturbation in nature, to receive at once the benefit of sleep, and do the effects of watching" (V.i.9-10). Being awake, able to speak and write letters and at the same time being unconscious and absentminded is a proof of her isolation and alienation. Her famous gesture of washing her hands may be interpreted as a sign of remorse but also her fear of being convicted of the murder:

> Out damned spot – out I say. One – two –
> Why then 'tis time to do't – Hell is murky. Fie, my lord,
> fie, a soldier, and afeard? What need we fear who knows
> it, when none can call our power to account? Yet who would have thought the old man to have had so much
> blood in him.
> [...]
> Here's the smell of blood still – all the
> Perfumes of Arabia will not sweeten this little hand. O,
> O, O. (V.i.33-50)

"In her loss of power and self-control, in her alienation even from her husband, and in her desperate suicidal death [...], Lady Macbeth appears to be womanized at the end of the play – [... which] restores gender balance and psychological realism, disturbed earlier in the play by [...] presenting a female character with a mind more masculine [...] than the most manly man."[174]

Macbeth, the "butcher"

As mentioned above, the beginning of the play portrays Macbeth as a virtuous soldier, acting in accordance with his society's codes of proper male behaviour not only in battle but also towards the king. However, it becomes clear quite quickly that Macbeth is torn between honour, conscience and loyalty on the one hand and ambition and lust for power on the other.

Being faced with the witches' prophecy plunges Macbeth in a moral dilemma. Where Banquo prudently rejects the prophecy as a mere temptation and is not

---

[173] Sadowski, *Dynamism of Character in Shakespeare's Mature Tragedies*, 290.

[174] Sadowski, *Dynamism of Character in Shakespeare's Mature Tragedies*, 291.

entirely sure whether the witches' words were real or just a hallucination caused by the consumption of an "insane root" (I.iii.84), Macbeth's ambition is roused.

Macbeth is constructed as a pawn to female characters: the witches' prophecy confirms his subconscious desire for domination and power, and as in the course of the play the prediction is actually fulfilled, he acts according to their will. Lady Macbeth's influence on her husband is perhaps even more important since she is the one who, by questioning his masculinity, compels him to regicide. The letter, in which he tells his wife about the weird sisters' predictions shows that he wants to share his feelings with his wife but it may also be seen as an indication that Macbeth is psychologically dependent on her and that she is –as the play subsequently reveals- the more mature and dominant partner in their marriage.[175] Lady Macbeth knows that her husband is "too full o' th' milk of human kindness" (I.v.16) and it is the moment in Act I, scene v when Macbeth refuses to plan Duncan's murder that she realizes that he has to be manipulated into committing the crime. Since Lady Macbeth constantly faces him with her masculinity, and his own effeminacy, he feels the need to prove his manliness. His reaction to the brutal image of her, killing her own child, overawes him and he is so impressed that he admiringly says:

> Bring forth men-children only:
> For thy undaunted mettle should compose
> Nothing but males. (I.vii.73-75)

For Macbeth the regicide is the only way to prove his manliness, to live up to his wife's expectations and to climb up the ladder of success. Immediately before the murder, he is extremely nervous and sees "[a] dagger of the mind, a false creation / Proceeding from the heat-oppressèd brain" (II.i.39-40) but decides that this vision is just a hallucination expressing his unease over the murder. After the deed is done, Macbeth's peace of mind is gone:

> Methought I heard a voice cry 'Sleep no more;
> Macbeth does murder sleep, the innocent sleep,
> Sleep that knits up the revelled sleeve of care,
> The death of each day's life, sore labour's bath,
> Balm of hurt minds, great nature's second course,
> Chief nourisher in life's feast.' (II.ii.34-39)

---

[175] Cf. ibid., 278, f.

For Lady Macbeth, the traces of the crime are easily washed away with water but for Macbeth the blood has symbolic connotations which "great Neptune's ocean" (II.ii.59) can never wash away. Macbeth is afraid of the discovery of the king's body but immediately after its uncovering he puts aside his guilty conscience and acts like a real man with a clear eye towards his purpose. He calls upon the nobles to "put on manly readiness" (II.iii.135) and do their duty. In murdering the king, Macbeth reduces human virtue to courage by identifying courage and manliness.[176] With the death of the king and Macbeth's subsequent ascension to the Scottish throne, the old order of gracious king and loyal subjects is eliminated and replaced by a tyrannous rule.

After the murder Macbeth acts according to the rules of manliness defined by his wife. From scene to scene his violence and remorselessness increase. For Macbeth Banquo is dangerous since he is the only one to know about the witches' prophecy and the only one whom he really fears and thus he has to die. It is remarkable that Macbeth's first act as king of Scotland is to commission Banquo's murder. He adopts the same rhetoric his wife used in Act I, scene vii to convince two murderers to kill Banquo. He questions their manliness and bases his hopes on their need to prove that they are men and they react exactly the way Macbeth has hoped them to.

Despite his determined manner and his displays of fearfulness his inner agitation is expressed through his language. Saying

> We have scorched the snake, not killed it:
> She'll close, and be herself, whilst our poor malice
> Remains in danger of her former tooth (III.ii.14-16)

he shows that he is still afraid of Banquo although the latter's death was already decided upon. Besides, his he complains to his wife that his mind is "full of scorpions" (III.ii.39-40) and that, at the moment, there is no comfort for him.

Now that his reign of terror is in full swing he no longer needs his wife since he has internalized her "bloody instructions" (I.vii.9) and does not even want to let

---

[176] Cf. Davis, Michael. "Courage and Impotence in Shakespeare's *Macbeth*". Eds. Alulis, Joseph and Sullivan, Vickie. *Shakespeare's Political Pageant: Essays in Literature and Politics.* (London: Rowman and Littlefield Publishers, Inc., 1996) 223.

her in on Banquo's murder. He tells her to "[be] innocent of the knowledge, dearest chuck, / Till thou applaud the deeed" (III.ii.48-49) and thus exhibits a "patronizing and stereotyped point of view"[177].

The banqueting scene, Macbeth's hour of triumph, is in fact the beginning of his downfall as he is "unmanned in folly" (III.iv.74) and confesses his bloody deeds to those present. His moral degeneration becomes obvious since he appears to be mad. Banquo's ghost represents the fears and limits of his own powers and his alienation from human society. "This encounter is a moment of truth in which Macbeth clearly sees his affinity with and power over the inhuman world; his ability to summon the ghost, even inadvertently, proves how far he has stepped beyond the limits of humanity."[178] Counter to his wife's reproachful rebuke "Are you a man?" (III.iv.57) he confirms that he even is "a bold one, that dare look on that / Which might appal the Devil" (III.iv.58-59). In the course of the play for Macbeth "'being a man' has become synonymous with being invulnerable to conscience, fear, or compassion, [...] with assuming [...] Godlike qualities and powers"[179]. The murders of the Macduffs and Banquo show that with every murder Macbeth commits or commissions, he is more and more psychologically removed from his victims, his scruples become fewer and his motivation more and more political.[180] Macbeth seems to be aware of his alienation from all humanity and that a return to his former virtuous life is no longer possible since he says about himself: "I am in blood / Stepped in so far, that should I wade no more, / Returning were as tedious as go o'er" (III.iv.137-139).

Security is all Macbeth has ever wanted but never achieved. After the disastrous banquet he seeks assurance with the witches and Hecate, the goddess of witchcraft. The visions they conjure up convey a false sense of security since he is told that "none of woman born / Shall harm Macbeth" (IV.i.94-95) but he does not know that this description is true for Macduff, one of the Scottish nobles. So, this promise of security is his greatest enemy since the latter will eventually kill him.

---

[177] Asp, "Be bloody, bold and resolute: Tragic Action and Sexual Stereotyping in Macbeth", 386.

[178] Ibid., 387.

[179] Ibid., 388.

[180] Sadowski, *Dynamism of Character in Shakespeare's Mature Tragedies*, 282.

The death of Lady Macbeth is the next step in his alienation from society and life. He greets the news seemingly indifferently, coolly and resignedly and seems to be barren of all human feeling:

> She should have died hereafter;
> There would have been a time for such a word –
> Tomorrow, and tomorrow, and tomorrow,
> Creeps in this pretty pace from day to day,
> To the least syllable of recorded time;
> And all our yesterdays have lighted fools
> The way to dusty death. Out, out, brief candle,
> Life's but a walking shadow, a poor player
> That struts and frets his hour upon the stage,
> And then is heard no more. It is a tale
> Told by an idiot, full of sound and fury
> Signifying nothing. (V.v.17-28)

"After a brutal career of striving 'manfully' to impose his own consequentiality upon the future, Macbeth now foresees a future of mere repetitive sequence – 'time and the hour' do *not* 'run through the roughest day' but are stuck fast in it (I.iii.146.7)."[181] The last lines of this speech now show a nihilistic approach to life: "Life's but a walking shadow, [...] full of sound and fury [,] signifying nothing". It can also be read in the light of a self-justification, though. If everything is meaningless, Macbeth's cruelties are so, too. Although Macbeth has realized the uselessness of his crimes (cf. III.i.64-70), he does not repent. In the end, he gives way to despair for his deeds have not brought him what he has expected them to. He has to live with the knowledge of having killed his king, an innocent family, and a former friend, that his wife has committed suicide, and that the game of his life is almost over. Trying to grasp all that life could offer him, he has lost everything and is now pitying himself. In the final battle, taking place after Birnam Wood has moved to Dunsinan, Macbeth resolves to die fighting, to die a hero's death. He decides not to "play the Roman fool, and die / On [...his] own sword" (V.vii.31-32). In their last encounter on the battlefield, Macduff disillusions Macbeth by telling him that he was "from his mother's womb / Untimely ripped" (V.vii.45-46) and thus Macbeth has to give up the illusion of his own immortality. Wanting to escape humiliating captivity and knowing that he is doomed, Macbeth

---

[181] Ramsey, Jarold. "The Perversion of Manliness in Macbeth". In: *Studies in English Literature, 1500-1900*, Vol. 13, No. 2, Elizabethan and Jacobean Drama. (Spring, 1973), 298.

keeps on fighting like young Siward and is eventually killed by Macduff. Macbeth has become "a monster of degenerate 'manliness'"[182] who fought "bear-like" (V.vii.2) for his life but nevertheless lost the struggle. In the course of the play, Macbeth has become less than man, his downfall is a dramatized perversion of manly virtues.

Macbeth – an inversion of gender roles?

The Macbeths' role as tragic heroes has its cause in the tension between the gender roles they think they have to assume and the limits their actual role imposes on them. Having examined the characters of the two protagonists with regard to traditional gender structures, the question now rises whether Shakespeare has intentionally inverted the gender roles in *Macbeth* or whether the old patriarchal order is despite all appearances never questioned. In order to answer that question, I will in the following take a look at Lady Macbeth's character in more detail.

A first reading of *Macbeth* seems to confirm the assertion that the gender roles are reversed since Lady Macbeth appears to be a fully rounded female villain. Her portrayal runs counter to the characterization of women as tender, loving, and incapable of all evil and thus also counter to the common stereotype as described above. Compared to Lady Macduff, who represents the natural femininity in the play, Lady Macbeth has a surprisingly active role for a woman. She has internalized male values like power and ambition and is prepared to use manly violence to reach her aims. She is the one who pushes Macbeth to action and who, at least in the beginning, is powerful at the expense of her husband and stronger than him but it is she who breaks down first. Calling on spirits to "unsex" (I.v.40) her she puts her natural femininity aside and asks the "murd'ring ministers" (I.v.47) to bestow upon her all the male qualities necessary to seize the Scottish crown.

Admittedly, Lady Macbeth's sexual status is ambiguous. There are, however, several points that are contradictory to the theory of an inversion of gender roles. Lady Macbeth is a woman who has internalized the values of the male warrior society and acts according to them. In the world of *Macbeth* men have things firmly under control. It may even be argued that Lady Macbeth holds no real power although the opening scenes convey a different impression. Her preoccupation with and constant references to manhood may be interpreted as an equation of masculinity and power and femininity and powerlessness respectively.

---

[182] Ibid., 299.

A close reading of several scenes Lady Macbeth appears in shows that she is not as evil as she seems to be and not capable of infinite evil. When taking a closer look at the metaphors Shakespeare makes use of it becomes obvious that some of them are gender related like, for example "milk", which is typically associated with femininity. Lady Macbeth complains that her husband is "too full o'th' milk of human kindness" (I.v.16); here especially it becomes clear that "milk" is always equated with characteristically female qualities and virtues like kindness, tenderness and compassion. In Act IV, scene iii, Malcolm wants to "[p]our the sweet milk of concord into Hell" (IV.iii.98); here again "milk" is associated with a female quality, that of concord. Lady Macbeth has to invoke supernatural powers to "unsex" (I.v.40) her. Apparently it is not possible for her to just ignore her biological sex; she needs help to "[s]top up th'access and passage to remorse" (I.v.43), help which no human being can offer her. Only through the loss of her femininity is she able to forget her traditional role as nurturing and life-giving mother and has her "woman's breasts" (I.v.46) filled with gall instead of milk. Macbeth admires her for her manly virtues, her "undaunted mettle" (I.vii.74) as he calls it, since she apparently would be cruel and ruthless enough to kill her own child had she promised to do so.

Lady Macbeth's character is contradictory. At first sight she seems to be cruel and pitiless, acting in complete accordance with her utterances. But if her actions and speeches are examined more closely, the image of the cold-blooded female villain shows signs of breaking up. Unlike her self-proclaimed ruthlessness she is not capable of committing regicide herself since Duncan resembled her father while he was asleep. Maybe she even was afraid since the king is a figure of authority and it is her duty as a subject to be loyal to him. So, her public and her private persona are not identical.

In the sleepwalking scene Lady Macbeth is shaken by the "compunctious visitings of nature" (I.v.44) she feared in Act I and which she considers to be typically female. Duncan's blood now has symbolic connotations and she constantly tries to wash away an imaginary bloodstain from her hand. In Act V she unconsciously gains back her femininity since she says that "all the / perfumes of Arabia will not sweeten this little hand" (V.i.48-49), "sweet", "little" and "perfumes" being habitually associated with the female sex.

When regarding Macbeth it is not possible to speak of a reversal of gender roles, either. It is true that Macbeth needs the impetus of his wife to give in to his ambition and act in accordance with the male values, as defined by himself and his wife. Having achieved what he always wanted Macbeth no longer needs his wife and does not let her in on his plan to murder Banquo which is intended to bring security, something he will never achieve, though.

Thus he assigns her to her traditional role as a woman or wife and deprives her of the possibility to exercise power. Lady Macbeth's desire has to be denied since it does not reflect his wishes.

Even the deaths of the two protagonists are typical for their sex: Lady Macbeth dies at home, in private, through the female act of suicide and Macbeth dies fighting on the battlefield like a virtuous soldier. With such an ending Shakespeare probably wanted to hint at the fact that a society in which gender roles are polarized into masculine action and feminine passivity is doomed.

Some critics consider *Macbeth* as misogynistic because of Lady Macbeth and the witches, the play's four temptresses. This view may be justified because Lady Macbeth oversteps the boundaries of normal female behaviour and the witches stir Macbeth's enormous ambition with their prophecy. When regarding Lady Macbeth's "unsex me here" soliloquy, however, this view is no longer justified since it becomes obvious that she is a product of the society she lives in. She has just accepted the values of her culture and applied them to herself and her husband. Misogyny in *Macbeth* is not as strong and apparent as in *Hamlet*, where the Prince of Denmark says "Frailty, thy name is Woman" (I.ii.146).

Malcolm's coronation at the end of the play is a restoration of the old patriarchal order and simultaneously a total exclusion of the female. Alexander Leggat says that the ending of *Macbeth* leaves a chill in the air since the "moral judgements of Macbeth and Lady Macbeth, though perfectly valid, have missed the point."[183] They are portrayed as human despite their cruel ambition and it is with the help of the two tragic heroes that Shakespeare shows that even in a warrior society like medieval Scotland deep human bonds between husband and wife do exist and that a marriage does not necessarily have to be reduced to a relationship like the one between the Macduffs in which the wife is portrayed as merely helpless and reduced to passivity.

---

[183] Leggat, Alexander. *Shakespeare's Tragedies: Violation and Identity*. (Cambridge: CUP, 2005) 208.

Conclusion

As shown above, *Macbeth* is play that hugely builds on gender stereotypes. It is one of the few plays in which a woman wields power over a man, even if only for a limited period of time. The very power Lady Macbeth holds is the trigger of the tragedy which takes its course after the murder of Duncan. She oversteps the boundary of appropriate female behaviour by indirectly compelling her husband to murder. Since Lady Macbeth equals masculinity not only with violence but also with male potency, Macbeth feels the need to prove his manhood by killing the king. For the Macbeths the regicide is a first turning point in the play since immediately afterwards Macbeth gains the lead and Lady Macbeth is assigned the traditionally passive role of a woman. She is no longer his confidante; he plots the murders of Banquo and the Macduffs without her knowledge. Lady Macbeth's tragedy is that she has internalized a certain ideology, the male values and virtues of her culture. Her descent into madness and the disintegration of her character are a proof that her former violent claims were only intended to push her husband to action. The blood she so pragmatically washed away after the regicide has now become symbolic: she cannot deal with the knowledge of being responsible for the king's death and indirectly also for the murder of Lady Macduff and her children. Had she not compelled her husband to murder, it would not have been necessary to commission more murders just for the sake of security, something they never achieved. Her suicide restores the gender balance since it is a typically female way of dying. She no longer is more manly than her husband but womanised again.

At the beginning of the play, Macbeth is portrayed as a virtuous and loyal soldier since he killed the treacherous Macdonald who cooperated with the Norwegians against the Scottish king. In accordance with the values of the society, he is awarded the title of the Thane of Cawdor as a reward for his prowess in battle. The witches' prophecy stirs Macbeth's ambition since they address him with his newly awarded title even before he is aware that he was "promoted". He takes this as a proof that the prophecy is true and is in the following pushed to action by his wife. Her violent images with which she wants to push him to action show that she is more manly than he is and he commits the regicide out of the need to demonstrate his masculinity. Immediately after the murder Macbeth is mentally distressed and afraid of the impending discovery of the king's body. But immediately after the uncovering of the murder he puts on "manly readiness" (II.iii.135) and his effeminacy is forgotten. Only at the banqueting scene does he suffer a relapse and has to put up with his wife's questioning of his manhood. The banqueting scene is also the turning point in the play since Macbeth unconsciously reveals the murders he has committed or commissioned in order to secure his power. In the following, his wife's suicide still adds to his mental distress and he dies a manly death, defending his honour and name on the battlefield.

Although Lady Macbeth's sexual status is ambiguous and Macbeth needs to be pushed to action by a woman, I would not support the thesis that Shakespeare has inverted the gender roles. The sexual stereotyping apparent in *Macbeth*, the two protagonists' ways of dying, and the ending of the play, in which the patriarchal order is restored and the female totally excluded proves that the society has not changed.

There are remarkable parallels between the ending and the opening scenes of the play, "indicating society's continued acceptance of the values and stereotypes that paradoxically both threaten it and guarantee its continuation"[184]. Each time a treacherous criminal is destroyed, his head severed and soldierly valour, bravery and manhood placed above feeling and womanly virtues. Malcolm, the rightful heir is made king of Scotland and the short interval of Macbeth's tyrannous reign is almost forgotten since the living proves of tyranny, Macbeth and his wife have been eliminated.

---

[184] Asp, "'Be Bloody, bold and resolute': Tragic Action and Sexual Stereotyping in *Macbeth*", 392.

Bibliography

Adelman, Janet. "'Born of Woman': Fantasies of Maternal Power in Macbeth". Eds. Shirley Nelson Garner and Madelon Sprengnether. Shakespearean Tragedy and Gender. Bloomington and Indianapolis: Indiana University Press, 1996. 105-134.

Asp, Carolyn. "'Be bloody, bold and resolute': Tragic Action and Sexual Stereotyping in Macbeth". Ed. Samuel Schoenbaum. Macbeth: Critical Essays. London and New York: Garland Publishing, Inc., 1991. 377-395.

Bear, R. S. "Pamphilia to Amphilanthus". Renascence Editions: An Online Repository of Works Printed in English Between the Years 1477 and 1799. Homepage: http://darkwing.uoregon.edu/~rbear/mary.html. Called up on 24 February 2008.

Callaghan, Dympna. Woman and Gender in Renaissance Tragedy: A Study of King Lear, Othello, The Duchess of Malfi and The White Devil. London: Harvester Wheatsheaf,1989.

Dash, Irene G. Women's Worlds in Shakespeare's Plays. London: Associated University Presses, 1997.

Davis, Michael. "Courage and Impotence in Shakespeare's Macbeth". Eds. Joseph Alulis and Vickie Sullivan. Shakespeare's Political Pageant: Essays in Literature and Politics. London: Rowman and Littlefield Publishers, Inc., 1996. 219-236.

Leggat, Alexander. Shakespeare's Tragedies: Violation and Identity. Cambridge: Cambridge University Press, 2005.

León Alfar, Christina. Fantasies of Female Evil: The Dynamics of Gender and Power in Shakespearean Tragedy. London: Associated University Presses, 2003.

Middleton, Thomas and Rowley, William. The Changeling. Ed. Trevor R. Griffiths. London: Nick Hern Books, 2000.

Rackin, Phyllis. Shakespeare and Women. Oxford and New York: Oxford University Press, 2005.

Ramsey, Jarold. "The Perversion of Manliness in Macbeth". In: Studies in English Literature, 1500-1900, Vol. 13, No. 2, Elizabethan and Jacobean Drama. (Spring, 1973), 285-300.

Sadowski, Piotr. Dynamism of Character in Shakespeare' Mature Tragedies. London: Associated University Presses, 2003.

Shakespeare, William. Hamlet. Eds. Ann Thompson and Neil Taylor. London: Thomson Learning, 2006.

Shakespeare, William. Macbeth. Ed. Nicholas Brooke. Oxford and New York: Oxford University Press, 1990.

Shakespeare, William. The Taming of the Shrew. In: Eds. Richard Proudfoot, Ann Thompson and David Scott Kastan. The Arden Shakespeare: Complete Works London: Thomson Learning, 2001. 1041-1069.

Traub, Valerie. "Gender and Sexuality in Shakespeare". Eds. Margareta de Grazia and Stanley Wells. The Cambridge Companion to Shakespeare. Cambridge: Cambridge University Press, 2001. 129-146.

Körper- und Spiegelmetapher und ihre Funktion in ausgewählten Sonetten William Shakespeares

Stephanie Schnabel, 2005

Einleitung

Diese Hausarbeit behandelt die Funktion der Körper- und Spiegelmetaphern in den Sonetten William Shakespeares anhand ausgewählter Beispiele.

Im ersten Teil geht es um den allgemeinen Hintergrund der Sonette als Gedichtform. Es wird kurz auf die Übertragung des Sonetts in den englischsprachigen Kulturraum eingegangen, um danach den Höhepunkt seiner Entwicklung in England am Ende des 16. Jahrhunderts vorzustellen. Shakespeares Sonettzyklus fällt ein wenig aus diesem zeitlichen Rahmen heraus, da seine Gedichte erst 1609 veröffentlicht werden. Auch er arbeitet jedoch mit Bildern und Metaphern, die in der Tradition Petrarcas stehen. Wie aber sehen diese aus?

Worin unterscheidet sich Shakespeares Werk möglicherweise von dem seiner Zeitgenossen?

Da mir bei der Durchsicht der Literatur zum Thema Metapher aufgefallen ist, wie schwer sich einzelne Metapherntypen trennen lassen, werde ich in meiner Untersuchung ausgewählter Sonette Shakespeares auf zwei Metapherntypen eingehen. Als Grundlage hierfür dienten mir die folgenden Monographien:

Speculum, Mirror und Looking-Glass – Kontinuität und Originalität der Spiegelmetapher in den Buchtiteln des Mittelalters und der englischen Literatur des 13. bis 17. Jahrhunderts von Herbert Grabes und Ernst Robert Curtius' Werk *Europäische Literatur und lateinisches Mittelalter*.

Es geht in diesem zweiten Teil als erstes um die literarische Entwicklung und Verwendung der zwei Metapherntypen vor der elisabethanischen Zeit. Danach werden der Gebrauch und die Weiterentwicklung bei den Schriftstellerkollegen Shakespeares beschrieben, um anschließend den Blick auf drei ausgewählte Sonette des Dichters und Dramatikers zu richten, die auf unterschiedliche Art und Weise mit diesen Metaphern spielen.

Die Entwicklung des Sonetts bis in die elisabethanische Zeit

Das Sonett kam das erste Mal in Italien zur Blüte. Vermutlich wurde es von dem Notar Giacomo da Lentini entwickelt,[185] jedoch machten erst Dante Alighieri und nach ihm Francesco Petrarca diese Gedichtform populär. Vor allen Dingen war Petrarca schon zu seinen Lebzeiten in England bekannt. Er wurde von seinem jüngeren Zeitgenossen Geoffrey Chaucer gleich zweimal in dessen Werken erwähnt bzw. übersetzt.[186]

Petrarca und seine ‚Übersetzer' Wyatt und Surrey

Die ersten Sonette in englischer Sprache waren keine eigenständig verfassten Werke, sondern recht freie Übersetzungen bzw. Übertragungen der Sonette Petrarcas durch Sir Thomas Wyatt und Henry Howard, Earl of Surrey. Teilweise hielten sie sich ziemlich genau an den Wortlaut dieser Gedichte, teilweise veränderten sie ihn und führten so einen aktiven Dialog mit der italienischen Vorlage.[187] Durch diese Übertragungen wurden die Gedichte Petrarcas für ein englischsprachiges, gebildetes Publikum verfügbar gemacht.

Da jedoch das Englische nicht so viele Reimpaare enthält wie das Italienische,[188] veränderte erst Wyatt, dann auch Surrey die Form seiner Sonette:

Wyatt führte den Paarreim ein, der das Sonett in Zukunft abschließen sollte.[189] Die Folge von Oktave und Sextett mit einem gedanklichen *turn* dazwischen verwandelte dann Surrey in vier Quartette mit Kreuzreim und dem abschließenden *couplet*. Er erfand auch den *blank verse*, den unter anderem Shakespeare später benutzen sollte.

Die „Surreysche Normform"[190] sieht also folgendermaßen aus: abab cdcd efef gg. Diese Form wird auch ‚englisches Sonett' genannt.

---

[185] Vgl Kapp, Volker (Hg.): Italienische Literaturgeschichte. Stuttgart, Weimar: Verlag J. B. Metzler 1994 (2. Auflage), S. 13

[186] Vgl. Edmondson, Paul und Stanley Wells: *Shakespeare's Sonnets*. Oxford: Oxford University Press 2004, S. 13

[187] Vgl. Seeber, Hans Ulrich (Hg.): *Englische Literaturgeschichte*. Stuttgart, Weimar: Verlag J. B. Metzler 1999 (3. Auflage), S. 94

[188] Petrarca konnte so in den zwei Quartetten wie auch den beiden Terzetten jeweils nur zwei Reime verwenden. Das von ihm am häufigsten verwendete Schema sieht folgendermaßen aus: abba abba cdc cdc.

[189] Seine Form wurde zu abba abba cdc cdd.

[190] Vgl. Tetzeli von Rosador, Kurt: „Die nichtdramatischen Dichtungen.", S. 581

Durch diese Anordnung der Reime kann mehr Variation innerhalb der Quartette erzeugt werden. Im *couplet* ist häufig ein Gegengewicht zu der in den ersten zwölf Versen aufgestellten These zu finden. Man kann eine gewisse Tendenz zu einer überraschenden Wendung oder einer Schlussfolgerung innerhalb dieser zwei Verse feststellen.[191]

Diese Variationen wurden durch die Übertragungen vom italienischen in den englischen Kulturkreis und dessen Dichtungs- und Liebeskonventionen noch beschleunigt. Wyatt und Surrey gehörten beide dem Hof Heinrichs VIII. an. Sie lebten und schrieben dort.[192]

Es fand außerdem eine Polarisierung des Dichtens statt. Nicht nur höfische Wertvorstellungen wurden miteinbezogen, man berücksichtigte auch bürgerliche Weltanschauungen. Die Sonnetiers wurden zu so genannten *poet-courtiers*. Sie buhlten mit ihren Gedichten gleichzeitig um die Gunst der Geliebten und die des Monarchen bzw. des Mäzens.

Der Höhepunkt der Sonettdichtung in England

Obwohl Surrey und Wyatt die großen Vorbilder für die 60er und 70er Jahre des 16. Jahrhunderts blieben,[193] kam das Sonett als Form der Dichtung erst in den 90er Jahren „in Mode".[194]

Beginnend mit dem posthum veröffentlichten Sonettzyklus *Astrophel and Stella* von Sir Philip Sidney wurden zwischen 1591 und 1597 eine ganze Reihe anderer Zyklen und Sonettsammlungen veröffentlicht, so zum Beispiel *Delia* von Samuel Daniel, *Diana* von Henry Constable, Michael Draytons *Ideas Mirrour*, Barnabe Barnes *Parthenophil and Parthenophe* und Edmund Spensers *Amoretti*. Die meisten dieser Zyklen tragen Titel, in denen ein Frauenname oder –pseudonym genannt wird.

Der immer noch andauernde Dialog mit Petrarca verknüpft auch alle Sonette dieser Zeit. Dieser wird nicht nur im positiven Sinn geführt. Einige der Dichter wen-

---

[191] Vgl. Tetzeli von Rosador (2000), S. 580

[192] Viele ihrer Sonette, die vorher nur in Manuskripten zugänglich waren, wurden 1557 in *Tottel's Miscellany*, einer Sammlung von Gedichten, veröffentlicht.

[193] Vgl. Standop, Ewald und Edgar Mertner: *Englische Literaturgeschichte*. Heidelberg: Quelle & Meyer 1983 (4.Auflage), S. 184

[194] Baumann, Uwe: *Shakespeare und seine Zeit*. Stuttgart: Ernst Klett Verlag 1998, S. 32

den sich sogar gegen die petrarkistischen Ideale und beginnen, diese zu verspotten. Zu diesen Idealen zählen unter anderem „the magic attraction of the adored but cruel and distant lady, the sufferings of the male lover, and the expression of passion and the wish to die".[195]

Schon bei Wyatt und Surrey zeichnet sich ebenfalls ab, dass die englischen Dichter mit der Werbung um die Geliebte anders umgehen, als dies Petrarca in seinen Sonetten tat. Petrarca geht von einer Liebesphilosophie aus, die die körperliche Schönheit der Geliebten als „Ausdruck ihrer inneren Vollkommenheit, ihres Geistes und ihrer keuschen Tugend"[196] ansieht. Die Dame ist ein Idealobjekt, eine Geheiligte, und der um sie Werbende muss sein körperliches Begehren in ein reines, platonisches Verehren umwandeln. Die Werbung um die Dame wird daher zu einem Werben um das göttliche Prinzip in ihr.

Diese Liebeskonzeption konnte aufgrund anderer Voraussetzungen nicht genau so in die englische Dichtung übernommen werden. Dem petrarkistischen Ideal stand der in England vorherrschende Protestantismus entgegen, und mit Elisabeth I. war nun eine weibliche Herrscherin auf dem Thron, die dem Werbungsspiel immer auch einen politischen Anstrich verlieh.

Dies zeigt sich zum Beispiel in Sidneys Zyklus *Astrophel and Stella*. Die Liebe ist nicht mehr nur die ganze Welt der beiden Titelfiguren, sie ist vielmehr eingebettet in das normale gesellschaftliche Leben der elisabethanischen Zeit. „Die Selbstvergessenheit des absolut Liebenden wäre demgegenüber pflichtvergessene Verantwortungslosigkeit".[197] Auch bricht dieser Zyklus nicht wie bei Petrarca mit dem Tod bzw. der geistigen Vereinigung der Liebenden nach dem Tod ab, sondern mit ihrer gegenseitigen Entfremdung. Sidneys Astrophel hat außerdem damit zu kämpfen, dass das platonische Liebesideal immer wieder an einem nicht bezähmbaren Begehren scheitert. Dies äußert sich in einer erregt wirkenden Sprache, einem aus konkreten Situationen erwachsenden Sprechakt und in wiederholten Beteuerungen, dass er es mit seiner Werbung ernst meine.

Dem gegenüber steht zum Beispiel in den *Amoretti* Edmund Spensers eine ruhige Sprache, die von dem Liebenden in bedächtigen Rückblicken auf vergangene Ereignisse verwendet wird. In diesem Sonettzyklus ist das Ziel der Werbung um die

---

[195] Wagner, Hans-Peter: *A History of British, Irish and American Literature*. Trier: Wissenschaftlicher Verlag 2003, S. 14

[196] Seeber (1999), S. 95

[197] Ebd., S. 98

Geliebte etwas Konkretes, nämlich die christliche Ehe. Es scheint, als herrsche dadurch im gesamten Zyklus eine Ruhe und Gelassenheit, die man in den Sonettsammlungen anderer Dichter wie zum Beispiel bei Sidney etwas vermisst. Zwar müssen die Liebenden etliche Prüfungen, Widerstände und Verleumdungen überstehen, doch dies festigt ihre Zuneigung und damit ihre Liebe nur noch mehr.

Wie alle Modeerscheinungen geht jedoch auch die Sonettmode am Verschleiß durch Überproduktion zugrunde. „Zur Endphase eines solchen Verschleißprozesses gehört auch das Umkippen der Konventionen in die Parodie".[198] Die petrarkistischen Topoi werden in der Dichtung aufgenommen, nur damit sie abgelehnt und verworfen werden. „Als Form des erotischen Diskurses hat das Sonett nach der Jahrhundertwende offensichtlich ausgespielt".[199]

---

[198] Vgl. Seeber (1999), S. 101

[199] Ebd., S. 101

Das Sonett bei William Shakespeare

Shakespeares Sonette fallen aus dem oben erwähnten Zeitrahmen heraus: Sie erschienen erst 1609, zu einem Zeitpunkt also, an dem die „kurzlebige elisabethanische Sonettmode"[200] ihren Höhepunkt schon überschritten hatte. Sie haben keinen wirklichen Titel. Außerdem hinterlassen viele der Sonette den Eindruck, als würde das lyrische Ich einen Mann verehren.

Shakespeares Sammlung war in der Renaissance allerdings mit 154 Sonetten die umfangreichste ihrer Art.[201]

Aus der Verehrung des jungen Mannes erwächst in einigen Sonetten auch eine recht unruhige und ungestüme Sprache, wenn das lyrische Ich den Geliebten mit heißen Worten lobpreist, aber auch kritisiert. Es möchte ihn vor allen Fährnissen des Liebeslebens schützen. Dies gelingt ihm jedoch nicht immer: Der Geliebte wendet sich ebenfalls einem *rival poet* und einer *dark lady* zu.

Die Verbindung von Biographie und Werk

Die einzige Verbindung von Biographie und Werk findet man in der Widmung. Da diese sehr vieldeutig abgefasst ist, wirft sie einige Fragen auf.

Die Widmung ist nicht, wie man zunächst annehmen könnte, von Shakespeare selbst unterzeichnet. Es handelt sich vielmehr um eine persönliche Widmung Thomas Thorpes, dem Verleger der Quarto-Ausgabe von 1609. Einige Forscher schließen aus dieser Tatsache, dass Shakespeare zur Zeit des Druckes nicht in London war oder möglicherweise gar nicht an der endgültigen Drucklegung beteiligt wurde. Thorpe unterzeichnete normalerweise nur, wenn der Autor außer Landes weilte oder schon verstorben war.[202]

Als nächstes fällt der „onlie begetter [...] Mr. W.H." auf. Was ist damit gemeint? Und wer könnte „Mr. W.H." sein? Hier gibt es wiederum verschiedene Möglichkeiten: Mit „onlie begetter" könnte derjenige gemeint sein, der Shakespeare zu den Sonetten inspiriert hat; vielleicht sogar der Freund der ersten 126 Sonette. Als „onlie begetter" kann aber auch die Person bezeichnet werden, die Thorpe das Manuskript zur Verfügung stellte. Legt man die zweite Annahme zugrunde, hat

---

[200] Baumann (1998), S.32

[201] Zum Vergleich: Sidney bringt es mit seinem Zyklus ‚nur' auf 108 Sonette. (vgl. Edmondson (2004), S. 14)

[202] Vgl. Shakespeare, William: *The Complete Sonnets and Poems* – edited by Collin Burrow. Oxford: Oxford University Press 2002, S. 99

„Mr. W.H." nichts mehr mit den Sonetten selbst zu tun. Nimmt man dagegen an, dass „Mr. W.H." der Inspirator war, trifft man wieder auf unzählige Vermutungen und Annahmen.

Eine der zwei wahrscheinlichsten Möglichkeiten für ‚Mr. W. H.' wäre der Earl of Southampton, Henry Wriothesley, dem Shakespeare seine beiden Versepen *Venus and Adonis* und *The Rape of Lucrece* widmete. Eine mögliche Verbindung mit dem jungen Mann der Sonette scheint nicht mehr so ungewöhnlich, wenn man die Widmung zu *The Rape of Lucrece* betrachtet, die schon zu einer größeren Vertraulichkeit neigt als die *Venus and Adonis* vorangestellte Widmung. Vielleicht findet diese Vertraulichkeit in den Sonetten eine weitere Steigerung? Auffällig ist vor allem, dass die beiden letzten Worte „all happinesse" ebenfalls in der Widmung der Sonette vorkommen.[203]

Argumente gegen Wriothesley sind die nötige Umkehrung der Initialen und die Sonette selber: In einigen *Dark Lady*-Sonetten wird in mehreren Variationen mit dem Namen Will gespielt. Dies nehmen einige Forscher zum Anlass, Wriothesley als Kandidaten für „Mr. W.H." abzulehnen.

William Herbert, Earl of Pembroke, einer der beiden dedicatees der First Folio, wird von vielen als der zweite Kandidat angesehen. Er hat die richtigen Initialen, wurde als Mäzen Shakespeares erwähnt und hatte eine Heirat immer notorisch abgelehnt, obwohl er Frauen generell nicht abgeneigt war. Davon zeugt seine Affäre mit Mary Fitton. Vielleicht drängen ihn die ersten 17 Sonette zum Heiraten? Genau kann man heute nicht mehr beweisen, wer sich hinter „Mr. W.H." verbirgt.[204]

Die Figuren im kompletten Sonettzyklus

Obwohl sich nicht mehr feststellen lässt, wem Shakespeare seine Sonette widmete, finden sich einige Motive und Figuren, die im gesamten Zyklus vorkommen.

Als erstes wäre hier das lyrische Ich zu nennen. Man kann es nicht mit Shakespeare gleichsetzen. Die Sonette sind also keine autobiographischen Gedichte, und doch gibt es einige Informationen über diese Figur.

---

[203] Vgl. Muir, Kenneth: *Shakespeare's Sonnets*. London: George Allen & Unwin LTD 1979, S. 153

[204] Andere Möglichkeiten sind weniger wahrscheinlich, beispielsweise William Harvey, William Hatcliffe, William Hughes oder William Himself.

Das lyrische Ich ist unverheiratet, hat jedoch einen weiblichen Partner. Und doch geht es soweit, anzudeuten, dass seine Beziehung zu dem jungen Mann ähnlich der einer Frau zu ihrem Mann wäre. Der Sprecher ist älter als der junge Mann und stellt immer wieder seine eigene Unwürdigkeit dem Geliebten gegenüber heraus. Außerdem fühlt er sich als Opfer eines Skandals. Vielleicht ein Hinweis auf eine angedeutete homosexuelle Beziehung? Einige der Sonette beinhalten ein Gefühl des Sich-Sehnen nach dem Geliebten, der für das lyrische Ich fast unerreichbar scheint. Die Gründe hierfür könnten in einer geographischen Trennung, einem sozialen Standesunterschied oder in der Tatsache, dass beide männlich sind, liegen.

Der junge Mann der Sonette ist ebenfalls unverheiratet und macht anscheinend auch keinerlei Anstalten zu einer Heirat. Dadurch zieht er den Zorn des lyrischen Ichs auf sich. Dieses wirft ihm vor, er handle egoistisch, indem er seine Schönheit für sich behalte und sie nicht an mögliche Kinder weitergebe. Später stellt das lyrische Ich fest, dass der junge Mann ihn mit einer Frau betrogen und sich einem anderen Dichter zugewendet habe, der ihn über alle Maßen lobe.

Auch wenn der geliebte junge Mann in mehreren Sonetten des Zyklus kritisiert wird, so lässt sich doch die Tendenz feststellen, ihn zu einem Idealbild zu erheben und seine Schönheit, sein ganzes Wesen zu preisen, wie es in den Sonettsequenzen der elisabethanischen Zeit üblich war.

Die dritte Figur ist die so genannte *dark lady*. Obwohl sie in keinem der Sonette so bezeichnet wird, kann man in einigen der Gedichte eine Beschreibung finden, die auf ihren dunklen Charakter hinweist. Außerdem ist sie im Gegensatz zu den beiden bisher erwähnten männlichen Figuren verheiratet. Das lyrische Ich beklagt in mehreren Sonetten, dass sie seinen Geliebten zum Bruch verführt und ihn sozusagen durch ihre Reize gefangen nimmt. Dies wirft es jedoch auch dem *rival poet* vor:

Der Dichter-Rivale preist den jungen Mann sehr. Dieser fühlt sich geschmeichelt und wendet sich von nun an ebenfalls diesem Mann zu. Der *rival poet* ist gebildet und versteht es, durch seine Worte den jungen Mann zu verführen. Das lyrische Ich ist erzürnt und kritisiert den *rival poet* und vor allen Dingen auch den jungen Mann sehr.

Aus diesen Situationen gibt es jedoch in den Sonetten keinen wirklichen Ausweg. Fast scheint es „as if Shakespeare were providing us with all the ingredients necessary to make our own series of narratives about love".[205]

---

[205] Edmondson (2004), S. 46

Körper- und Spiegelmetapher in der Literatur

Ursprünge der Metaphern in der Literatur

Genau wie für die Verwendung von Topoi in der Literatur liegen die Anfänge für die Verwendung der Metaphern in der griechischen und römischen Antike. Metapher bedeutet ‚Übertragung'.[206] Meistens werden Substantive metaphorisch gebraucht, jedoch kann man auch Verben benutzen. „In a metaphor, a word or expression which in literal usage denotes one kind of thing or action is applied to a distinctly different kind of thing or action, without asserting a comparison".[207]

Körpermetaphern sind schon bei Platon in der altgriechischen Literatur zu finden. Er prägte zum Beispiel das Bild vom „Auge der Seele", das seitdem immer wieder gerne verwendet wurde. Die Sehkraft des Auges wird auf „das geistige Erkenntnisvermögen"[208] angewendet, d. h. „den äußeren Sinnen werden innere Sinne zugeordnet".[209] Vor allen Dingen in der Bibel lassen sich zahlreiche Verwendungen dieser Metapher feststellen. Aber auch andere Körperteile, wie zum Beispiel die Ohren, der Bauch, die Zunge, das Herz werden zu Metaphern. Teilweise reicht ihre Verwendung bis in die karolingische Dichtung sowie bis zur Dichtung Dantes in Italien.

Eine besonders hervorstechende, über das Maß hinaus einprägsame und beliebte Metapher sind die „Knie des Herzens" aus der apokryphen *Oratio Manassae*. Dieses Schriftstück ist vermutlich um 70 nach Christus verfasst und befindet sich im Anhang der Vulgata. Die Metapher wurde in die kirchliche Liturgie übernommen und taucht in der mittelalterlichen Poesie wieder auf.

Auch die Spiegelmetapher geht auf die Antike zurück. Erste Verwendungen finden sich bei Aischylos, Platon, Aristoteles und anderen Schriftstellern. Später wird sie dann von Cicero und Terenz aufgegriffen. Cicero nennt zum Beispiel die Komödie „imitatio vitae" oder „speculum consuetudinis".[210]

---

[206] Vgl. Curtius, Ernst Robert: *Europäische Literatur und lateinisches Mittelalter*. Bern und München: Francke Verlag 1984 (10. Auflage), S. 138

[207] Abrams, M. H.: *A Glossary of literary terms*. Fort Worth: Harcourt Brave Jovanovich 1993 (6. Auflage), S. 67

[208] Curtius (1984), S. 146

[209] Ebd., S. 146

[210] Vgl. Curtius (1984), S. 340, Anmerkung 1

Der metaphorische Spiegel weist verschiedene Funktionen auf, die sich je nach dem Anliegen der Autoren in ihren Werken wiederfinden.

Er ist in der Bibel und der christlichen Literatur ebenfalls sehr beliebt. Hier wird zum Beispiel der menschliche Geist mit einem Spiegel verglichen. Ab dem 12. und 13. Jahrhundert taucht das Wort ‚speculum' immer häufiger in Buchtiteln auf. Diese Schriften sehen sich selbst als Spiegel. Sie wollen zur Besserung und Belehrung dienen. Wer sie liest, bekommt seine schlechten Eigenschaften vor Augen geführt, er soll sich durch den Blick in diesen Spiegel als Instrument der Erkenntnis möglichst bessern.

Parallel dazu gibt es Spiegelmetaphern innerhalb einzelner literarischer Schriften. So kann beispielsweise der menschliche Körper bzw. eine bestimmte Person als guter oder warnender Spiegel dienen. Hier wären für den vorbildlichen Spiegel zum Beispiel aus der christlichen Literatur Maria,[211] Christus und die Heiligen zu nennen, für den warnenden Spiegel besonders eitle oder böse Menschen. Die Wurzeln für diese spezielle Verwendung reichen ebenfalls bis zu Platon in der altgriechischen und Cicero in der lateinischen Literatur zurück. Diese Verwendung setzt sich in der Zeit Shakespeares fort.

Aber auch einzelne Körperteile können zum Spiegel werden. Das Gesicht eines Menschen besitzt als Spiegel eine gewisse, das Auge eine beachtliche Kontinuität innerhalb der Literatur.[212]

Das Antlitz als Spiegel wird in der englischen Literatur schon von Chaucer verwendet, gewinnt aber erst in der elisabethanischen Zeit mehr und mehr an Bedeutung.

Die Tradition vom Auge als Spiegel wurde seit der Wahrnehmungstheorie des Augustinus[213] immer wieder benutzt. „Es kam darauf an, das Bild im Sinnesorgan vom Bild, das die Seele schafft, zu differenzieren und es gleichzeitig ihm gegenüber abzuwerten".[214] Damit verbunden sind mehrere Übereinstimmungen von

---

[211] Heinz-Mohr, Gerd: *Lexikon der Symbole – Bilder und Zeichen der christlichen Kunst.* Freiburg, Basel, Wien: Herder 1991 (6. Auflage), S. 293 (Eintrag ‚Spiegel')

[212] Vgl. Grabes, Herbert: *Speculum, Mirror und Looking-Glass – Kontinuität und Originalität der Spiegelmetapher in den Buchtiteln des Mittelalters und der englischen Literatur des 13. bis 17. Jahrhunderts.* Tübingen: Max Niemeyer Verlag 1973, S. 86

[213] Nach dieser Theorie senden die Dinge Strahlen aus, die – wenn man sie betrachtet – in das Auge fallen und so ein (Spiegel-) Bild im Auge erzeugen.

[214] Grabes (1973), S. 87

Auge und Spiegel im Gegensatz zur Seele als Spiegel: Auge und Spiegel können nur solange ein Bild abbilden, solange das zu Spiegelnde vorhanden ist; sie können nur passiv spiegeln. Erst in der Seele kommt zu dem Spiegelbild die wirkliche Wahrnehmung hinzu. Für das Entstehen eines inneren Bildes in der Seele muss das Auge den Gegenstand so spiegeln, wie er wirklich ist. Es darf ihn nicht verzerren, entstellen oder verändern. Genau dies ist aber auch eine grundlegende Eigenschaft des Spiegels. „Die in der skizzierten Wahrnehmungstheorie[215] angenommene große Nähe von Seele und Auge, von innerem Bild und körperlichem Abbild, förderte zugleich die Vorstellung vom Auge als Spiegel des Herzens, der seelischen Gestimmtheit und Liebe".[216]

Jedoch gibt es noch andere Tendenzen: „Neben dem Auge ist das Herz derjenige Teil des Körpers, der am meisten metaphorisch zum Spiegel erklärt wurde".[217] Sowohl in der Antike wie zu Beginn des Christentums wurde diese Metapher hauptsächlich zur Bezeichnung von etwas Göttlichem bzw. von Gott verwendet. Im Mittelalter wurde sie weiterentwickelt und gelangte über italienische Autoren in die englische Renaissanceliteratur. Hier kommt jedoch noch ein entscheidendes Detail hinzu: Auch die Geliebte kann im Spiegel des Herzens zu sehen sein.

Die Metaphern bei den Zeitgenossen William Shakespeares

Wie schon im vorherigen Kapitel angedeutet wurde, setzt sich die Verwendung der zwei Metaphern in der Literatur bis in die englische Renaissance fort. Man kann sie nur schwer voneinander trennen, da sie vielfach gemeinsam verwendet wurden.

Die Verwendung der Spiegelmetapher kann man auch mit dem tatsächlichen Aufkommen des realen ‚Gebrauchsspiegels' begründen. Ab dem 12. Jahrhundert wurden wieder Spiegel hergestellt. Ab dem Ende des 15. Jahrhunderts[218] gab es eine regelrechte Massenproduktion, die kleinere Spiegel für jedermann erschwinglich machte.

Nach H. Grabes weist die Spiegelmetapher in der englischsprachigen Literatur des 13. bis 17. Jahrhunderts in ihrer Verwendung eine große Originalität auf, die

---

[215] Hier ist die Wahrnehmungstheorie des Augustinus gemeint.
[216] Ebd., S. 90
[217] Ebd., S. 92
[218] Nach 1500 waren vor allem die Venezianer damit beschäftigt, Spiegel in größerer Zahl herzustellen, ab dem frühen 16. Jahrhundert begannen die Engländer ebenfalls damit.

er in einen nicht unwesentlichen Zusammenhang mit dem Aufkommen der realen Spiegel stellt. Er schränkt den von ihm gewählten Untersuchungszeitraum sogar noch weiter ein: Für ihn liegt der Höhepunkt der Verwendung dieser Metapher zwischen 1550 und 1650.[219]

Die Spiegelmetapher begegnet dem Leser hier immer im Bereich des Menschen, ist also eng mit der Körpermetaphorik verknüpft. Aufgrund der Fülle des Materials aus dieser Zeit kann man hier eine noch weiter in die Tiefe gehende Unterteilung vornehmen.[220] Eine Kontinuität in der Verwendung weist vor allen Dingen der Liebende als Spiegel der Geliebten bzw. die Geliebte als Spiegel des Liebenden auf, obwohl der Mensch als Spiegelbild des Menschen zum Beispiel auch auf Kinder und Eltern, Mann und Frau, Geschwister und Freude angewendet wird. Hier kommt die Ähnlichkeit von Ab- und Urbild zum Tragen, die man zum Beispiel bei John Milton und Andrew Marvell wiederfindet.

Seit dem frühen 14. Jahrhundert erscheinen ebenfalls Könige, Fürsten und Ritter als Spiegel in der englischen Literatur. Zusammen mit dem Motiv der edlen und schönen Dame als Spiegel bilden sie in der elisabethanischen Zeit ein literarisches Gemeingut. Die Renaissance-Dichter bedienen sich häufig dieses Spiegels, vor allem in Zusammenhang mit der neu entstehenden Liebesdichtung petrarkistischer Prägung.

Durch diese Art der Dichtung kommt noch ein weiteres Element hinzu, durch das sich nun Spiegel- und Körpermetaphern ganz besonders vermischen: Der Dichter ist sehr darauf bedacht, seine angebetete Geliebte in einem positiven Licht darzustellen. Er beschreibt ihre Schönheit oft anhand eines sogenannten Katalogs des Körpers. Sinne oder Körperteile werden einzeln aufgezählt und mit anderen edlen Dingen verglichen oder gleichgesetzt.

George Gascoigne nennt zum Beispiel den gesamten Körper seiner Geliebten „tender"[221]

---

[219] Auf seine Untersuchung der Spiegelmetapher im Titel literarischer Werke möchte ich hier nicht weiter eingehen. Ich werde mich im Folgenden auf den Gebrauch dieser Metapher innerhalb einzelner Werke der Zeitgenossen Shakespeares beschränken.

[220] Vgl. Grabes (1973), S. 78 ff.

[221] In seinem Sonett "That self-same tongue which first did thee entreat", in: Levin, Phillis (Hg.): *The Penguin Book of the Sonnet – 500 Years of a Classical Tradition in English*. Harmondswoth: Penguin Books. 2001, S. 9

oder das Gesicht der Angebeteten „a lovely nutbrowne face"[222]. Ein gutes Beispiel findet sich in „There is a Garden in Her Face" [223] von Thomas Campion, sieht man einmal von den letzten beiden Versen jeder Strophe ab:

> There is a garden in her face
>   Where roses and white lilies grow;
> A heavenly paradise is that place,
>   Wherein these pleasant fruits do flow.
> There cherries grow much which none may buy,
> Till 'Cherry-ripe' themselves do cry.
>
> These cherries fairly do enclose
>   Of orient pearl a double row,
> Which when her lovely laughter shows,
>   They look like rose-buds filled with snow;
> Yet them no peer nor prince can buy,
> Till 'Cherry-ripe' themselves do cry.
>
> Her eyes like angels watch them still;
>   Her brows like bended bows do stand,
> Threatening with piercing shafts to kill
>   All that presume with eye or hand
> Those sacred cherries to come nigh;
> Till 'Cherry-ripe' themselves do cry.

Auch Edmund Spenser zählt in der Darstellung der Dame Una im ersten Canto der *Faerie Queen* nach und nach mehrere Körperteile auf, die er mit verschiedenen Dingen vergleicht: Er nennt ihre Haut zum Beispiel „much whiter then snow".[224] Christopher Marlowe bezeichnet in *Hero and Leander* den Atem Heros als „sweet smell"[225] und ihre Hände als „so white".[226]

---

[222] In seinem Sonett "A Sonet written in prayse of the browne beautie,...", in: Levin (2001), S.9

[223] Hollander, John und Frank Kermode: *The Literature of Renaissance England*. New York, London, Toronto: Oxford University Press 1973, S. 512

[224] Vgl. ebd., S. 172

[225] Ebd., S. 400

[226] Ebd., S. 400

Das Auge spielt in der Literatur dieser Zeit eine besondere Rolle: Es ist sowohl ein Spiegel[227] als auch ein Körperteil der Geliebten.[228] Hier vermischen sich ebenfalls Körper- und Spiegelmetapher. Jedoch muss man das Bild, das im Auge entsteht, von dem im Herzen und in der Seele trennen.

In der Dichtung der Renaissance wurden zwei verschiedene Wahrnehmungstheorien miteinander vermischt. Hierunter fallen die schon erwähnte Theorie des Augustinus und die des Euklids. Nach Euklid sendet das Auge eine Kraft aus, die von dem angeblickten Gegenstand aufgenommen wird. „So kann in der Liebesdichtung das Auge der Geliebten Spiegel sein, es kann aber zugleich auch feurige Strahlen aussenden, die vom Auge des Geliebten rezipiert, gespiegelt werden, in sein Herz dringen und es entzünden".[229] In Sonett 3 aus Henry Constables Zyklus *Diana* werden die vom Auge ausgehenden Strahlen mit den Pfeilen des Liebesgottes Amor gleichgesetzt. Auf dieses *conceit* wird schon im Titel angespielt: „Of the conspiracie of his Ladies eyes and his owne to ingender Loue".[230]

Die Spiegelung des Liebenden im Auge der Geliebten ist die am häufigsten verwendete Funktion. Sie ist zwischen 1590 und 1602 besonders beliebt. Hierbei spiegelt sich die eigene Person im Auge eines anderen Menschen und wird so zum Ausdruck der Zuneigung und des Liebeswerbens. Das Verhältnis der beiden Liebenden zueinander hat sich jedoch geändert: War die Dame früher höhergestellt als ihr Liebhaber, so sind sie in der Renaissance einander gleichberechtigt. Die Geliebte kann sich nun auch in den Augen ihres Liebhabers spiegeln. Das Betrachten im gegenseitigen Augenspiegel ist zu einem Zeichen gleichberechtigter Partner in der Liebe geworden.

---

[227] Vgl. hierzu Chapman: For as a glasse is an inanimate eie, And outward formes imbraceth inwardlie: So is the eye an animate glasse that showes Informes without us, ... (vgl. Anmerkung in Grabes (1973), S. 90, Anmerkung 180)

[228] Samuel Daniel nennt in seinem Zyklus *To Delia* in Sonett 50 die Augen seiner Geliebten „those faire eyes", in: Levin (2001), S. 32

[229] Grabes (1973), S. 89

[230] Vgl. ebd., S. 89 (in Verbindung mit Anmerkung 178 auf derselben Seite)

Betrachtung einzelner Sonette[231]

In diesem Kapitel werden drei Sonette William Shakespeares untersucht, zwei aus dem ersten Teil der Sammlung (Nr. 20 und 24) und eines aus dem zweiten Teil (Nr. 130).

Die Reime in Sonett 20 sind durchgängig weiblich, vielleicht wegen der Weiblichkeit des Geliebten. Außerdem ist es „a poem which has caused a good deal of unneccessary embarrassment"[232] wegen der Anspielungen auf die männlichen Geschlechtsorgane. Es ist das erste Gedicht Shakespeares, das nicht in irgendeiner Weise auf die Vergänglichkeit der Zeit eingeht. Hier steht der Unterschied von physischer und spiritueller Liebe im Vordergrund.

In Sonett 24 stellt Shakespeare eindeutig die Augen und ihre Funktion in der Beziehung zwischen lyrischem Ich und dem Geliebten in den Vordergrund. Shakespeare spielt hier mit der Metapher des Auges als Spiegel. Am Ende übt er aber auch Kritik: Das Auge kann nicht die gesamte Wirklichkeit spiegeln, man muss ebenfalls das eigene Herz befragen.

In Sonett 130 geht es um die sogenannte *dark lady*. Shakespeare beschreibt sie in aller Ausführlichkeit, sie ist aber vollkommen anders ist als andere in der Liebesdichtung der Zeit beschriebenen Frauen. Ihre Reize entsprechen der Realität.

Sonett 20

> A woman's face with nature's own hand painted,
> Hast thou, the master mistress of my passion;
> A woman's gentle heart, but not acquainted
> With shifting change as is false women's fashion;
> An eye more bright than theirs, less false in rolling,
> Gilding the object whereupon it gazeth;
> A man in hue, all hues in his controlling,
> Which steals men's eyes and women's souls amazeth.
> And for a woman wert thou first created,
> Till nature as she wrought thee fell a-doting,
> And by addition me of thee defeated,
> By adding one thing to my purpose nothing.

---

[231] Text der Sonette nach: Burrow (2002), S. 421, S. 429, S. 641

[232] Muir (1979), S. 54

> But since she pricked thee out for women's pleasure,
> Mine be thy love, and thy love's use their treasure.

In diesem Sonett beschreibt das lyrische Ich den Geliebten, der eindeutig ein Mann ist. Dies kann man daraus ableiten, dass er Frauen oder Frauentypen gegenübergestellt, an ihnen sozusagen gespiegelt wird. Andererseits wird hier mit verschiedenen Metaphern auf den männlichen Penis angespielt. Außerdem lässt sich aus diesem Sonett ableiten, dass die Beziehung des lyrischen Ich zu dem Freund keineswegs sexueller Natur ist, sondern sich eher einer Liebe zuneigt, die in der Seele verwurzelt ist.

Im ersten Quartett wird der Vergleich eingeführt: Der Freund hat ein Gesicht, das dem einer Frau ähnelt (V. 1). Daher auch die Bezeichnung „master mistress" im zweiten Vers. Der Freund ist männlich, doch hat ihn die Natur einer Frau ähnlich geschaffen. „His androgyny is part of his appeal".[233] „With nature's own hand" kann jedoch auch bedeuten, dass der Freund natürlich ist und sich nicht wie viele Frauen der Kosmetik bedient. Vielleicht macht dies seinen Reiz aus.

Der Freund hat ein sanftes, gütiges Herz (V. 3), jedoch unterscheidet es sich in einem wesentlichen Punkt von dem einer Frau, wie es im vierten Vers beschrieben wird: Es ist nicht flatterhaft. Frauen wird der Renaissance eine große Unbeständigkeit in ihren Entscheidungen vorgeworfen, die bis zu fehlender Vorsicht und mangelndem Urteilsvermögen reicht. Der Freund besitzt jedoch alle diese Eigenschaften, er ist weder unvorsichtig noch unbeständig.

Auch im zweiten Quartett wird er mit dem weiblichen Geschlecht verglichen. In den beiden ersten Versen geht das lyrische Ich näher auf die Augen bzw. das Auge des Freundes ein. Da das Auge sowohl „bright" als auch weniger „false in rolling" ist als das einer Frau, werden die angeschauten Gegenstände vergoldet. Dies steht in Zusammenhang mit der oben erwähnten Sehtheorie des Euklids. Weil das Auge des Freundes keinerlei falsche Strahlen aussendet, überträgt sich der Glanz der Augenstrahlen auf die Gegenstände. Diese werden noch schöner.

In Vers 7 fällt in der Quarto-Ausgabe das kursiv gedruckte Wort *Hews* auf. Es ist möglicherweise eine Anspielung, die für Shakespeare als Dichter und für den Adressaten dieses Sonetts eine besondere Bedeutung hatte. Vielleicht ist es auch eine Anspielung auf den Namen Hughes. Jedoch lassen sich diese Vermutungen heute nicht mehr verifizieren.

---

[233] Edmondson (2004), S. 73

„Hews" oder „hew" kann aber auch ‚colour', ‚external appearance of the face and skin' oder ‚form, shape, figure' bedeuten, was diesen zwei Zeilen eine andere Bedeutung gäbe. Entweder ist der Freund so hübsch, dass ihm alle Farben unterstehen oder dass er alle Farben kontrollieren kann. Mit Farben sind hier vor allen Dingen die Farben des Gesichts gemeint, wie zum Beispiel Erröten oder Erbleichen. „Hew" wäre dann eine Metapher. Diese „hews" lenken die Blicke aller Männer auf sich und überwältigen die Frauen (V. 8). Der Freund wird durch das Lob des lyrischen Ich über alle anderen erhoben und als etwas Besonderes herausgestellt.

Im dritten Quartett kann man den Grund für das besondere Aussehen des Freundes finden: Die Natur wollte ihn eigentlich als Frau erschaffen, hat sich jedoch in ihre eigene Schöpfung verliebt (V. 9 und 10). Die Natur als weibliche Personifikation konnte sich unmöglich in eine Frau verlieben. Ihrer Schöpfung schenkte sie daher einen Reiz mehr (V. 11). „Addition" (V. 11) oder „one thing" (V. 12) sind Metaphern für den Penis. Durch diesen Zusatz hat sie den Freund dem lyrischen Ich weggenommen (V. 12). Der Penis des Freundes hat für das lyrische Ich keinen Sinn (V. 12), weil beide männlich sind.

Eine Lösung für dieses Problem findet sich in dem abschließenden *couplet*. Die Natur hat dem Freund den Penis beigegeben, damit sich Frauen mit ihm vergnügen können (V. 13). Deshalb gehört dieser „Schatz" den Frauen, dem lyrischen Ich aber die wirkliche Liebe, die in der Seele verankert ist (V. 14).

In diesem Sonett finden sich vor allen Dingen in den letzten vier Versen mehrere Metaphern für den Penis. Entweder wird auf ihn direkt mit „addition", „one thing", oder „pricked thee out" angespielt oder sein Zweck wird mit einer Metapher bezeichnet. Beispiele hierfür sind „women's pleasure" und „thy love's use their treasure".

Auch die Spiegelmetapher findet sich in diesem Sonett indirekt. Shakespeare bzw. das von ihm geschaffene lyrische Ich haben die Vorstellung einer Frau, an der sie den jungen Mann, den Freund spiegeln. Sie beginnen den Vergleich mit dem Gesicht oder Antlitz, dann kommt das Herz an die Reihe und schließlich enden sie mit dem Auge. Frauen sind hier keine Vorbilder. Sie sind etwas Negatives, Falsches, von dem sich der Freund vollkommen unterscheidet. So kann das lyrische Ich ihn denn auch auffordern: „Mine be thy love".

Sonett 24

> Mine eye hath played the painter and hath stelled
> Thy beauty's form in table of my heart;
> My body is the frame wherein 'tis held,
> And perspective it is best painter's art,
> For through the painter must you see his skill
> To find where your true image pictured lies,
> Which in my bosom's shop is hanging still,
> That hath his windows glazèd with thine eyes.
> Now see what good turns eyes for eyes have done:
> Mine eyes have drawn thy shape, and thine for me
> Are windows to my breast, wherethrough the sun
> Delights to peep, to gaze therein on thee.
>   Yet eyes this cunning want to grace their art:
>   They draw but what they see, know not the heart.

In diesem Sonett betrachten das lyrische Ich und der Geliebte sich gegenseitig in den Augen des anderen. Hier hat neben den Anspielungen auf den Körper als Objekt der Betrachtung die Spiegelmetapher einen zentralen Stellenwert. Am Ende wird jedoch auch der Unterschied zwischen den Augen als Spiegel und dem Herz deutlich hervorgehoben.

Im ersten Quartett wird die Ausgangslage dargestellt. Das Auge des lyrischen Ich hat sich in einen Maler verwandelt (V. 1) und entwirft das Bild des Geliebten auf eine Leinwand. Das Herz des lyrischen Ich ist diese Leinwand (V. 2). Sein Körper ist der Rahmen für dieses Gemälde (V. 3). Gleichzeitig erfüllt dieser Rahmen noch eine andere Funktion (V. 4). Mit „perspective" ist in der damaligen Zeit eine besondere Form der Malerei gemeint: „an art which involved the painting of a distorted image which when viewed through a small aperture placed at the side converted the image into something more normal".[234] Der Körper bzw. die Augen des Ich bilden demnach diese „aperture", durch die der Geliebte bzw. auch andere das Bild des Geliebten richtig betrachten können. Darauf weisen auch die Verse 5 und 6 hin: Durch den Maler, das heißt durch seine Augen, ist das „true image" erst zu sehen. Das Bild ist immer noch im „bossom's shop" vorhanden (V. 7). Der Geliebte schaut wie durch einen Glasspiegel in die Augen des lyrischen Ichs: Der Geliebte kann sich nämlich in ihnen spiegeln. Sie sind die Fenster des Herzens. (V. 8).

---

[234] http://www.shakespeares-sonnets.com/xxivcomm.htm

Im nächsten Quartett geht es um die Funktion der Augen des lyrischen Ich und des Geliebten in der gegenseitigen Betrachtung. Fast scheint es so, als ob in diesen vier Versen noch einmal die positive Seite der Augen als Spiegel, ein Wechselspiel der Spiegelung,[235] herausgestellt werden soll, bevor im *couplet* der negative Aspekt im Vordergrund steht.

Die Augen des lyrischen Ichs haben das Bild des Geliebten gemalt (V. 10). Dessen Augen sind Fenster in seiner Brust (V. 10, 11), durch die die Strahlen der Sonne auf das Bild des Geliebten schauen (V. 11, 12).

Mit dem Beginn des *couplets* beginnt jedoch die Kritik an den Augenspiegeln.[236] Sie können nur reine Äußerlichkeiten widerspiegeln, erkennen aber nicht den Wert einer Person (V. 13, 14).[237] Die Seele des Geliebten kann einerseits noch schöner sein als sein äußerer Anblick, andererseits kann der Anblick des Geliebten schöner sein als die Seele.

Wie schon seine Dichterkollegen vermischt Shakespeare in diesem Sonett die verschiedenen Bereiche, für die das Auge stehen kann. Es ist der Körperteil des lyrischen Ich und des Geliebten, aber auch ein Spiegel. Fast dasselbe gilt für das Herz: Es ist sowohl die Leinwand, auf die das Gemälde des Geliebten gemalt wird, aber auch ein wirklicher Teil des menschlichen Körpers. Der gesamte Körper des Ich erfüllt auch eine Funktion. Er ist der Rahmen für das Bild des Geliebten. Durch den Körper als Rahmen bzw. durch die Augen des „painters" kann alles, sogar die Sonne, das „image" des Geliebten erst in der richtigen Perspektive sehen.

In diesem Sonett spiegeln sich beide Partner in den Augen des anderen. Dies ist ebenfalls typisch für die Tradition der Metapher wie auch der Liebesdichtung. Die beiden Liebenden stehen auf der gleichen Ebene, keiner ist höher als der andere, denn sie können sich gegenseitig in die Augen sehen.

Auch der Vorwurf an die Spiegel, sie könnten nur das offen Sichtbare wiedergeben, findet sich in diesem Sonett. Die (Spiegel-)Bilder in den Augen der beiden Liebenden zeigen nur das, was nach außen sichtbar ist. Das Bild, das sich die Seele von einem Menschen macht, trifft man in diesem Sonett nicht an. Wie schon oben angesprochen, kann man daraus zwei verschiedene Schlüsse ziehen.

---

[235] „Mine eyes...thy shape, and this for me"
[236] „Yet..."
[237] „the heart"

Sonett 130

> My mistress' eyes are nothing like the sun,
> Coral is far more red than her lips' red;
> If snow be white, why then her breasts are dun;
> If hairs be wires, black wires grow on her head.
> I have seen roses damasked, red and white,
> But no such roses see I in her cheeks,
> And in some perfumes is there more delight
> Than in the breath that from my mistress reeks.
> I love to hear her speak, yet well I know
> That music have a far more pleasing sound.
> I grant I never saw a goddess go:
> My mistress when she walks treads on the ground.
>   And yet, by heaven, I think my love as rare
>   As any she belied with false compare.

In diesem Sonett werden die Reize der *dark lady* beschrieben. Sie ist jedoch keine Frau, wie sie normalerweise in den Sonetten der Zeit beschrieben wird. Wie in vielen Sonetten Shakespeares gibt es im *couplet* eine überraschende Wendung.

Als erstes werden die Augen der „mistress" beschrieben. Sie sind nicht der Sonne ähnlich (V. 1), so wie das Rot der Lippen nicht dem der Koralle gleicht (V. 2). Ihre Brüste sind nicht weiß wie Schnee, sondern haben eine graubraune Farbe (V. 3). Die Haare sind nicht goldfarben wie „wire", sie sind schwarz (V. 4).

Im zweiten Quartett werden die Wangen und der Atem der „mistress" beschrieben. Das lyrische Ich kennt rote, weiße und „damasked" Rosen, aber die Wangen seiner Geliebten sind nichts von alledem (V. 5 und 6). Auch ist ihr Atem nicht wie Parfüm (V. 7 und 8). „Reek" wird in dieser Zeit mit dem Rauch des Schornsteins bzw. dem Geruch von Blut in Verbindung gebracht, ist also kein schöner Vergleich für eine Geliebte.

In den nächsten vier Versen werden weitere Eigenschaften der „mistress" beschrieben: Das Ich hört sie zwar gerne sprechen, ist sich aber auch bewusst, dass der Klang ihrer Stimme durch Musik noch übertroffen wird (V. 9 und 10). In Vers 11 räumt das lyrische Ich ein, dass sie keine Göttin ist, weil ihre Füße den Boden berühren.

Alle Vergleiche werden anhand des so genannten Körperkatalogs aufgezählt: Erst werden die Augen, dann die Lippen, die Brüste, die Haare, die Wangen erwähnt, schließlich der Atem und die Stimme, als letztes die Art zu gehen. In der Dichtungstradition Petrarcas sowie in den Werken anderer Schriftsteller wird durch die Übertragung der Eigenschaften edler und strahlender Dinge wie der Sonne, der Koralle, des Schnees und ähnliches auf diese Körperteile die Schönheit der Geliebten herausgestellt und über alles andere erhoben.

Shakespeare stellt sich mit diesem Sonett dem entschieden entgegen. Er beschreibt seine Geliebten nicht mit überzogenen Vergleichen, sondern realistisch. Die Tradition der Lobpreisung der Geliebten dient Shakespeare als eine Art Spiegel. Nur durch diese schon vorhandenen Metaphern kann er seine „mistress" anders beschreiben. Die *concetti* in den Quartetten zusammen mit dem abschließenden *couplet* werden dadurch für den Leser noch schockierender.

Im *couplet* stellt das lyrische Ich nämlich fest, dass, obwohl seine Geliebte keine Schönheit ist, keine andere Frau an ihre Reize heranreicht. Diese werden durch verlogene Vergleiche[238] falsch dargestellt. Fast hört man hier das lyrische Ich wie Touchstone in *As You Like It* ausrufen: „an ill-favor'd thing, sir, but mine own!"[239]

---

[238] „false"

[239] Greenblatt, Stephen (Hg.): *The Norton Shakespeare – Based on the Oxford Edition*. New York, London: W. W. Norton & Company 1997, S. 1653, Akt 5, Szene 4, Vers 55

Zusammenfassung

Die vorliegende Arbeit zeigt, dass Shakespeare einerseits sehr den petrarkistischen Dichtungskonventionen der Zeit verhaftet ist. Dies wird besonders deutlich in den zwei untersuchten Sonetten aus dem ersten Teil seiner Sammlung: „Sonnet 20 is rather conventional in form, subject, and language"[240] und Sonett 24 hinterlässt beim modernen Leser auch keinen negativen Nachgeschmack.

Shakespeare preist hier die Schönheit des Geliebten über alles andere. Dieses Herausstellen ist an sich nichts Ungewöhnliches. Shakespeare fällt jedoch schon aus dem üblichen Rahmen der Renaissancedichtung heraus, weil er einen Mann preist.

In Sonett 130 aus dem zweiten Teil seiner Sammlung geht es um das ‚Lob' einer Frau. Dies ist wieder konventionell, ganz im Sinne der Tradition. Auffallend ist hier allerdings, dass diese Frau in den Quartetten nicht gepriesen wird, sondern im Gegensatz zu den sonst üblichen Vergleichen verspottet und lächerlich gemacht wird. Im *couplet* wird dieses Vorgehen jedoch noch zu einem positiven Ergebnis geführt. Shakespeare parodiert hier eindeutig die bisher geltenden Dichtungstraditionen.

Shakespeare stellt somit mit seinen Sonetten einen Wendepunkt in dieser Art der Dichtung dar.

---

[240] Wright, Eugene Patrick: *The Structure of Shakspeare's Sonnets*. Lewiston/Queenston/Lampeter: The Edwin Mellen Press 1993, S. 78

Literaturverzeichnis

Primärliteratur

Shakespeare, William: The Complete Sonnets and Poems – edited by Collin Burrow. Oxford: Oxford University Press 2002.

Shakespeare, William: Sonette und Versepen. Düsseldorf/Zürich: Artemis und Winkler Verlag 2001.

Sekundärliteratur

Abrams, M. H.: A Glossary of literary terms. Fort Worth: Harcourt Brave Jovanovich 1993 (6. Auflage).

Baumann, Uwe: Shakespeare und seine Zeit. Stuttgart: Ernst Klett Verlag 1998.

Curtius, Ernst Robert: Europäische Literatur und lateinisches Mittelalter. Bern und München: Francke Verlag 1984 (10. Auflage).

Edmondson, Paul und Stanley Wells: Shakespeare's Sonnets. Oxford: Oxford University Press 2004.

Grabes, Herbert: Speculum, Mirror und Looking-Glass – Kontinuität und Originalität der Spiegelmetapher in den Buchtiteln des Mittelalters und der englischen Literatur des 13. bis 17. Jahrhunderts. Tübingen: Max Niemeyer Verlag 1973.

Greenblatt, Stephen (Hg.): The Norton Shakespeare – Based on the Oxford Edition. New York, London: W. W. Norton & Company 1997.

Heinz-Mohr, Gerd: Lexikon der Symbole – Bilder und Zeichen der christlichen Kunst. Freiburg, Basel, Wien: Herder 1991 (6.Auflage).

Hollander, John und Frank Kermode: The Literature of Renaissance England. New York, London, Toronto: Oxford University Press 1973.

Kapp, Volker (Hg.): Italienische Literaturgeschichte. Stuttgart, Weimar: Verlag J. B. Metzler 1994 (2. Auflage).

Levin, Phillis (Hg.): The Penguin Book of the Sonnet – 500 Years of a Classical Tradition in English. Harmondswoth: Penguin Books. 2001.

Muir, Kenneth: Shakespeare's Sonnets. London: George Allen & Unwin LTD 1979.

Seeber, Hans Ulrich (Hg.): Englische Literaturgeschichte. Stuttgart, Weimar: Verlag J. B. Metzler 1999 (3. Auflage).

Standop, Ewald und Edgar Mertner: Englische Literaturgeschichte. Heidelberg: Quelle & Meyer 1983 (4.Auflage).

Tetzeli von Rosador, Kurt: „Die nichtdramatischen Dichtungen." In: Schabert, Ina (Hg.): Shakespeare-Handbuch., Stuttgart: Alfred Kröner Verlag 2000 (4. Auflage).

Wagner, Hans-Peter: A History of British, Irish and American Literature. Trier: Wissenschaftlicher Verlag 2003.

Wright, Eugene Patrick: The Structure of Shakspeare's Sonnets. Lewiston/Queenston/Lampeter: The Edwin Mellen Press 1993.

Internetquellen:

http://www.shakespeares-sonnets.com/xxcomm.htm

http://www.shakespeares-sonnets.com/xxivcomm.htm

http://www.shakespeares-sonnets.com/130comm.htm (Autor/Besitzer der Seite: Oxquary Books Ltd, 27 Western Road, Oxford 4LF; erstellt zwischen Januar 2000 und Januar 2001; regelmäßige Updates; eingesehen am 03.04.2005)

http://www.literaturwissenschaft-online.unikiel.de/veranstaltungen/ringvorlesungen/liebesdichtung_antike_barock.asp (hieraus: Dietrich Jäger „Die Sonette William Shakespeares" (Beitrag zur Ringvorlesung am 24.06. 2003; eingesehen am 03.04.2005)

Einzelbände

Vinzent Fröhlich: The construction of femininity and masculinity in Shakespeare's *Macbeth*.
ISBN: 978-3-638-94917-0

Katharina Herrmann: Gender Politics in *Macbeth*.
ISBN: 978-3-640-77125-7

Verena Ludwig: Monstrous Bodies – Körper und Männlichkeit bei Shakespeare.
ISBN: 978-3-640-15601-6

Stephanie Schnabel: Körper- und Spiegelmetapher und ihre Funktion in ausgewählten Sonetten William Shakespeares.
ISBN: 978-3-638-69255-7